What Ot'   Are Saying A.   ...gy and Spiritual
Awakenin

"This valuable book explores the essential purpose of astrology: To serve as a beacon that can illuminate our individual road to enlightenment. I highly recommend this book to astrologers, psychologists, and other fellow travelers on the Path.
　　　　Dennis Harness, Ph.D.,
　　　　Director, Institute of Vedic Astrology

"Greg's book fills a long neglected need in astrological literature. He brings astrology alive! *Astrology and Spiritual Awakening* explains the birth charts of famous spiritual teachers and literary figures in order to show us the possibility of realizing the evolutionary potential of our own lives. His astrological expertise, coupled with his psychological acumen make for an outstanding contribution to our field.
　　　　Jonathan Tenney, M.A., MFCC
　　　　Psychotherapist and Astrologer

"In this fresh and innovative volume, Greg Bogart builds upon and carries forward Dane Rudhyar's work while also finding his own voice. It is a beautifully written book that demonstrates Greg's talent in applying astrological knowledge to the practice of counseling and spiritual guidance. *Astrology and Spiritual Awakening* secure's Greg's place among the dynamic new practitioners of the stellar art."
　　　　Neil Marbell
　　　　NCGR Advisory Board

"A ground-breaking book, featuring lucid explanations of basic astrological material, plenty of sample horoscope interpretation, and an insightful review of Dane Rudhyar's main ideas. All students will profit from reading an astrologer whose insights are backed up by thorough research and balanced judgment.
　　　　Tim Lyons
　　　　Review in *Planet Earth* Magazine

ASTROLOGY AND

SPIRITUAL AWAKENING

Gregory C. Bogart

Foreword by Shelley Jordan

DAWN MOUNTAIN PRESS
BERKELEY, CA

Astrology and Spiritual Awakening
By Gregory C. Bogart

Published by
Dawn Mountain Press
Post Office Box 9563
Berkeley, CA 94709-0563
U.S.A.

Portions of this book previously appeared in The Mountain Astrologer, NCGR Journal, Aspects, and Considerations.

Book Design: Paul Hoffman
Cover Design: Andrea Duflon
Graphics: Jim Tucker, Syllogy Consulting
Editors: Nancy Grimley Carleton, Diana Syverud

10 9 8 7 6 5 4 3 2

First Edition
Printed in the United States of America
Printed on acid-free, recycled paper

Library of Congress Catalog Card Number 93-73696
Bogart, Gregory C.
1. Astrology 2. Spiritual Growth 3. Biography
4. Yoga 5. Transpersonal Psychology
6. Mysticism

ISBN 0-9639068-3-6 (pbk.)

Table of Contents

Key To Symbols

Planets

⊙ Sun

☽ Moon

☿ Mercury

♀ Venus

♂ Mars

♃ Jupiter

♄ Saturn

⚷ Chiron

♅ Uranus

♆ Neptune

♇ Pluto

☊ North Node

☋ South Node

Signs

♈ Aries

♉ Taurus

♊ Gemini

♋ Cancer

♌ Leo

♍ Virgo

♎ Libra

♏ Scorpio

♐ Sagittarius

♑ Capricorn

♒ Aquarius

♓ Pisces

Aspect Lines

——————— 180°   Opposition

— · — · - 150°   Quincunx

— — — 135°   Sesquiquadrate

~~~~~~~~ 120°   Trine

——————— 90°   Square

·············· 60°   Sextile

——————— 45/30° Semisquare/Semisextile

Houses

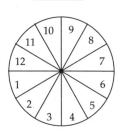

This book is dedicated to my spiritual teachers:

Swami Muktananda Paramahamsa

and

The Venerable Dane Rudhyar

About the Author .

Greg Bogart, Ph.D is a licensed Marriage, Family, and Child Counselor and maintains a private psychotherapy practice in Berkeley, California. He has taught and practiced astrology professionally since 1981 and is certified as an astrological counselor by the National Council for Geocosmic Research. Greg is also a musician, a song-writer, and a yoga teacher. He currently lives in Richmond, California.

Greg received his B.A. in Religious Studies from Wesleyan University, his M.A. in Counseling Psychology from the California Institute of Integral Studies, and his Ph.D. in Psychology from Saybrook Institute. He has published articles in publications such as *The Mountain Astrologer, Considerations, NCGR Journal, Aspects,* and *The Astrological Journal.* His psychological writings have appeared in the *Journal of Transpersonal Psychology, American Journal of Psychotherapy, The California Therapist, Journal of Humanistic Psychology, Dreaming: The Journal of the Society for the Study of Dreams,* and *Yoga Journal.*

To contact Greg, write to him c/o Dawn Mountain Press, P.O. Box 9563, Berkeley, CA 94709–0563. Please enclose a self-addressed, stamped envelope for reply.

Acknowledgements

I owe an inestimable debt to my parents, Leo and Agnes Bogart, and my sister, Michele Bogart, who have always encouraged me to find and follow my own path.

I would like to thank Chakrapani Ullal, one of the world's great living astrologers, who has offered me so much encouragement over the years. I am grateful to my astrology teacher, KHM9 Andres Takra, the Wildman of Karakas, who taught me the craft. Many thanks to David Spangler, Allan Bateman, and Judith Lasater for their skillful spiritual guidance.

Nancy Grimley Carleton, Linda Cogozzo, Andrea DuFlon, Gayle Peterson, Paul Hoffman, Shelley Jordan, and Jim Tucker offered invaluable assistance without which this book would never have been completed. My special thanks to them, and to five people who helped make the publication of this volume possible: Michael Gliksohn, David Kesten, Karl Knobler, Ken Parker, and Richard Rosen.

I am filled with gratitude to the following friends, mentors, and allies, all of whom have supported me in innumerable ways: Chris Abajian, Rick Amaro, Kim Anderson, Stephanie Austin, Bob Bartner, Anushka Bliss, Stephen Bodian, Mikl Brawner, Jamila Buckley, Marka Carson, Rob Chambret, Carolyn Cherry, John Clausen, Cathy Coleman, Katherine & Roger Collis, Dominic D'Ambrosio, Mike Dakaota, Scott Drengsen, Cathy Esser, Donna Fone, Bob Forte, Karen Fry, Nur and Drolma Gale, Rob Gellman, Lynn Geosits, Stuart Gold, Satpreet Grewal, Vern Haddick, Dennis Harness, Andy Hendrickson, Judy Hess, Hilarion, Joann Horton, Evaleah Howard, John Demian Kennedy, Arthur Kilmurray, Stanley Krippner, Greg Kowalsky, Dan Johnson, Janene Jurgensen, David LaChappelle, Kim Lacy, Cate Laughran, Ian LeCheminant, David Lukoff, Judy MacMurray, Neil Marbell, Roger Marsden, Kathi & Milenko Matanovic, Barbara McEnerney, Michel Meiffren, Mary Metz, Nicki Michaels, Tom Miller, Chris Mondloch, Patricia Moore, Barbara Morgan, Donald Moyer, Maryann Mulvihill, Nicole Normandeau, Evan O'Malone, Robyn Sean Peterson, Robert Powell, Martin Priest, Leyla Rael, Tony Rogers, Donald Rothberg, Karyn Sanders, Bill Sargent, Dick Schuettge, Ken Seastrom, Gray Shaw, Laura

Shekerjian, Kate Sholly, Harry Sirota, Barbara Somerfield, Stuart Sovatsky, Julie Spangler, Marcia Starck, Sara Strand, Kimberly Sylvan, Coke Swanston, Jonathan Tenney, Tem Tarriktar, Michele Thelen-Steere, Linda Trageser, Stephen Van Zandt, Robert Walker, Stuart Walker, Rodney Yee, Heather Wakefield, Intz Walker, Bryan Wittine, Peggy Wright, Ren Zaugg, and Jeremy Zwelling. Thank you one and all.

Special thanks to Charles Mintz, my hometown buddy; to Richard Cook, who, in a spirit of service and generosity, allowed me to conduct classes at his Sunrise Bookshop; and to Diana Syverud, the bright Sun in my life, the star I'm steering by.

Foreword

Astrology has been in a state of transition ever since the 1936 publication of Dane Rudhyar's seminal work, *The Astrology of Personality*. Dane Rudhyar could be called the Copernicus of astrology. Like Copernicus, who stated that the Sun was in the center of the solar system, Rudhyar observed that it was the individual, not the planets, that control the astrological birth chart. His perspective radically challenged the ancient claims that astrology could predict the future, and that there were "good" birth charts and "bad" birth charts. Gradually, as a result of Rudhyar's innovation, astrology has been extricating itself from its eons-old association with fortune-telling. Particularly during the astrological renaissance of the past three decades, astrology has been releasing more and more the idea of predestination from its group of essential assumptions, replacing these erroneous claims with concepts of holism, humanism, and depth psychology.

It took 100 years for Copernicus' ideas to catch on. Fortunately, it hasn't taken astrologers nearly as long to begin assimilating these new concepts. In recent years, the focus in the astrological literature has shifted from a judgemental, predictive style to one that is more psychologically and philosophically mature and realistic. Thus, the birth chart is increasingly employed as a valuable tool for self-improvement, insight, and personal transformation.

Among those who stand at the forefront of this trend is Dr. Greg Bogart, one of the most educated and intelligent voices in the field of astrology today — an impeccable role model for the New Astrologer. The advantages of his years of extensive study, training, and discipline are made obvious in this especially creative, innovative, and insightful work.

In *Astrology and Spiritual Awakening*, Greg Bogart has taken astrological biography — the blending of astrology, psychology, and biographical studies — to new levels of excellence. Using profoundly perceptive and sensitive biographies of spiritual teachers, Greg demonstrates chart analysis with a high degree of technical and psychological sophistication. His dramatic, story-telling method of recounting the stories of their lives while examining their birth charts is both highly entertaining and inspiring. The book is also full of fascinating case examples written with a depth of insight new to astrology.

This book exemplifies the philosophy that life is not predestined and that an individual can use astrology to take control of his or her life and development. Greg uses his expertise and personal experience in spiritual and yogic traditions to suggest practices that each of us may choose as appropriate ways of catalyzing our personal evolution. The suggested paths and techniques are contemporary and can be followed by anyone, not just those interested in meditation, yoga, or other traditional spiritual practices.

Astrology and Spiritual Awakening is one of the most clearly written and practical works on astrology I've ever seen. It is a pleasure for me to recommend a book that is technically excellent, intellectually mature, and exciting to read, one that will enrich any reader's understanding of astrology.

Shelley Jordan, M.A.
Madison, Wisconsin
October 15, 1993

Introduction

This book is for those who seek a deeper understanding of how astrology illuminates the process of spiritual growth and awakening. Its goal is to help you follow the path of astrological self-study to discover your unique spiritual path. My fundamental premise is that the process of transformation spoken of by humanity's great spiritual traditions is a structured process, the nature of which can be clearly discerned through intelligent study of the birth chart. Moreover, in an era in which many sources of spiritual and moral authority have come into question, the stellar art provides an invaluable means of guiding ourselves through our own initiatory processes.

These essays are derived from classes and workshops I conducted between 1986 and 1992. They are presented in three parts, each self-contained, yet each exploring from different perspectives the theme of astrology and spiritual awakening. Part I offers practical guidelines for utilizing the birth chart to find a spiritual path. Part II explores the transpersonal approach to chart interpretation. Part III illustrates these practical and theoretical principles through a series of astro-biographical studies.

Chapter 1 is a concise review of the foundations of astrology, which will be useful background material for newcomers to this subject. Chapter 2 describes how the twelve zodiacal signs and houses of the birth chart can be viewed as symbols of twelve dimensions of the path of awakening. I discuss "The Twelve Yogas of the Zodiac" and offer guidelines for interpreting the birth chart with a spiritual orientation. This chapter includes numerous examples and will help you discern the form of spiritual practice that is most appropriate to your natal chart, and to the transits and progressions operative during a particular period.

Chapters 3, 4, and 5 examine the theoretical foundations of humanistic and transpersonal astrology, as described by the great modern astrologer, Dane Rudhyar. My intention is not to present a complete survey of Rudhyar's work, a task that Leyla Rael admirably carried out in her book, *The Essential Rudhyar*. Instead, I explore a few of his important ideas and attempt to demonstrate their practical relevance to contemporary astrologers. My hope is that this material will contribute to a renaissance of interest in his original writings. It is important to note that at times I amplify Rudhyar's ideas and utilize them as a springboard to develop ideas of my own. I am fully responsible for any misunderstandings of Rudhyar that may have resulted in the process.

Chapters 4 and 5 also contain a detailed case study illustrating the use of astrological principles for guiding a person through an intensive period of spiritual crisis and awakening. This includes a discussion of the initiations catalyzed by the trans-saturnian planets, Uranus, Neptune, and Pluto. I also note the importance of integrating astrology with spiritual teachings concerning the process of transformation. Thus, I introduce some concepts from the ancient yogic tradition of Kashmir Shaivism, which shed additional light on the metamorphosis of consciousness that transpersonal astrology attempts to facilitate.

Chapters 6-12 feature "astrological biographies" of seven widely acknowledged spiritual teachers, each of whom confronted in varying ways the quest for enlightenment and the challenges of transpersonal living. These astrobiographies examine the various tests, crises, and turning points of their lives in relation to their natal charts. It is important to note that these studies are not definitive biographical sketches but *life interpretations* that emerged from my interaction with students and workshop participants with particular concerns and interests. They are intended to be entertaining and practical illustrations of the insights that astrology can provide into the process of human transformation.

The biographies examined here are simply those of individuals I find interesting and who have influenced me in some way. My choices reflect my own interest in mysticism, yoga, contemplative life, and comparative religions and literature. While I have chosen to focus on men's lives here, I discuss numerous women in Parts I and II. (See Rodden, 1979, for astrological studies of five hundred women).

Also, while it may seem to be redundant to explore the lives of seven persons in some way connected with the spiritual traditions of India, the striking contrasts in their personalities and life-histories should be evident. Their lives demonstrate greatly varying modes of pursuing, and giving expression to, the process of spiritual awakening: service to the poor (Meher Baba), establishment of spiritual communities (Bhagwan Rajneesh, Sri Kriyananda), historical reflection, scholarship, and romantic relationships (Mircea Eliade), Kundalini Yoga (Swami Muktananda), love, service, and devotion to a Guru (Ram Dass), contemporary reinterpretation of ancient spiritual teachings (Rajneesh), and inspired creativity and political activism (Rabindranath Tagore). I do not wish to offend anyone with the comments I have made about any of these individuals, but neither do I hide my opinions.

The goal of these biographical studies is threefold. First, they provide detailed examples of the application of basic astrological methods such as transits and secondary progressions. This is the best way to learn to refine our chart interpretion skills. My approach here is in keeping with Rudhyar's statement that students of astrology should devote themselves to,

> [no less than] a few years of concentrated study not only of the elements of the language of astrology per se, but even more, of well-known people's birth-charts, progressions, and transits in connection with their detailed year-by-year biographies — *the only way of intelligently studying the intricacies of actually applying and using astrology.* (1980, p. 121, emphasis mine)

Secondly, in-depth astrological biographies enable us to understand the coherent pattern of the lives of the individuals studied, and to perceive each event as a necessary and significant phase of the process of transformation. These explorations thus illustrate Rudhyar's concept of "eonic consciousness," through which we discern the unity of the life-cycle.

Thirdly, study of these "famous lives" illuminates our own processes of spiritual growth and metamorphosis, and can inspire our own efforts on the path of awakening. Studying such astrological biographies may not only fill us with admiration for the attainments of great personages, but can also teach us important lessons that help us navigate the sometimes turbulent waters of our own spiritual journeys more wisely and courageously. While studying these lives we have the opportunity to reflect upon how we might respond to similar placements of natal planets, or analogous transits and progressions. By reading these astro-biographies, our own struggles and strivings come into perspective, and we begin to better understand our own multi-dimensional transformations.

My purpose in presenting these biographies is to suggest how we might actualize our distinctive birth potentials and evolve spiritually. Each of these famous individuals passed through struggles and tests quite similar to those that you and I experience. Their quests did not lead them directly into transcendent realms of divine light, but straight into the heart of some of the most highly charged, emotionally turbulent dimensions of human life: dilemmas about money and sexuality, ostracism by the family, confusing visions, fear of becoming insane, difficult relationships with mentors, and questions about how to actualize a spiritual vocation in the world. Their biographies demonstrate that spiritual life is a battle with numerous psychological and material obstacles, terrors, and uncertainties. It is my hope that these astrological portraits may also serve as examples of the luminous victory that is possible.

PART I

Astrology and Spiritual Awakening

Astrology is the Yoga of Time. It is a form of sacred knowledge that teaches us to live consciously as embodied beings in a temporal world. Study of the birth chart enables us to find our next step in evolution — whether this means choosing a career, forming a relationship, physical or emotional healing, building a business, social activism, or deepening our meditation practice. It can be a reliable guide through life's changes, a means of sanctifying earthly existence and fulfilling its challenges with courage, clarity, and joy.

The purpose of this book is to show how astrology may be utilized to understand the stages and facets of the spiritual path, the process of awakening to the presence of a more encompassing reality or consciousness — God, Atman, Buddha Mind, the pure Light. Toward this end, we will discuss the theory and practice of humanistic and transpersonal astrology and study many examples of persons in the midst of deep psycho-spiritual transformations. Before embarking on our journey, however, I would like to begin by surveying some basic astrological information that will serve as a shared language and a foundation for understanding the material that follows.

CHAPTER 1

Astrological Symbols and the Birth Chart

Astrology is the study of the ever-changing pattern of the planets and stars in relation to human experience. Astrologers examine planetary positions at the moment of a person's birth in order to discern themes, characteristics, and interests that may be emphasized over the course of that person's life. Dane Rudhyar (1976a) taught that the birth chart is a "seed pattern," a set of "celestial instructions" revealing what an individual potentially can become and the kinds of experience and actions that may be necessary to fulfill one's life purpose.

The astrological birth chart can be viewed as a roadmap provided by the Creator. This roadmap provides individualized guidance through life's changes and challenges — the sharp turns, steep climbs, and occasional plateaus that all of us experience. To understand your birth chart, it is important to grasp the meaning of five basic factors: planets, signs, houses, cycles, and aspects. We will examine each of these topics briefly, as well as transits and progressions, two methods astrologers use to determine the timing of events and experiences.

The Planets

The planets represent the many facets of the personality: the **Sun** symbolizes the core of the personality, the basic life purpose, the conscious sense of self, a quality that must be developed and expressed by an individual. The **Moon** represents one's moods, and needs, the quality of one's emotional and feeling life. **Mercury** symbolizes how one speaks, thinks, analyzes, and communicates verbally. **Venus** signifies one's way of interacting with others, the manner in which one relates, expresses love, and seeks to be loved by others. It is also a symbol of what one values and finds desirable, beautiful, and attractive. **Mars** symbolizes one's way of asserting oneself and pursuing whatever is considered desirable and attractive. It is the symbol of the will, the vital energy that fuels activity and achievement. It also signifies how we express our anger, desires, and sexuality. Sun, Moon, Mercury, Venus, and Mars are called the "personal planets."

Jupiter and Saturn are the two "social planets." **Jupiter** represents one's capacity for planning and aspiration, and the urge for expansion, growth, improvement, conceptual understanding, adventure, and social participation. **Saturn** represents the urge for stabilization of our lives through focused and sustained effort. It symbolizes the maturity and the hard work needed to meet the pressures of material existence and to actualize the aspirations of Jupiter. Saturn also represents the desire for security and tangible accomplishment, social adjustment, conformity to tradition, and our ability to adapt to and function within larger social institutions.

Uranus, Neptune, and Pluto are called the "transpersonal planets." Physically, they are outside the orbit of Saturn and symbolically they operate beyond the laws of Saturn — defined by family, tradition, and cultural institutions. These planets are often felt to disrupt and transform the structures developed by Saturn. **Uranus** impacts the life through rebellion, defiance, unconventional behavior, expression of uniqueness, scientific pursuits, progressive or radical politics, and sudden changes of attitude or direction. **Neptune** operates through expansion, transcendence, religion or spirituality, development of intuitive or psychic capacities, or through avoidance and escapist behaviors. **Pluto** transforms through catharsis, purgation of outmoded attitudes or behaviors, and elimination of psychic impurities such as hatred, greed, resentment, or jealousy.

The Signs of the Zodiac

Each planet is placed in a sign, which shows the quality of energy with which the planet expresses itself. The signs are divisions of the ecliptic, the path of the Sun's *apparent* motion around the Earth (from the Earth's perspective; in actuality the Earth orbits around the Sun). Imagine the ecliptic as a band of light surrounding the Earth with twelve colors, with each color representing one of the twelve zodiacal signs. Now visualize a planet like Mars passing through red, blue, green, yellow, orange, purple, or black zones. Mars will express itself with a particular modality, quality, or style depending on which sign it is placed in at a given time. Signs modify and give a specific coloration to each planet. They also symbolize the cyclic passage of the seasons, with Aries, Cancer, Libra, and Capricorn corresponding respectively to the beginning of Spring, Summer, Autumn, and Winter.

Most people know their Sun sign and a few, popular phrases describing the qualities associated with that sign. Taureans, for example, are said to be stubborn, Leo natives to be vain, proud, and theatrical, and so forth. However, the zodiacal signs must be understood as a whole, as a sequence of symbols that describe twelve phases of the cycle of evolution. Let me briefly describe the story described by the zodiac.

Imagine a condition of formlessness, a vast ocean of potentialities in which no distinct entities exist, a condition of expansiveness, emptiness, and nothingness. This is the phase called **Pisces**. It is an oceanic condition that is shrouded in mist, uncertainty, and peace. It is the state of quiescence that precedes creation.

Then, a discrete, individual form begins to crystalize and seeks to become autonomous and to distinguish itself from the collective, the undifferentiated ocean of potentiality symbolized by Pisces. This phase of **emergence** of individual identity is called **Aries**. Aries, considered the first zodiacal sign in Western astrology, represents the moment of spring, the birth of individual identity. Symbolically, we could compare it to the moment of a child being born and crying out, as is to announce, "I am here!" In Aries one cultivates the strength of the physical body and personal will and focuses on oneself and one's desires.

Subsequently, the child must learn to stand on its own and, eventually, to procure food and shelter. This is the **Taurus** phase of **substantiation** of personality. In Taurus, the person must concretize the identity that emerged in Aries through concrete, productive, pragmatic activities that enable him or her to survive and sustain herself biologically. In this phase, the capacity for sensory experience evolves and brings the person into physical contact with the world.

In the next phase of growth, called Gemini, one becomes curious to explore one's surroundings, and to investigate and name the many objects one perceives. It is thus considered the phase of **extension** of the personality out into its environment. In Gemini, the mind develops and linguistic ability emerges, enabling one to communicate and to acquire and exchange information.

Next, in **Cancer**, one becomes tired of roaming in search of new experiences and begins to seek to orient oneself by putting down roots in a particular location. One now feels the nesting instinct and seeks to establish a home, a sense of family, a safe environment, and to focus one's attention on some limited area of of activity. Cancer is thus the phase of **orientation** or **focalization**. It is also the phase in which one evolves the capacity to **feel**, to care, and to build emotional bonds with others.

Then, having established a home, during the **Leo** phase of the life-cycle one becomes ready to play, take risks, and demonstrate the full powers of one's personality. This is the phase of self-expression and creativity, the dramatic **externalization** of the self. Here one seeks enjoyment, celebration of life and of one's capacities, and expression of one's love and one's individual talents in a visible manner that will be appreciated, praised, and admired by others.

In the next phase, **Virgo**, one begins to step back, analyze oneself, and recognize one's imperfections. Here one develops self-reflectiveness and may become intensely dissatisfied with oneself, often growing anxious and self-critical as a result. This is the phase in which one seeks **purification**, self-improvement through discipline or technique, training, employment, or apprenticeship. Here personal crises catalyze adjustments of one's actions in preparation for the new challenges of the second six signs.

The first six signs, Aries through Virgo, are focused on the process of individual growth, the development of individual potentials. However, the second six signs mark a new phase, focused on the tasks of social integration of the individual. In **Libra**, one begins to recognize the existence of others, to perceive them as attractive, and to seek to love, share, cooperate, and relate harmoniously and congenially. Thus, this stage focuses on **interaction** and **connection**. At this stage one experiences attraction to others and begins to learn about the dynamics of courtship. This is the phase of relationship and appreciation of beauty, and marks the entry into the social hemisphere of existence.

However, after the initial phase of loving, joyous, interaction in which relationships form and grow, a new stage is reached when two individuals attempt to not just court each other, but to actually live and work together and to find a social purpose for their relationship. In the phase of the life-cycle called **Scorpio**, the energies of relationship become productive as the two individuals attempt to work toward some common end. However, joint financial or emotional investments and commitments create new challenges; for as two people try to cooperate and work together, conflicts of will and differences of opinion inevitably arise. In Scorpio one experiences the subtle dynamics of power, anger, control, mistrust, jealousy, resentment, dominance, hostility, and aggression that arise in many deep and committed human interactions. Scorpio is concerned with the profound process of **regeneration** the individual may experience as a consequence of interpersonal crisis and the adjustments that all relationships require. The regeneration may also stem from traumatic events or a brush with death.

Subsequently, in **Sagittarius**, one steps back from the prior modes of experience and tries to understand it all. This is the phase of **comprehension** or **conceptualization**; for here one is concerned with defining beliefs, theories, and moral or philosophical doctrines that can guide one's way through life and make one's varied experiences meaningful. Sagittarius is the phase of learning, education, travel, pilgrimmage, or other experiences that expand one's intellectual and cultural horizon.

In the phase of **Capricorn**, the challenge is then to apply the principles defined in Sagittarius within the domain of social structures and institutions. Here the predominant concern is to find one's appropriate place within the social hierarchy. This is the stage at which one attempts to rise in stature and to achieve great things that will win recognition in the world. In Capricorn one strives for success by actualizing some personally meaningful project. It is the phase of **accomplishment**, and of **incarnation** of one's ideals.

In **Aquarius**, one begins to look beyond personal ambitions and achievements and to recognize oneself as a member of a collective, a member of a society at a particular moment of time and history. A new concern arises with furthering the welfare of the group, the society as a whole, and to envision new ideals and goals for the future. To pursue these ideals and goals, it is important to join together with other like-minded individuals in groups, political parties, communities, collectives, cooperatives. This is the pinnacle of the process of social integration, just as Leo, the opposite sign, was the pinnacle of the process of individualization. Here one is challenged to broaden one's awareness beyond personal concerns to social and historical issues. Thus, this is the phase of **participation**, and involvement in all activities promoting **innovation**, social change, or scientific discovery.

Finally, returning to the phase of **Pisces**, the evolutionary movement leads beyond even this socially focused activity and identification with a group and toward union with the source of all life: God, Spirit, the infinite, the divine being, the void. Here one is asked to relinquish control and all personal concern and to become one, once again, with the great ocean from which our existence as individuals emerges. During this phase of **expansion** or **universalization**, one has the opportunity to transcend oneself, and move into an expanded consciousness, awareness of God, Emptiness, or the infinite. At times this loss of individual control may be associated with experiences of powerlessness, helplessness, or victimization. However, Pisces may also in some cases be the phase of enlightenment through merging into consciousness, the formless Spirit, the source or matrix of existence.

In later chapters we will examine many examples that illustrate how to interpret a planet in a particular sign. In addition, there are numerous books available that systematically explore this topic (for example, Arroyo, 1989, and Forest, 1984).

The Astrological Houses

Each planet is placed not only in a sign but also in a house of the birth chart. The houses are divisions of the space that surround an individual at the moment of birth. Using the exact date, place, and time of birth, astrologers determine the position of the point directly overhead at the moment of birth (the "midheaven" or "MC"), the point exactly opposite the MC (the "nadir" or "IC"), the point on the Eastern horizon (the "ascendant," often called the "rising sign") and the point on the Western horizon (the "descendant"). These four angles define four quadrants of the sky, which are then further subdivided into the twelve divisions of the sky that we call the astrological houses. The houses represent specific situations and fields of life, and cover the full spectrum of human experience. Each of the twelve houses has some correspondence with one of the twelve signs. For example, in house 10 one deals with situations and concerns related to those that are the focus of the tenth sign, Capricorn.

House 1 concerns self-image and the formation of identity. House 2 concerns survival issues, money and other personal resources. House 3 concerns one's ability to communicate, think, speak, and one's capacity for mobility and free interchange with the environment and with siblings, neighbors, or other people whom one encounters in the course of daily life. House 4 concerns family life, domestic/housing issues, personal memory, one's sense of stability and orientation, and deep emotional responses. House 5 concerns self-expression, creativity, play, enjoyment, and children. House 6 concerns health, employment, training situations, self-purification, and self-analysis. House 7 is the realm of significant relationships with other persons, such as friendship and marriage. House 8 concerns the deepening of relationship through exchange of financial, emotional and sexual energies, and development of the capacity for intimacy, commitment, and responsibility to another. House 9 concerns the formation of concepts and belief systems that bestow meaning upon experience, especially as these are cultivated through study and travel. House 10 is the realm in which we apply our beliefs and principles in profession, vocation, career, contribution to society. House 11 concerns our awareness of our social and historical circumstances and our response to them, as well as participation in collectives, cooperatives, community affairs, political movements, professional organizations, or any group concerned with the future and human welfare. House 12 is the realm of solitude, voluntary retreat, introspection, altruistic activity, awareness of ancestral or karmic forces and the collective unconscious, and exploration of the inner, psychological world through meditation, dreams, or fantasy.

Each house is said to have a "dispositor," a planetary ruler determined by the sign on the cusp of the house. For example, if Leo is the sign on your 10th house cusp, then the Sun (ruler of Leo) is the dispositor of your 10th house.

Cycles

A central astrological concept is the principle of the cyclic nature of existence. All of life follows a cyclic pattern of birth, growth, decay, and new beginnings. Dane Rudhyar popularized the metaphor of the vegetation cycle to illustrate this point: in spring seeds sprout, put down roots, and grow stalks and branches. During summer flowering, fruits are produced. In autumn, leaves wither and fall to the ground to become raw material for future cycles. Finally, seeds are released that lie dormant through the winter, waiting to sprout in the subsequent spring, when a new cycle begins.

The monthly phases of the Sun and Moon exemplify this cycle of growth, decay, and rebirth. At New Moon, an impulse is released as the Moon receives new light from the Sun. This impulse develops during the first half of the lunation cycle, which emphasizes *growth of form*. A turning point is reached at the First Quarter, which Rudhyar called a "crisis in action," a moment when decisive action is required to overcome the inertia of the past and to carry forth the new impulse into actuality. At the Full Moon phase the process culminates in an illumination of purpose, leading to an objective awareness of the meaning of this cycle of existence. The plant, or the cycle of development, has reached its symbolic and existential fruition.

Subsequently, during the second half of the cycle there is a completion and reevaluation of the structures developed in the first half. A process of *dissolution of form* begins now, based on the realizations of the Full Moon phase; and this dissolution of form may be accompanied by a *growth in awareness*. At the Third Quarter phase, a "crisis in consciousness" occurs. Aspects of the past may need to be repudiated, and old beliefs may be adjusted or relinquished. Finally, as the cycle nears completion during the Balsamic Moon phase (the waning crescent Moon), there is a release of the past, a letting go, and a period of waiting in preparation for a new cycle that will commence at the next New Moon.

A human life follows a similar pattern of development. The entire lifetime constitutes the individual's cycle of existence, in which there are beginning, middle, and ending phases. The first half of life, for example, is often a process of struggling to establish a stable personal identity and material existence and can be broadly characterized as a process of growth of form. Later in life, while growth of form may indeed continue, it is also common to reevaluate the pursuits and achievements of youth and to give greater attention to questions of meaning and growth of awareness.

The birth moment is the inception of a new life-cycle, containing an implicit pattern of development that can potentially unfold during the remainder of the life-cycle. Thus, the birth chart is said to operate as a "seed pattern" for the person's life. More specifically, the birthmap helps us identify themes and areas of activity that are likely to be emphasized over the course of a lifetime. It also enables us to understand the numerous, interconnected subcycles, operating within the life-cycle as a whole, defined by the transits of the planets — each of which has a particular purpose and intention.

All events and experiences gain heightened significance when situated within the context of cycles. Just as each month there is a New Moon, a First Quarter Moon, a Full Moon, and a Third Quarter Moon, so, too, there are identifiable phases in all human experience. Thus, some periods can be interpreted as moments of new beginnings, while others may be viewed as moments requiring decisive action or changes of attitude, or as moments of completion and preparation for a new cycle.

Through reflection on astrological symbolism we come to understand that everything is cyclic and occurs in phases. From this perspective, enlightenment means understanding these cycles of development and cooperating with them. Knowledge of astrology teaches us when to act and when to wait, when to plant and when to harvest, when to dig in at home and when to set forth in pilgrimage, when to meditate or remain silent, and when to step forward and speak.

Interplanetary Aspects

Just as the lunation cycle has a number of major phases, all of the other planets enact cyclic relationships with one another. The significant phases of these relationships are called "aspects." Aspects show how the planetary functions link up and work together within the personality. Two planets placed together (like the New Moon) are said to be in "conjunction," whereas if they are directly opposite one another (180 degrees), they are in "opposition" (like the Full Moon). If they are 90 degrees apart, they form a "square" aspect. The "trine" is a 120 degree aspect, and the "sextile" is a 60 degree aspect between two planets. Other important aspects include the "quincunx" (150 degrees), the "semi-square" (45 degrees), and the "sesquiquadrate" (135 degrees). Each aspect has a slightly different flavor, with the trine and sextile showing inherent skills, talents, and the harmonious interplay of planetary energies. The other aspects represent areas where change and adjustment are necessary to allow expression of facets of the self that may at times be in conflict with one another. Even if planets are not in a classical aspect, they are also related to one another through their midpoints, the point midway between their two zodiacal placements. Tierney (1983) provides a thorough explanation of aspects. For discussion of midpoints, refer to Harding & Harvey (1990).

Transits

Examination of the signs, house placements, and aspects of the planets in the birth chart yields a symbolic portrait of the full complexity of the individual. Astrology also enables us to understand the timing of our experience of the many potentials indicated in the birth chart. The birth chart is brought to life, as it were, by transits, the continuing movements of planets through the sky, which activate the planets and angles of the birthmap. The Moon's transit through the twelve signs each month symbolizes our constantly changing emotional lives. The Sun, Venus, and Mercury pass through the entire chart every year; the transits of these inner planets show, respectively, the changing focus of our vital energy, our affections, and our mental attention. Mars takes two years to transit through the entire birth chart; its movement through the signs and houses shows where we need to take the initiative and assert ourselves vigorously to promote movement and change, even if this leads occassionally to minor frictions, irritations, and tensions. Jupiter takes twelve years to transit through the twelve signs and houses and brings growth of aspirations, plans, and desire for improvement and expansion. Saturn, Uranus, Neptune, and Pluto are slower-moving planets, and their transits are considered more momentous and more productive of deep changes in an individual's life. These transits are discussed at length in later chapters (also see Arroyo, 1978). The study of transits enables us to understand the kinds of developmental pressures and growth processes an individual may be experiencing at any given time. For example, Saturn transits (such as its return to its birth position) are always processes of maturation asking us to become more responsible in a particular area of life. In contrast, Uranus transits challenge us to break free and take chances in ways that may seem a bit wild and reckless.

An important dimension of transits mentioned frequently in this book is the study of interplanetary cycles, which examines the phasic aspects formed by pairs of transiting planets. Just as the New Moon and Full Moon represent the monthly conjunction and opposition of the Sun and Moon, the transiting cycles of other planetary pairs also have great significance. For example, the cycle of Venus and Mars helps us understand the process of joining our affections and our passions into the experience of romantic, sexual love.[1] One interplanetary transit mentioned frequently in Part III of this book is the twenty-year cycle of Jupiter and Saturn, which symbolizes the process of forming and actualizing a sense of social destiny, one's goals for accomplishment within the domain of society and culture (Ruperti, 1978). In studying interplanetary cycles, instead of following the transit of one planet in relation to natal planets and houses, one follows the movement of two transiting planets in relation to one another, from their conjunction, to their first quarter square, to opposition, to third quarter square, to their subsequent conjunction. The phases of the Jupiter-Saturn cycle measure important stages in the maturation and growth of a career or a calling in life. This principle is illustrated in detail in the biography of Tagore in Part III.

---

[1] See "Coyote's Web: The Astrological Dynamics of Relationships," in **Selected Essays** by Greg Bogart, available from Dawn Mountain Press.

Progressions

Transits are concerned with how environmental pressures activate the inherent psychological characteristics or personality traits indicated by the natal chart. However, most astrologers do not view human beings as fixed and static entities, but rather as persons who are continually growing and changing. The birth pattern is like a snapshot of the sky frozen in time, which contains an implicit continuation and resolution of the birth moment. Astrologers posit a correspondence between the planetary positions in the days after birth and developments in the corresponding years of the individual's life. Thus, if we examine the positions of the planets in the days immediately after birth, we observe changes in the birth pattern, showing the continuation or "follow through" of the birth moment. This is the method astrologers call "secondary progressions," using the formula *one day after birth equals one year of life* to measure changes occurring within the birth pattern and the individual life-world that it symbolizes. The combination of transits and progressions give astrologers two powerful means of measuring the kinds of experiences and evolutionary development an individual may face during a particular period.

The Appropriate Attitude Toward Astrological Symbolism

An ongoing topic of debate in the field of astrology is the question of whether or not we are fated to experience certain events. It is clear to most people who engage in a serious study of astrology that a great deal of predictive accuracy is indeed possible using methods such as transits and progressions (Tyl, 1991). Nevertheless, this does not necessarily imply that all events are predestined or can be foreseen astrologically.

Liz Greene's book *The Astrology of Fate* is an extended meditation on the nature of fate, prediction, and destiny in astrology. Greene describes the story of King Henri II of France, who went to two different astrologers, both of whom predicted that on a certain date the King would die in a duel from a blow to the head. Sure enough, his death occurred exactly as predicted. Greene examined the king's chart to see if she could figure out what the astrologers had looked at to predict his death. She concluded that they had focused on the king's Sun in Aries square Saturn (Aries rules battles, duels, and the head). However, she reasoned, she herself had done many charts of people with the same configuration but not one of them had suffered a fate similar to that of King Henri.

How could this be? Could it be that the predestined, "fated" quality of planetary combinations no longer holds for modern persons? Could the modern psyche have changed in such a way that we longer need to exteriorize events in order to experience the energies and archetypes of planetary combinations? Greene contends that through the mediation of symbols we can overcome the compulsion to externalize events as an expression of planetary forces and can instead internalize, and thereby transform, these energies through the magical power of symbols. She writes,

> Psychic energy tends to transform from instinctual compulsion to meaningful inner experience through the mediation of the symbol. In other words, psychic energy "introverts" if the image which corresponds to the outer compulsion emerges within the individual and if he [sic] is able to contain that compulsion through the mediating power of the image. . . . We are ultimately the inheritors of Ficino and the alchemists, who believed that the transformation of one's own substance was the only possible answer to fate. Paradoxically, this entails an embrace of one's fate. (pp. 151, 153)

I believe that this is the kind of understanding that is most useful in the study of natal astrology. Chart interpretation becomes increasingly subtle as we learn to work cooperatively with the planetary archetypes and view each of their tests as means of embracing our fate and transforming our inner substance. The magnificence of astrology is that it enables us to see such internal psychological and spiritual evolution come to life vividly in events that can be timed quite accurately using transits, progressions, and other methods.

Finally, consider these words of Hazrat Inayat Khan, a great Sufi master who lived earlier in this century:

> Be firm in faith through life's tests and trials. . . . It matters little whether you are on the top of the mountain or at the foot of it, if you are happy where you are. . . . The one who is able to keep his [her] equilibrium without being annoyed, without being troubled, gains that mastery which is needed in the evolution of life. . . . Stand through life firm as a rock in the sea, undisturbed and unmoved by its ever-rising waters (Inayat Khan, 1978).

When practiced wisely, astrology teaches us to live through each event and experience consciously, viewing it as a test or initiation, with the noble attitude toward the changes of time invoked by Inayat Khan. Through reflection on astrological symbols and the nature of cycles, we learn to remain even-minded, hopeful, and composed under all conditions, to make appropriate responses and well-timed choices, and to meet all experiences with which life presents us as initiatory lessons leading to transformation. Study of the birth chart suggests how we might express the many different components of the personality (the planets) and navigate wisely all phases of the wheel of life symbolized by the twelve signs and houses. Moreover, astrology can not only guide us toward actualization of our individual potentials, but also depicts the steps we may need to take to pursue the path of self-transcendence and spiritual awakening. That is the topic of the remainder of this book.

CHAPTER 2

Finding a Spiritual Path: The Twelve Yogas of the Zodiac

All spiritual traditions speak of a condition of enlightenment, of expanded consciousness or fully actualized spiritual potential. This has been called by many names, including *Atman, nirvana, moksa* (liberation), *satori*, cosmic consciousness, and God realization; but all traditions agree that this condition of enlightenment represents a state of inner freedom and the highest stage and goal of human evolution. To reach this condition, nearly all spiritual teachings state that we must do a *sadhana*, a discipline or practice of some kind, such as meditation. However, finding a spiritual path can be a complex affair in our era due to the wide range of options and teachings available. Seekers are confronted with an almost overwhelming array of alternatives for spiritual growth, for example, channeling, yoga, body-work and movement therapies, brain-wave synchronization audiotapes, Tantra, rebirthing, ayurvedic medicine, mystical Judaism and Christianity, Buddhism, Sufism, shamanism, out-of-body travel, lucid dreaming, macrobiotics, fasting, and transpersonal psychotherapies. While contemporary spiritual seekers have more access to information about various traditions and practices than ever before, the sheer volume and diversity of the teachings now available can be confusing, making it difficult at times to know which path to follow.

Astrology can provide invaluable guidance in the process of finding and following a road to spiritual growth and awakened consciousness. The birth chart can be viewed as a non-sectarian map of the path, containing images of the goal that is possible, and perhaps even *intended*, for us. The purpose of this chapter is to help you utilize your birth chart to discern what approach to spiritual awakening is most suited to your individual nature, both on a long-term basis and for the duration of particular transits or progressions. Above all, it is intended to inspire you to practice sadhana and thus to take conscious steps to advance spiritually.

Astrology teaches that every aspect of our incarnations as human beings is sacred and an aspect of the spiritual path — not just meditating, following a guru, or studying ancient metaphysical texts. From an astrological perspective, every event, every circumstance, and every relationship in our lives may be viewed as an opportunity for personal growth and expansion of consciousness. Astrology provides confirmation of the fact that extraordinary spiritual pursuits (Kabir, the Indian poet-saint, calls them "spiritual gymnastics") are not always necessary; and that perennial, and seemingly "ordinary," aspects of human existence — such as childbirth, earning a livelihood, or working the earth — may be complete spiritual paths. Any road, followed with consciousness and reverence, can take us to the Light. Study of the birth chart reveals that our individual lives are enactments of universal principles and thus enables us to transcend the limitations of our particular biographical perspectives. Yet it also enables us to clearly define our purpose as incarnated beings in a particular place and period of history, and thus to discern the nature of our unique spiritual paths.

In many spiritual traditions, a teacher prescribes contemplative practices that match a student's personality and stage of development. Similarly, our birth charts can help us determine for ourselves which methods or paths we could most fruitfully pursue. This application of astrology may be especially useful for those who do not adhere to traditional religious doctrines yet who feel drawn toward a life of transformation. Moreover, the complexities of the birth chart accurately reflect the way that many facets of our lives and our personalities can be integrated to develop an individualized sadhana, a uniquely appropriate path. In many cases this will indicate a need to blend several different pursuits, for example a combination of music, meditation, parenting, and martial arts.

Study of the birth chart can help us understand the nature and stages of the path leading to transformation of awareness. Some of the great sages of ancient India understood this, and there was a strong connection between astrology and contemplative practices such as yoga in their spiritual traditions (Braha, 1986; Frawley, 1991). In fact, in Indian astrological scriptures certain planetary combinations are known as *yogas*, suggesting that particular natal configurations represent karmically determined patterns that are to serve as an individual's evolutionary path toward enlightenment. (Those interested in studying the system of planetary yogas in Hindu astrology should consult books such as Raman (1972) and an experienced teacher). The ancient Indian sages recognized that no single approach to spiritual growth is suitable for everyone, that there are numerous yogic paths that all lead to God, enlightenment, or higher consciousness, and that astrology may be used to assist each person in finding the most suitable path. Thus, the planetary yogas in the natal chart were utilized to discern the proper approach to yoga or spiritual life for that individual.

The Twelve Yogas of the Zodiac: A Model for Spiritual Development

This chapter takes a contemporary approach to this dimension of astrology, describing how the most fundamental astrological symbols, the twelve zodiacal signs, may be viewed as demarcating twelve essential yogas or paths of spiritual development. I associate the twelve signs with Sanskrit terms from the Indian yogic tradition because I feel these terms describe many dimensions of the spiritual path with unique subtlety.

The symbols of the zodiac have been explained by innumerable authors and can be understood in an almost infinite variety of ways. Figure 1 summarizes some of the keywords I used in the previous chapter to describe the zodiacal signs. Please take some time to study Figures 2 and 3, which provide several sets of additional keywords that can be used to understand the signs. Note that I purposely avoid using traditional, stereotypical descriptions of the qualities of each sign, such as equating Taurus with stubbornness or Leo with vanity and egotism, to suggest alternative ways of understanding these perennially fascinating symbols.

In the pages that follow I link the meanings of the signs with their ruling planets and the twelve houses of the birth chart in a manner similar to the "astrological alphabet" popularized by Zipporah Dobyns, one of the great astrologers of this century. In this system (Dobyns & Roof, 1973), the first sign, Aries, house 1, and the planetary ruler of Aries, Mars, all refer to similar themes, which she describes as "self will in spontaneous action; initiative, impulse, . . . pioneering spirit, vitality, . . . enthusiasm for the new. . . ." Taurus, its ruler Venus, and the 2nd house comprise the second letter of the alphabetical alphabet: "Pleasure in manipulating the physical sense world; comfort, . . . contentment, love of beauty in tangible possessions. . . ." Dobyns' model is a clear way of breaking down the complexity of the birth chart into basic themes.

Similarly, in the model of "The Twelve Yogas of the Zodiac" presented here, the signs, their planetary rulers, and the house corresponding to each sign are interpreted as symbols of twelve dimensions or phases of the journey of awakening (Figure 4). This model suggests some of the approaches to spiritual growth that you might pursue if you have emphasis in your birthmap on particular signs, houses, or planets. An example of such natal emphasis would be having the Sun in Taurus and Saturn in the 2nd house; or the Moon in Pisces and Neptune (ruler of Pisces) conjunct the ascendant; or having several planets placed in the same sign or house. Any planet closely aspecting the Sun, Moon, or ascendant ruler, or conjunct an angle of the birth chart may be said to be accentuated.

This chapter utilizes many case examples to convey the flavor of these twelve yogas. As you read through the examples, reflect on your own birthchart and what it might say about the path, or combination of paths, that is most appropriate for you. According to the makeup of your particular horoscope, one or more of the yogas described below will be emphasized more than others. If one's natal chart features a strong aspect of Sun and Saturn, the Moon in Capricorn, and several planets in the 10th house, there would obviously be a significant emphasis on the Capricorn/10th house yoga. More typically, the natal chart will indicate a need to focus on several of these paths. Moreover, due to the influence of transits and progressions, you will need to grapple with (and hopefully master)

Figure 1: Zodiac as 12 Phases of Evolution

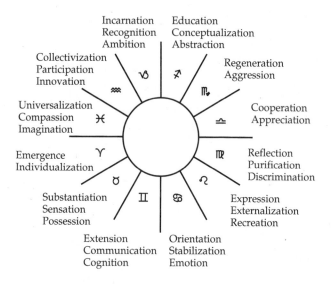

Figure 2: Mandala of 12 Modes of Activity

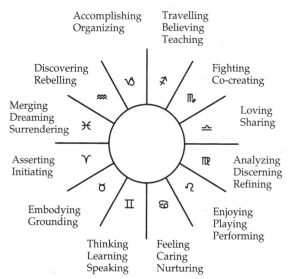

Figure 3: Mandala of Central Human Concerns

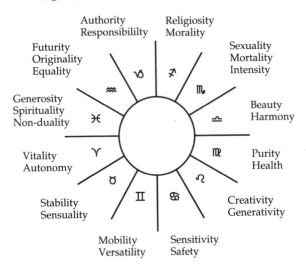

Authority
Responsibililty

Religiosity
Morality

Futurity
Originality
Equality

Sexuality
Mortality
Intensity

Generosity
Spirituality
Non-duality

Beauty
Harmony

Vitality
Autonomy

Purity
Health

Stability
Sensuality

Creativity
Generativity

Mobility
Versatility

Sensitivity
Safety

Figure 4: Mandala of the Twelve Yogas of the Zodiac

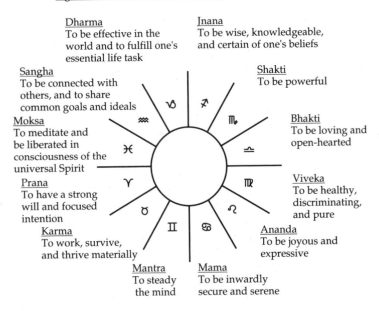

Dharma
To be effective in the
world and to fulfill one's
essential life task

Jnana
To be wise, knowledgeable,
and certain of one's beliefs

Sangha
To be connected with
others, and to share
common goals and ideals

Shakti
To be powerful

Moksa
To meditate and
be liberated in
consciousness of the
universal Spirit

Bhakti
To be loving and
open-hearted

Prana
To have a strong
will and focused
intention

Viveka
To be healthy,
discriminating,
and pure

Karma
To work, survive,
and thrive materially

Ananda
To be joyous and
expressive

Mantra
To steady
the mind

Mama
To be inwardly
secure and serene

all of them at some point in the course of life. In Part III, we will apply these principles to the study of the birth charts of seven renowned twentieth century spiritual teachers.

Please note that each natal planetary placement refers to issues deriving from both the planet's sign and house. To understand the meaning of a placement of the Sun in Scorpio in the 5th house, refer to the issues pertinent to both Leo/5th house and Scorpio/8th house.

The charts of some famous people are noted below. These charts are found at the end of this chapter.

Aries/Mars/1st House: Awakening Prana: The Yoga of Vitality and Identity

If your birth chart emphasizes the sign Aries, its ruler Mars, or the 1st house, your spiritual path may focus on defining your personal identity, asserting your will, and acting on your desires. While at other stages of the evolutionary process you are challenged to transcend identification with a particular self-construct or self-image, at this stage your personal qualities, characteristics, and behaviors must be clearly recognized and expressed. For it is only through the particular form and vehicle of a well defined personality that spiritual energies can express themselves. As American spiritual teacher Ram Dass says, "You have to be somebody before you can be nobody." Therefore, give your attention here to the need for a clear sense of what and who you are as an individual.

Planets in the 1st house symbolize important facets of our identity and self-image, behaviors and personal characteristics that we present spontaneously to the world. For example, Ram Dass (see Chapter 12) has Jupiter and Pluto in his 1st house, an apt symbol for a powerful, influential (Pluto) teacher (Jupiter). A man with Uranus conjunct his ascendant gradually outgrew the "oddball" self-image of his youth and emerged as a highly inventive computer science wizard. A young woman with Mars in her 1st house pursued a career in gymnastics and thrived on the excitement of competition. Another woman, with Neptune in her 1st house, had many prophetic, psychic dreams.

A man whose unconventional parents raised him in a 1960s hippie commune had Saturn placed in his 1st house. He vehemently rejected his parents' values and lifestyle, was a highly serious student of history, became a dentist, and got involved with several conservative (Saturn) political and religious organizations. His central priority in life was to achieve financial and professional stability.

Gordon Michael Scallion, a well known psychic and futurist, has Uranus and Saturn in the 1st house (Chart 1). Before becoming a psychic he was an engineer, and he has maintained a strong interest in science and new technologies (Uranus). In his lectures and writings he presents channeled information and prophecies of earthquakes and other Earth Changes in a very believable, credible way. His visible identity (1st house) is that of a unique person who expresses innovative, original ideas (Uranus in Gemini) in a clear, organized, sensible manner (Saturn in Gemini).

Prominent placement of Mars or planets in Aries may suggest that it is important for you to strengthen or restructure your physical body through vigorous exercise or practices like *hatha yoga* (physical postures) and *pranayama* (breathing exercises), Postural Integration, or Bioenergetics. All of these can help you express your identity through a stronger, more vital and balanced, and less obstructed physical vehicle. Yoga postures and pranayama are particularly important means of awakening and steadying the **prana** (vital energy) or "quieting the vital" (to use Sri Aurobindo's phrase) in order to still the mind and enter deeper states of consciousness. With an emphasis here, you may also feel a strong need to transform your expression of passions and instinctual drives, or to learn to either curb your desires or to act on them more directly and assertively. It may also indicate a need to develop a strong personal will to actualize your essential identity.

A 45 year-old man with Sun in Aries in the 5th house (which often concerns performance and athletics), gave up his meditation practice because it made him feel "dead." Instead he took up acting classes and weight lifting, both of which, he said, made him feel "energetic and alive."

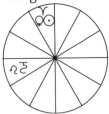

A teenager with natal Saturn in her 1st house in Leo and a Sun-Venus conjunction in Aries in her 10th house is physically beautiful (Venus conjunct Sun), exceptionally gifted as an artist and musician (Venus), and at times performs and paints with an inspired exuberance and vitality that is awesome to witness. However, she also has a painfully shy streak and a negative self-image (Saturn in 1st house) that inhibit her creativity (see Leo). I anticipate that her spiritual path will focus on resolving these issues of personal identity so that she is ultimately able to perceive and express herself freely as a spirited, lively, passionate individual (Sun in Aries).

Dane Rudhyar, whose Aries Sun was placed in the 3rd house (thinking, writing), was an intellectual and spiritual pioneer, a voice for original ideas that emerged through him in the form of inspired poetry and philosophical concepts (Chart 2). His dynamic personal identity was expressed in his voluminous writings.

Sexuality is a central issue for Aries and its ruler Mars, less because of the intense interpersonal dynamics and transformations that result (see Scorpio), but because of the feeling of vitality and aliveness that this dimension of life can awaken. Wilhelm Reich, whose psychological theories and therapeutic practices focused on sexual healing, the development of the capacity for full orgasmic potency, and the dissolution of "character armor" at the level of physical musculature, had the Sun placed in Aries square to Mars in Cancer.

John Lennon married Yoko Ono in 1969 while transiting Uranus and Jupiter in Libra were passing over his natal Mars (Chart 3). Soon after their marriage John and Yoko held a "bed-in" for peace. They lay in bed, made love, and gave interviews in which they talked about peace and war. This open display and celebration of sexuality was intended to be a revolutionary act, a proclamation of sexual freedom and liberation (Uranus conjunct Mars).

Persons with strong natal aspects between Mars and Saturn may be attracted to hatha yoga because of the increased strength and concentration of vital energies that this practice promotes. Persons with strong aspects of Mars and Uranus may prefer a more exuberant or vigourous practice such as a martial art. Persons with prominent Mars-Jupiter aspects are often drawn to adventurous, outdoor activities, or situations requiring bravery, heroism, and valor. For example, a man who has spent years involved with many spiritual practices, said his most powerful enlightenment experience occurred while fighting a major forest fire, while transiting Uranus was conjunct his natal Mars-Jupiter conjunction. Regardless of the exact aspect involved, if the planet Mars is prominent in your chart, an important spiritual task is to strengthen or redirect the expression of physical and sexual energies. Yogi Amrit Desai, founder of the Kripalu community and an inspired teacher of hatha yoga, has Mars (ruler of Aries) placed on his midheaven (Chart 4). His teachings emphasize awakening and directing vital energy (*prana*) through yoga postures (*asanas*) and breathing practices. He also recommends regular aerobic exercise such as running. (For more on Amrit Desai, see Pisces section below).

Taurus/Venus/2nd House: Karma Yoga and the Path of Money and Enjoyment

With a natal emphasis on Taurus, its ruler Venus, or the 2nd house, money and physical comfort may be important priorities. You may need to make sustained efforts to substantiate your personal identity by working to achieve a stable, secure material existence, and by developing self-esteem and a sense of solidity, competence, or abundance. Here the path may be to enjoy the serenity that comes from material stability and sensuous enjoyment. Although these aspects of human life are much reviled by some spiritual teachings, they are an important facet of our incarnate existence. It is important not to become totally preoccupied with glutting oneself with sensual experience and to remember that, as the Buddha taught, everything is impermanent, including pleasure. But that is not to say that moderate enjoyment and satisfaction do not have a place in a balanced spiritual life.

Taurus and the 2nd house are both concerned with finding means of right livelihood; evaluating and defining your material needs and your life's fundamental values; and using resources appropriately. Emphasis here may also indicate that you need to develop a non-clinging, non-avaricious attitude. You may experience considerable inner growth through the path of *karma yoga*, the path of effort and action; for in Taurus and the 2nd house the inexorable law of karma (action and reaction) gives us immediate feedback about the quality of our actions or attitudes. The Taurus and 2nd house yoga is a process of learning to generate abundance through what spiritual teacher David Spangler has called "the laws of manifestation."

A man with Sun in Taurus and in the 2nd house gradually drifted away from his involvement with psychic readings and channeled teachings, and became more focused on the pursuit of a lucrative job. He now proclaims, "Making money is my spiritual path."

A woman with Mars, Sun, and Moon in the 2nd house in Capricorn works for a large international bank. Because these planets are square to Neptune in the 11th house (groups), she has often dreamed of quitting her job and living in a rural spiritual community. However, as she is a single mother with two small children 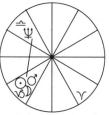 (Mars, ruler of 5th house, conjunct Sun), she recognizes that for the time being her path is to sustain her family materially, and to pay occasional visits to the ashram. Thus, she has effectively handled the tension between her 2nd house needs to be a strong provider and her neptunian spiritual ideal.

A man with a Sun-Mercury conjunction in Gemini in the 2nd house has earned his livelihood through a variety of business activities and is fascinated with money and finance.

A man with Sun, Moon, and Venus in Taurus and a Saturn-Pluto conjunction in Leo in the 2nd house is a multi-millionaire with a large stock portfolio who worries constantly about losing all of his money through bad investments. He has had to overcome his financial anxiety and learn how to spend and enjoy his wealth! However, as his Sun-Moon in Taurus are placed in the 12th house (altruism), he is also a philanthropist who secretly gives away large sums of money to others.

A socially conscious woman with a Sun-Mars conjunction in Taurus in the 8th house (joint resources), square to Saturn and Pluto in the 11th house (social awareness, organizational involvements) is married to a very wealthy man. While she enjoys the comfort that this marriage affords her, she is also profoundly troubled by the contrast between their opulent, luxurious, suburban lifestyle and her awareness of the pervasive poverty and suffering in the world (Saturn-Pluto in the 11th). She has had many arguments with her husband because of her desire to contribute money to social causes, and only agreed to stay in the marriage after he reassured her he would make regular financial contributions to charitable organizations.

A man with Sun in Taurus opposite Neptune was quite spaced out and reported that he felt like he was "not in his body." He began to feel more grounded when he stopped smoking marijuana

(Neptune) and began practicing sensory awareness exercises that made him more aware of his body, and that helped him function more effectively in the world.

Major aspects to Venus often define or change a person's relationship to wealth and possessions. Financial tycoon Donald Trump has natal Venus conjunct Saturn and square Jupiter. During a major transit of Uranus to his natal Venus in Taurus, Rabindranath Tagore began to reevaluate his materialistic values.

Sufi Master Hazrat Inayat Khan had Saturn conjunct Neptune in his 2nd house (Chart 5). Although he longed for solitude and retreat from the world, his path was to ground his profoundly expanded awareness in the material world by establishing the Sufi Order. His teachings emphasize application of the principles of mysticism to everyday life as well as attunement to the splendor and sacredness of Nature (Neptune in Taurus).

Gemini/Mercury/3rd House: Mantra Yoga: Transformation of the Mind

Gemini and the 3rd house are concerned with development of the mind and mastery of language and communication skills. If you have prominent placements of planets here (or an accentuated Mercury), your spiritual path may focus on learning to form positive thoughts and mental images, practicing what the Buddhists call "right speech," or developing mental concentration. Most spiritual traditions emphasize techniques for cleansing of the mind, whether this means observation of the flow of thought through mindfulness practices like *zazen* or *vipassana* meditation; consciously forming thoughts of peace and compassion toward others; the practice of affirmations; or repetition and chanting of *mantras*, sacred sounds, and prayers. All of these are important spiritual practices associated with these areas of the chart. Moreover, since Gemini and the 3rd house refer to the narrative faculty, use your planets here to communicate your ideas and tell your story through speaking or writing. Gemini and the 3rd house correspond to what Kashmir Shaivism (a philosophy we will discuss further in Chapter 5) calls *maitrika shakti*, the power of language — which both creates and describes the manifest world of form, *and* ultimately leads to liberation from its grasp through the vibratory power of *mantra* (see Muller-Ortega, 1989 for discussion of *mantra yoga*).

For example, a woman with Venus, Mercury, and Jupiter in Gemini discovered that her favorite spiritual practices were story-telling and the Progoff Intensive Journal method. A man with Sun and Moon in the 3rd house opposite Neptune began to write poetry and fiction in his spare time, an activity he found extremely satisfying. A man with a Mercury-Saturn conjunction in the 10th house makes his living devising solutions to very complex practical problems; he is a landscape architect and an engineer. Another, with Mercury conjunct Neptune likes nothing better than to read mystery novels to relax his mind. A woman with Mercury square Neptune is deeply immersed in reading and writing poetry, and considers this her main spiritual discipline. A man with a Sun-Saturn-Neptune conjunction in his 3rd house experienced deep states of meditation through intense, concentrated practice of *mantra yoga*.

Dane Rudhyar, who published 52 books and wrote many other unpublished manuscripts, had Sun in the 3rd house and a conjunction of Mars, Jupiter, Neptune, and Pluto in Gemini (Chart 2).

Poet Gary Snyder has Mercury, Venus, and Jupiter in Gemini, and Saturn in the 3rd house trine the Sun. He is a master of naturalistic description, and his words are filled with a fierce, incantatory power (Saturn in 3rd opposite Pluto, square Mars-Uranus). Poet and translator Robert Bly has Mercury near his ascendant. Novelist Joyce Carol Oates has Sun and Mercury in Gemini. Andrew Harvey, who has written several books of translations of mystical poetry and descriptions of his own spiritual journey, has Sun, Moon, and Mars in Gemini. Poet Allen Ginsberg also has a Sun-Mercury conjunction in Gemini. His writings emphasize detailed, "close to the nose" descriptions of events, feelings, people, and places. William Butler Yeats, with a Sun-Uranus conjunction in Gemini in the 5th house (creativity), crafted words into completely original poetic utterances.

Cancer/Moon/4th House: Mama Yoga: The Path of Emotion, Memory, and Family

Cancer, its ruler Moon, and the 4th house concern one's capacity to feel, as well as one's sense of place, feelings of rootedness, and ability to draw sustenance and inspiration from local or traditional customs and one's family, racial, or national heritage. Many spiritual traditions denigrate the entanglements of family life and encourage detachment from emotions. Nevertheless, if you have an emphasis here in your birth chart, it may be important to follow the path of the householder, and to deal with the complex politics and intense emotions of family life. Or you may need to explore some form of "emotional yoga" by healing the past, developing the capacity for interpersonal bonding, nurturance, and tenderness, resolving family-of-origin issues, and understanding your family dynamics to gain insight into the inter-generational transmission of dysfunctional behavior. In many cases, such processes are greatly facilitated through psychotherapy. Cancer and the 4th house are the areas of the chart that focus on emotional dynamics, memory, and resolution of early developmental issues. Therefore, with natal placements here, your growth may require some form of "**mama yoga**," the yoga of clarifying emotions and establishing stronger, more harmonious relations with one's interior/emotional and exterior/family roots. You may also flourish through cultivation of what are traditionally known as the domestic arts, such as cooking and gardening. This is true for men as well as for women!

Wendell Berry, a great contemporary American novelist and essayist, writes extensively about agricultural issues and is a proponent of the "down home" values of family, farm, local community, and land conservation. He has natal Venus in Cancer, Mercury and Pluto in Cancer in the 3rd house (writing), and Sun in the 4th house (Chart 6).

Victor, a thirty year-old Buddhist, came into therapy during Saturn's return to its natal position in the 4th house. He had been estranged from his family for many years while he practiced meditation on retreat in India. He was beginning to recognize his need for greater stability, and was considering buying a home. He went to visit his family-of-origin and had a very meaningful exchange with his father, who agreed to loan him a large sum of money to make a down payment on a house. By the end of his Saturn return, he had managed to bring his parents and five siblings together for several sessions with a family therapist. Many "old scores" were settled, and, for the first time, he felt like he had a close family. He felt a dramatic increase in his emotional stability due to the new respect, acknowledgement, and support he felt from his family. This, in turn, helped his meditation practice.

A woman with Sun, Venus, and Mercury in Cancer complained that her boyfriend wanted her to participate in fire walks, psychedelic drug experiments, and intense breathing exercises. Only gradually was the boyfriend able to recognize and appreciate the fact that the spiritual path she felt drawn to involved gardening, studying herbs and flower remedies, cooking sumptuous meals, savoring memories, and understanding her rich emotional life.

A woman with Sun in Cancer in the 2nd house found fulfillment in drying, canning, and storing food grown in her garden.

A woman named "Barbara" with Sun, Venus, and Uranus conjunct in Cancer in the 8th house (the house of joint finances, interpersonal disagreements) had assiduously avoided marriage despite many proposals that had been offered. She had been particularly resistant to being trapped in traditional female roles as wife, 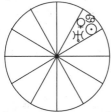 mother, and "homemaker" (Uranus, planet of freedom, rebellion, and independence, conjunct Venus-Sun in Cancer). She was particularly uncomfortable with the idea of caring for children and being expected to cook for a family. Now, at age 40, she was considering marriage and moved to a new city to live with her boyfriend, "Ed." Although Ed had planned to sell the house that he had lived in with his ex-wife and his children, he had been unable to do so, and Barbara was quite unhappy living in the same house that had been the scene of Ed's previous marriage. Strong feelings of insecurity (Cancer) about her centrality in Ed's life were aroused by the constant, nagging presence of Ed's ex-wife, "Laura," who constantly called and visited the house to make arrangements for child-care. Barbara was quite emotionally distraught as not only did she feel that this was not her home but she also had to be economically dependent (Cancer: dependency; 8th house: money received from another person) on Ed for several months while she found employment in the new location. A person with many planets in Cancer thrives in a warm, cozy, comfortable home, and with strong emotional bonds of family. However, this home felt to her like it was laden with the memories of Ed's prior marriage, and she experienced intense emotional conflicts about living with Ed's son, "William." Gradually, however, Barbara began to accept her stepson, and even Laura, as part of her family — unconventional a family as it was (Uranus in Cancer) — and adjusted to the inevitable tensions of family life. As she became clearer about her own feelings, she also began to be able to offer Ed her emotional support during this difficult transition. She realized that if she wanted to be the "woman of the household" she would have to make a home for herself and her new blended family. To her amazement, she found a deep reservoir of "mama" energy inside of her that grew as she nurtured Ed and William, and for the first time discovered that she truly enjoyed cooking and baking bread. She soon rebelled against the use of cookbooks, however, and began developing her own strange but unique recipes (Sun-Uranus in Cancer).

Leo/Sun/5th House: Ananda Yoga: The Path of Self-Expression, Creativity, and Joy

Leo represents the phase of evolution in which the full splendor, radiance, and grandeur of the self shine forth in celebration of one's individuality. With an emphasis on Leo or the 5th house one is asked not to transcend the self (as in Pisces/12th house) but to express oneself and demonstrate one's talents and creativity. If your chart accentuates these domains then highly serious and ascetic approaches to spiritual growth may not be appropriate for you. Instead you might prefer the paths of festivity, celebration, and play; parenting and relationships with children; or self-expression through artistic works, athletics, dance, drama, or other performance arts. Through all of these means, your inner transformation and realizations can be expressed outwardly in the world as **ananda** or joy. In Kashmir Shaivism, the *ananda shakti* refers to the inherent bliss of Supreme Consciousness, which needs nothing beyond itself and finds satisfaction in its own being. Similarly, emphasis here in the birth chart may refer to the capacity to feel pride, joy, and satisfaction in one's own being and activities, free of the need for admiration or adulation from others.

Since the natal Sun is a central symbol in every birth chart, the Sun's sign and house placement provides essential information about the context in which one is likely to seek expression of the self. See Part III for examples.

A woman with a Moon-Mars conjunction in Leo in her 10th house felt that her true calling in life was to have many children.

A woman with natal Pluto in her 5th house, opposite Sun, had a profoundly mystical experience while giving birth and felt that she herself was reborn in the process.

A woman with Jupiter and Mars in Leo in her tenth house leads workshops for children and adults on creativity, involving mask-making, dance, music, drawing, and the recovery of playfulness.

A woman with Venus and Mars in the 5th house decided at age 41 to take piano lessons and by age 48 was performing in jazz clubs.

Actress Liv Ullman has Sun and Mercury conjunct in the 5th house, and Pluto in Leo conjunct the ascendant (Chart 7). Many of her film performances depict the intense emotions of love, marriage, and family life (Mars and Venus in Scorpio in the 4th house; Moon in 4th house). She has also brought a profound philosophical reflectiveness (Sun in Sagittarius) to her work as a creative artist (5th house).

Musician Bruce Springsteen has Sun, Moon, Mercury, Venus, and Neptune in his 5th house (in Libra) and Mars-Pluto in Leo in his 3rd house. He is known for his intensely energetic and heart-felt concert performances (5th house), and for his passionate voice and song lyrics (Mars-Pluto in 3rd house). Guitarist Jerry Garcia of the Grateful Dead has Sun, Mercury, and Pluto in Leo. Mozart, a unique creative genius, had Sun, Mercury, and Saturn in the 5th house, in Aquarius. William Blake, the visionary poet and artist, had Sun, Mercury, and Jupiter in Sagittarius in the 5th house. Picasso had Moon in the 5th house. Poet Anne Waldman has Moon in Sagittarius in the 5th house trine her Sun in the 10th house; she is well known for her dramatic performances of her writings.

Virgo/Mercury/6th House: Viveka Yoga: The Way of Discrimination, and the Yoga of Apprenticeship or Discipleship

An emphasis in the birth chart on Virgo or the 6th house may show a strong need for self-analysis, self-purification, and self-improvement through technique, for example by practicing a *sadhana* or spiritual discipline. Emphasis here can suggest that physical illness may provide opportunities for transformation through adjustments in personal habits, diet, or exercise routines, and by learning the principles of mind-body healing.

Virgo and the 6th House are concerned with situations of training such as discipleship and apprenticeship, so these might be desirable to pursue with planets placed here. In many yogic traditions *guru seva* (service to the Guru) and mindful labor in general are considered complete spiritual disciplines. These areas of the chart also refer to one's skill in mastering job-related tasks and may point to the need to undertake some form of skill development or vocational training in order to procure better employment.

With planets here, you may need to develop **viveka**, i.e., discrimination. This may simply mean learning to discern for oneself what foods, habits, or activities are healthy and which are not. However, in a more subtle sense, viveka refers to the capacity to discriminate the real from the unreal, the eternal from the transitory, the true nature of mind and consciousness from the ever-changing flow of thought and perception. This essential element of spiritual practice enables consciousness to turn back upon itself, making possible the inner plunge signified by Pisces and the 12th house. To develop discrimination and inner purity it may be helpful to follow moral disciplines such as those described in Patanjali's Yoga Sutras, the Bible's Ten Commandments, and many Buddhist texts. As Hazrat Inayat Khan (1978) said, "A pure life and a clear conscience are like bread and wine for the soul." If your chart stresses Virgo or the 6th house, try to be discriminating and pure without becoming overly obsessive, anxious, or wracked by guilt about your imperfections or impurities.

A woman with three planets in Virgo, in the 6th house, suffers from Chronic Fatigue Syndrome. After becoming disillusioned with traditional medical treatment, she has reexamined her diet and experimented with nutritional supplements and alternative forms of medicine, such as acupuncture and herbology. The effort to regenerate her body has become a primary focus of her spiritual quest.

A 50 year-old man did an extended fast at a rural holistic health center during a transit of Jupiter through his 6th house.

A man with a conjunction of Mars-Jupiter and Sun in Leo in the 6th house was a juggler, whose highly precise routine required constant practice and rehearsal.

A woman with Saturn conjunct the Ascendant in Virgo was painfully self-critical, and often complained about the drudgery of having to work for a living. However, she also had a Sun-Jupiter-Venus conjunction in Aquarius in the 6th house and was always able to find employment in new and unusual fields that gave her a wide range of skills in a variety of trades.

A man with a Mars-Saturn conjunction in the 6th house became seriously ill while traveling in India. This experience caused him to radically change his diet and to learn about homeopathic medicine, in which he became quite skilled. During this time he also learned the disciplines of hatha yoga, which he has practiced with great vigor on a daily basis for over 25 years.

Carl Jung, who for an important period of his life was a disciple of Sigmund Freud, had a conjunction of Mercury and Venus in Cancer in the 6th house (Chart 8). In 1907, while transiting Neptune passed over Mercury and Venus, Jung first corresponded with Freud. At the time of their first meeting, during which they conversed for 13 hours without a break, transiting Jupiter was also in Cancer conjunct natal Venus. Their relationship intensified between 1908 and 1911 while transiting Neptune was conjunct Mercury-Venus and transiting Uranus opposed Mercury-Venus from Capricorn. The opposition of two transpersonal planets, Neptune and Uranus, symbolized a revelation of many new insights about the nature of religion, myth, symbols, the unconscious mind, and human consciousness itself that had a transformative effect on the thinking of these two men and consequently on all of humanity. The power of the Uranus-Neptune opposition was focused through Jung's Mercury-Venus in the 6th house, and thus this discipleship and training under Freud's guidance generated new ideas (Uranus and Neptune aspecting Mercury) that were a major contribution to the growth of modern psychology and twentieth century culture. This illustrates how transits of the outer, trans-saturnian planets (such as the 1992-1993 conjunction of Uranus and Neptune) operate through individual personalities and lives to bring about changes that impact all of humanity.

Libra/Venus/7th House: Bhakti Yoga and the Path of Love and Relationship

The sign of Libra represents the experience of love, harmony, and beauty. With planets placed in Libra or the 7th house, your spiritual evolution may in part occur through the dynamics of friendships and relationships. Simply put, you may need to have close friends or a partner in love if your horoscope emphasizes these areas. Indeed, while spiritual aspirants in some traditions were encouraged to live alone and to renounce the search for human love, learning to love and live with another person may be one of the most challenging and satisfying spiritual paths of all (See Vissell & Vissell, 1984). Following the couple's journey may be an important aspect of your path, challenging you to deepen your capacity to love as well as to recognize and withdraw projections upon others. Your path could also focus on developing **bhakti**, pure devotion to God, Spirit, or the Divine Being, and learning to open your heart through devotional practices as well as through worshipping the Light in your earthly Beloved. You may also draw great inspiration from appreciation of art, music, or other beautiful forms.

A 46 year-old woman with four planets in Libra in the 4th house has begun a new career in hotel management, giving her the opportunity for many friendly, pleasant interactions with others. She also finds great pleasure in painting.

A man with Venus in the 10th house is a popular recording artist who has had the conviction since his early childhood that he would one day be a famous musician.

Another man with Venus in the 10th house and Sun, Moon, Mercury, and Neptune in Libra in the 8th is a talented painter and computer graphics artist. His challenge has been to professionalize his art (Venus in 10th) and to create a business through which he can elicit financial investments from others (8th house) to fund his projects. His work as an artist is his way of attuning to, and expressing, his perception of divine beauty and perfection.

A woman who had spent eleven years as a monk got married when transiting Saturn passed through her 7th house, conjunct her natal Moon, Venus, and Jupiter.

A woman with Uranus conjunct the descendant in Cancer found that marriage inhibited her freedom too much, parted with her husband, and made a conscious decision to remain alone. Some years later, she and another woman decided they wanted to raise a child together, and, with her ex-husband's assistance, they eventually were able to do so.

Jean Paul Sartre, who had a famous long-term relationship with Simone de Beauvoir, had a Venus-Jupiter conjunction in his 7th house. Sufi Master Hazrat Inayat Khan, who had a close natal square of Venus and Neptune, began his career as a performing musician and had profound experiences of God-consciousness through music (Chart 5). He also married and was quite loving and devoted to his wife, as well as to his many *mureeds* (disciples).

Carl Jung had a Sun-Uranus conjunction in his 7th house (Chart 8). Returning briefly to the relationship of Freud and Jung, tension between the two men began to grow when transiting Uranus crossed Jung's ascendant in 1911 and Jung started to express a more independent viewpoint that was viewed as radical and rebellious by

Freud. The two men finally broke off all personal relations when transiting Uranus opposed Jung's natal Sun-Uranus in the 7th house. Ultimately Jung's development as an original thinker required freedom from this relationship.

John Lennon's Sun was placed in Libra, and near the cusp of the 7th house: Lennon's central life-purpose was to express his identity as a lover and musician (Chart 3). He also attended art school before he became a rock and roll musician. In 1967, during Saturn's transit opposite his Libra Sun, John became involved with Yoko Ono, an artist in her own right who encouraged the full range of John's artistic activity. Some years later, while transiting Uranus was conjunct his Libra Sun, John separated from Yoko and his experience of himself as a marital partner went through changes and major upsets. John returned to Yoko in 1975 when Jupiter transited opposite the Libra Sun. Transiting Saturn was squaring his natal Sun, which also indicated a need to focus on the primacy of his marital relationship. Although Saturn is often depicted as a planet that creates suffering, sorrows, and difficulties, it only does this if we are unable to accept responsibility, discipline, and commitments. If we are willing to embrace the virtues of sobriety and realism, and to straighten our lives out, Saturn can help us build structures that will endure. During this stabilizing Saturn transit to his natal Libra Sun, John settled down, reduced his drug use, began eating a macrobiotic diet, and became more mature as a husband and father.

Scorpio/Mars/Pluto/8th House: Shakti: The Yoga of Power, Sexuality, and Regeneration

Natal emphasis on the sign Scorpio, its rulers Pluto and Mars, or the 8th house may indicate a focus on transformation or generation of power through the intensities of human interaction and periodic experiences of interpersonal crisis. Traditional astrology books often state that Scorpio and the 8th house are concerned with death and rebirth or occult power, not making it sufficiently clear that experiences of death-rebirth or of the dynamics of power often occur in the context of interpersonal relationships. With major placements in Scorpio or 8th house, you may be deeply moved by encounters with others, have powerful confrontations with existential realities like death, or need to learn many lessons about cooperation and the ability to work together with others. Through situations involving joint finances, business ventures, and financial and emotional investments, you may come to better understand the dynamics of human aggression, disagreements, conflicts of will, resentment, hostility, possessiveness, and jealousy. These circumstances can give rise to a deeper maturity about sexuality, interpersonal commitments, and the capacity for intimacy.

Planets placed here may also indicate the importance of rites of passage, resolution of sexual issues, the need to transform your use of personal power, and transmutation of aggression and anger. With an emphasis here it may be very important for you to be committed to the principle of non-violence. It may also suggest that you should pursue a spiritual path focused on the generation of **shakti** or spiritual power, for example through sexuality, tantric practices, magic and ritual, *kundalini yoga,* or *shaktipat* initiation (described in Chapters 6 and 9).

A 33 year-old woman, with transiting Saturn conjunct her natal Sun in Scorpio in the 7th house, had been fighting with her husband for many months. Several sessions of marital counseling had only caused their conflicts and hostilities to escalate further. She had grave misgivings about letting negative feelings surface, as she was a deeply religious Christian and felt that she should be loving and forgiving. Over time, however, she realized that she indeed had many resentments toward her husband that she needed to express to feel at peace with herself and with God. She also needed to address many sexual issues with her husband.

A 45 year-old man with Mars in Aquarius and unaspected to any other planet, and Mars' dispositor, Uranus, in the 8th house was completely and voluntarily celibate and reported that he had never had the slightest interest in sex. In contrast, three men, one with Sun in the 8th house, the second with Sun in Scorpio in the 1st house, the third with a Moon-Mars conjunction in Scorpio, were all completely obsessed with their sexual lives and considered sexuality to be central to their spirituality.

A woman with Sun in Capricorn in the 8th house felt that the work she did in association with owning her own business was the most fulfilling thing she had ever done.

A woman with Saturn and Pluto in Leo in the 8th house had a dramatic near death experience during her Saturn return. She nearly died while giving birth, after more than 48 hours in labor. After a prolonged ordeal, her baby was finally born — completely healthy — and she herself felt that she had been reborn.

A man with Sun in Sagittarius in the 8th house owned a chain of stores, and felt that his greatest fulfillment came in applying his Taoist philosophical beliefs in the field of business. When transiting Saturn passed over his 8th house Sun, he experienced a falling-out with his business partner and a marital crisis that led 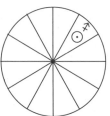 quickly to divorce. During this time, the man sold his stock in the business, and lost his home and savings in the divorce settlement. Nevertheless, he viewed this experience as one that led to renewal, for many latent conflicts in his marital and family relationships had finally been aired, and eventually he was able to make a fresh start in a new business.

American spiritual teacher Da Avabhasa (also known as Da Love Ananda) has the Sun in Scorpio in the 10th house, and a Moon-Pluto conjunction in the 7th house (Chart 9). He is widely known for his spiritual power, his capacity to shake up and transform others and to bless his devotees with dynamic energetic transmissions. During his career he has dealt continually with issues regarding power and sexuality, and his teachings describe in detail the transformative alchemy and intensity of the guru-disciple relationship.

Dr. Elisabeth Kubler-Ross, who has worked to promote more humane care for the dying, has Sun conjunct Pluto in Cancer, trine Saturn in Scorpio in the 8th house (Chart 10). With Saturn square Jupiter and Neptune, her writings describe how one must overcome the fear of death (Saturn in Scorpio) to arrive at an experience of peace, serenity, and wisdom (Jupiter and Neptune) through the dying process (Rodden, 1979, p. 111).

Dr. Stanislav Grof, the pioneer of psychedelic therapy and holotropic therapy, has a conjunction of Jupiter and Pluto in Cancer in the 8th house, opposite Moon and Saturn (Chart 11). His work emphasizes powerful, cathartic methods that often activate memories (Cancer) of the stages of biological birth. Grof's therapeutic methods are designed to help a person relive these sometimes traumatic memories (Pluto in Cancer) and to pass through a sequence of states of consciousness (called "perinatal matrices") that comprise a process of psychological death and rebirth.

A dramatic example of a death-rebirth process clearly symbolized by planetary aspects occurred in the life of Ramana

Maharshi (Chart 12). One day when he was 17 years old, Ramana Maharshi suddenly felt that he was dying, and soon passed suddenly and permanently into the highest state of enlightenment. Soon thereafter, he left home and left for Mount Arunachala in Southern India, where he lived for the rest of his life. At the time of this remarkable enlightenment experience, transiting Uranus and Neptune were in a close quincunx aspect between his natal 1st and 8th houses. Simultaneously transiting Saturn and Pluto were forming the exact same aspect. Thus, transiting Saturn-Uranus in the 1st house were quincunx transiting Pluto and Neptune in the 8th house, the house of death and rebirth. At this time, his progressed Sun was also trine Pluto, and transiting Mars and Pluto were conjunct in the 8th house.

Sagittarius/Jupiter/9th House: Jnana Yoga: The Path of Knowledge

Sagittarius, its ruler Jupiter, and the 9th house are concerned with defining concepts, theories, beliefs, cosmologies, and religious, philosophical, and ethical principles that enable us to find meaning in life. With an emphasis here, you may feel drawn to pursue a quest for meaning and purpose through philosophical reflection, travel, education, teaching, or publishing. Your spiritual path might focus on keeping the company of enlightened teachers; going on a pilgrimage or vision quest; or developing jnana, knowledge of the Real — also known in Western spiritual traditions as *gnosis*, sacred knowledge that bestows salvation. This is an important realm of the birth chart, for even if one has profound mystical experiences that transcend philosophical constructs one needs to be able to interpret these in the light of some guiding doctrine. Of course it is possible to become overly wrapped up in lofty, abstract concepts or dogmatic beliefs, but developing the higher intellect can be an important facet of spiritual growth.

A man with a Sun-Neptune conjunction in the 9th house was a physicist who specialized in cosmological theories. His reflections on the origins and structure of the universe were the core of his spiritual path.

A woman with Venus, Mars, and Sun in Sagittarius experienced a major illumination of the meaning of her life while on an extended voyage to Japan and China.

A woman with Sun and Mercury in Virgo in the 9th house was the head of the department of education in a large city.

A man met his guru when transiting Saturn passed into his 9th house, and traveled with this teacher on a national tour for two years, listening to his lectures and studying philosophical texts.

Anthropologist Margaret Mead, who had Sun, Mercury, and Uranus conjunct in Sagittarius and an exact conjunction of Mars and Jupiter, spent much of her life traveling around the world and writing about other cultures and anthropological theory. Many great writers with philosophical orientation have prominent placements of Jupiter. Novelist Thomas Mann had Sun in Gemini trine Jupiter. Herman Hesse had Jupiter in Sagittarius in the 1st house oppostite Mercury. D. H. Lawrence had a conjunction of Sun and Jupiter in Virgo. Philosopher Alfred North Whitehead had natal Sun opposite Jupiter.

Psychologist Stanley Krippner has Moon in Sagittarius and Jupiter conjunct Neptune and sesquiquadrate (135 degree aspect) Saturn in the 10th house (Chart 13). His pioneering research in parapsychology, dream telepathy, cross-cultural healing methods, and shamanism have helped bring studies of spiritual, mystical, and transpersonal dimensions of human consciousness and experience into the mainstream of psychology (Saturn aspecting Jupiter-Neptune). He completed his graduate studies while transiting Saturn was passing through his 9th house.

Sri Aurobindo, modern India's greatest philosopher and mystic seer, had Moon in Sagittarius, and Sun conjunct Jupiter in the 1st house, trine Neptune in the 9th (Chart 14). Spiritual philosopher Paul Brunton, who had a conjunction of Sun, Mercury, Venus, Saturn, and Uranus in Sagittarius, was famous for his descriptions of pilgrimages and the quest for knowledge in India and Egypt, and his studies of gurus like Ramana Maharshi.

Stanislav Grof has a Mars-Neptune conjunction in Virgo in the 9th house (Chart 11). He is a prolific author and teacher, and a theoretician (9th house) of great persuasive power (Mars) and imagination (Neptune) who describes the use of breathwork and other spiritual practices to explore the farthest regions of spirituality, mysticism, transpersonal psychology, and visionary experience.

Capricorn/Saturn/10th House: Dharma: The Yoga of Mastery Through Accomplishment

Emphasis on Capricorn, its ruler Saturn, or the 10th house may suggest a need to define and pursue your professional ambitions and to follow what Hazrat Inayat Khan calls the path of "mastery through accomplishment." Many spiritual seekers become sensitive and withdraw from the world and from personal ambitions. However, if you have prominent planets here you may feel impelled to become an incarnation of your ideals and to assume your appropriate position within the social and spiritual hierarchy of humanity, through tangible achievements. These areas of the chart emphasize the importance of embodying personally meaningful archetypes, applying your philosophical and moral principles in the world, defining and actualizing your **dharma** or personal vocation, and claiming authority or a position of leadership. ("Finding a Life's Calling" by Greg Bogart, available from Dawn Mountain Press, addresses these issues at greater length.)

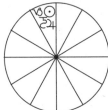

For example, a 29 year-old man with Sun, Jupiter, and Saturn in Capricorn in the 10th house, who had spent his twenties drifting around touring with the Grateful Dead, suddenly began to feel great anxiety because he had not accomplished anything or established a profession. During his Saturn return he became quite serious and focused about finding a career and eventually took a high-paying position as a corporate management trainee.

When Saturn transited over his midheaven, a man who had spent many years writing a historical novel began to stop waiting for the world to discover him, finished his novel, and systematically sought a publisher until he found one. He began to speak publicly and soon became widely recognized as an authority in his field.

When transiting Saturn and Pluto crossed over a woman's natal Jupiter-Neptune conjunction in Scorpio in the 10th house, she was appointed director of a school of metaphysical studies and became widely known as a psychic counselor and healer.

Clara Barton, founder of the American Red Cross, had Sun, Moon, Uranus, and Neptune in Capricorn *and* in the 10th house, as well as Saturn conjunct Jupiter in the 1st house (Chart 15). This highly capable, committed, and ambitious woman worked tirelessly to alleviate the sufferings of others (Sun-Neptune in 10th), risking death on the battlefields of the Civil War to care for the wounded. She served as the President of this large relief organization for twenty two years (Rodden, 1979, p. 272).

Former California Governor Jerry Brown has a Mars-Uranus conjunction in Taurus in the 10th house. He attempted to change governmental fiscal policies (Taurus), allocating funds to the development of new technologies (Uranus) such as alternative energy sources. Although, as a practicing Catholic and Zen Buddhist, Brown has a strong spiritual orientation, his *dharma* is to be a progressive, futurist politician.

Saturn's transit into Gordon Michael Scallion's 10th house in 1991 marked the beginning of a period of notoriety, fame, and recognition, during which he established his reputation as an educator and prophet (Chart 1).

Sri Aurobindo, with Pluto in the 10th house square Sun-Jupiter, experienced a "death-rebirth" crisis in which a period of imprisonment led him to completely relinquish his former ambitions and activities as a prominent journalist and social activist (Chart 14). Subsequently his powerful capacity for leadership (Pluto in 10th square Sun) was redirected into a new career as a spiritual teacher, who wrote extensively about the descent of "supramental" energies.

Aquarius/Uranus/11th House: The Yoga of Sangha

Aquarius and the 11th house are concerned with our responses to historical forces and social conditions through involvement with political issues, and participation in groups, communities, organizations, or cooperatives concerned with social change and creating a better future for humanity. With an emphasis here, you may find some form of political activism to be an important facet of your spiritual path. You may also want to seek to understand historical cycles and your place within them. Solitary spiritual pursuits may feel incomplete, and this may cause you to recognize the importance of **sangha**, (i.e., involvement in a spiritual community or affinity group), of addressing social issues, and of socially engaged forms of spirituality such as those based in the doctrines of Engaged Buddhism, Gandhi's "satyagraha" (non-violent civil disobedience), or Liberation Theology — the foundation of a movement that is an increasingly powerful force in some Third World nations. Scientific experimentation and interests in technological innovation may also be significant concerns if you have prominent placement of Uranus or planets in Aquarius or the 11th house.

A woman with Sun in Aquarius in the 4th house purchased property in order to found a new age community.

A woman with a Sun-Saturn conjunction in her 11th house found a new sense of purpose during her Saturn return when she joined an ashram community that practiced voluntary simplicity, and in which she assumed a position of responsibility.

 A highly successful black professional woman, with natal Sun in Taurus squaring a Saturn-Pluto conjunction in the 11th house, has repeatedly confronted institutionalized racism *and* sexism and is highly active politically in her local community. She is willing to invest her own money (Taurus Sun) in the struggle against hatred, discrimination, and oppression of minorities. She has jeopardized her own safety numerous times in order to confront militant right-wing organizations such as the Ku Klux Klan and the Aryan Nation, and to oppose violence against women.

A man with Uranus in the 10th house and Sun conjunct Pluto in the 11th house is a scientist and futurist who is also quite involved with professional organizations, the Grateful Dead community, and a large, cooperatively run household.

Jiddu Krishnamurti was the spiritual leader of a large organization within the Theosophical movement called the Order of the Star. He unexpectedly dissolved this order in August, 1929, while Saturn was transiting over his 11th house Moon.

President Franklin Roosevelt had Sun in Aquarius and Uranus conjunct his ascendant, and made part of his mark on history through the innovative policies of the New Deal. President Bill Clinton's Leo Sun is placed in the 11th house. He has been dedicated to progressive social causes since his youth. Physicist Albert Einstein, with Uranus in the 3rd house opposite Jupiter in the 9th house, revolutionized science and modern thought with his dazzling, revolutionary theories. Inventor and futurist Buckminster Fuller had a natal grand trine of Sun, Moon, and Uranus.

Tibetan Buddhist teacher Chogyam Trungpa Rinpoche was born on a Full Moon with the Sun in Aquarius closely squaring Uranus (ruler of Aquarius). He was an unpredictable, "crazy wisdom" teacher who broke with Tibetan traditions in many respects, whose actions sometimes shocked or outraged others, and who was dedicated to renewing Buddhist teachings by translating them into contemporary terms.

With Uranus in his 1st house, Gordon Michael Scallion is not only a clairvoyant, but also a futurist (Chart 1). If Neptune awakens us to a transcendental reality that is beyond the physical world, Uranus is concerned with *restructuring and reorganizing* concrete forms. Whereas some people respond to prophecies of Earth Changes with hopes of being rescued by extraterrestrials in spaceships (a neptunian response), Scallion encourages others to join together and create communities, to develop new technologies, and to prepare for new times and changing conditions.

Dane Rudhyar (Chart 2) had Moon in Aquarius, squaring Uranus in the 11th house. At the age of 21, while transiting Uranus was conjunct his natal Moon and square natal Uranus, Rudhyar cut himself loose from the past. He left his native France, sailed to America, and changed his name. He dedicated the rest of his life to cultural transformation through a unique, multi-faceted career as an avant garde musical composer, painter, philosopher, and astrologer (see Bogart, 1993). He was involved in numerous innovative artistic and spiritual movements and catalyzed a significant social trend by contributing to the growing popularity of astrology.

Pisces/Neptune/12th House: Moksa: The Path of Liberation and Self-Transcendence

In Pisces the individual is asked to open up and feel the stillness and ease of Being, the peace of existing as pure consciousness without form. The Pisces/Neptune/12th house yoga is to move beyond ego-centered awareness and to achieve **moksa**, liberation, a condition of interior spiritual freedom. This is the evolutionary stage at which one may pass into a state of enlightenment or mystical illumination, or realize the presence of God. Now one may experience what Buddhists call the "radiant light of consciousness," or what the Sufis call *fana* (annihilation of the ego) and *baqa* (Self-realization). The great Tibetan Buddhist guru Padmasambhava taught that the goal of spiritual practice is the remembrance of "intrinsic awareness." He said, "When you look into yourself. . . nakedly (without any discursive thoughts) since there is only this pure observing, there will be found a lucid clarity without anyone being there who is the observer. . . . This is the real introduction to the actual condition of things" (Reynolds, 1989, pp. 12–13). Pisces,

Neptune, and the 12th house are the astrological symbols associated with the awakening to this enlightened condition.

If your chart contains an emphasis on planets placed in Pisces or the 12th house (or accentuates Neptune) you may wish to explore many of the experiences and phenomena commonly associated with mysticism and spirituality: meditation; interiorization of consciousness; visions and trance states; dreams and dreamworking; altruism and selfless service; contemplative prayer; retreat and solitude; upsurgence of symbolic material from the deep unconscious; surrender; experiences of the void or of ecstasy; and an attitude of what Sri Aurobindo and Dane Rudhyar call "self-consecration."

For those who have not yet become conscious and wise navigators of the inner world, there may in some cases be less pleasant expressions of Pisces or 12th house planets: experiences of hospitalization, convalescence, delusions, loss of discriminative faculties, hallucinations, inflation, psychosis, or even institutionalization. This is also the realm of the dark night of the soul. More typically, one may need to grapple with addiction, codependency, loneliness, or feelings of victimization, ineffectiveness, powerlessness, abandonment, or grief. With planets here, you may find great satisfaction in exploring hypnosis, visualization, active imagination, symbolic amplification techniques, Jungian analysis, transpersonal therapies, shamanic journeys, past life regression, or use of psychedelics. Planets here can also indicate strong interest in mystical arts such as astrology.

Meditation may be an important spiritual practice with planets in Pisces or the 12th house, or with the Sun, Moon, or ascendant ruler in strong aspect to Neptune. Individuals with a strong Pisces/12th house emphasis may be drawn toward contemplative practices and periods of prayer, solitude, and retreat. These can be quite valuable unless they represent an avoidance of conflictual areas of your life (what psychologist John Welwood calls "spiritual bypassing"). As Pisces and the 12th house are concerned with transcendence of a limited, egoic perspective and the awakening of compassion, emphasis here may also give you a strong desire to express the spirit of service and loving-kindness in daily life.

A woman with Mars in Pisces in the 1st house has worked with disadvantaged children and as a nurse on an intensive care ward, and spends much of her spare time caring for an elderly neighbor.

Her sense of identity (1st house) is focused on her genuine desire to serve others through compassionate action (Mars in Pisces).

A man with Moon, Saturn, and Mars in the 12th house left his family to spend several months on retreat in the desert practicing strenuous austerities. During this time he experienced many visions, which convinced him that he was destined to become the Messiah, the World Saviour. Months of therapy and  disciplined meditation practice under skilled guidance brought this delusional belief under control. He did, however, have great psychic sensitivity and compassion, which he began to express through volunteer work, and through doing psychic readings.

A woman with Sun, Moon, Mercury, Venus, and Saturn in Pisces and in the 12th house opposite Mars, Uranus, and Pluto in Virgo in the 6th house experienced a dramatic religious conversion in her early twenties as transiting Uranus and Saturn squared all of these planets from Sagittarius. She had visions of Christ and 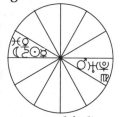 the Virgin Mary and oscillated between states of ecstasy and feelings of loneliness and abandonment. She also experienced a deep conflict between her spirituality (the Pisces planets) and her sexuality (Mars-Uranus-Pluto conjunction). She forced herself to undergo strict religious penances (Virgo-6th house emphasis), which she felt were necessary to purify herself and make herself worthy of God's presence and love.

A 24 year-old man, with natal Sun and Moon in the 12th house square a 3rd house Saturn, sought counseling during a period of profound confusion and disorientation. He was completely preoccupied with his dreams, and spent most of his time writing in his journal, meditating, and reading books about  spirituality, psychology, astrology, and mysticism. He also had no inclination to work or be involved in relationships. At the time, transiting Neptune was conjunct natal Saturn, while transiting Saturn was in the 12th house, conjunct his Sun-Moon. Many people thought there was something wrong with him and were worried by his tendency toward withdrawal and absorption in his inner world.

However, as he began to understand his birth chart it became clear that this was a crucial period of inner work, dissolution of prior identity and orientation in life, and preparation for the birth of a new self. Thus, he began to trust the appropriateness and necessity of this phase of inner exploration, and allowed himself to become fully immersed in it, knowing that eventually the period of confusion would come to an end. By the time Saturn transited over his ascendant, he had become much more grounded, willing and able to work, and began planning for his career as a writer (Saturn in the 3rd house). During his Saturn return he was appointed to a position as a religion reporter for a large metropolitan newspaper.

Astrologer and occultist Manly Palmer Hall had natal Sun in Pisces square Neptune, and Moon trine Neptune. Astrologer Evangeline Adams had Sun in the 12th house, Mercury, Jupiter, and Venus in Pisces, Pisces ascendant, and Neptune in the 1st house. Prophet and trance channel Edgar Cayce had a Moon-Neptune conjunction on his midheaven and the Sun in Pisces in the 9th house. Visionary philosopher-mystic Rudolph Steiner had Sun, Mercury, and Neptune in Pisces. Mystic-seer Sri Aurobindo had Sun trine Neptune, Mars-Uranus in the 12th house, and Mars square Neptune, all of which symbolized a powerful evolutionary pull toward enlightenment and a life of expanded consciousness (Chart 14).

Yogi Amrit Desai has natal Sun placed in the 12th house, symbolizing his life of dedication to God and meditation (Chart 4). His Sun is also involved in a Grand Cross with Pluto, Saturn, and Uranus. Sun square Pluto symbolizes the fact that he is a man of power whose presence can catalyze *kundalini* awakening in others; Sun square Saturn symbolizes his intense discipline, spirit of renunciation, and commitment to ancient yogic traditions; and Sun opposite Uranus symbolizes his innovative, experimental attitude, which has enabled him to present an approach to yoga that is vibrantly new and contemporary.

Psychic, Earth Changes prophet, and trance channel Gordon Michael Scallion has natal Sun and Neptune in conjunction (Chart 1). With these planets in the 5th house (performance), Scallion channels in front of large audiences, publicly proclaiming his message. In addition to his Sun-Neptune conjunction, his Moon in the 12th house also suggests psychic or intuitive abilities, contact with spiritual realms, and an orientation toward mystical experience. With Moon in Taurus, many of his inner visions and predictions focus on economics, stock market forecasts, and practical suggestions for survival and financial security.

Sri Ramakrishna, the great Bengali saint of the 19th century, had a Mars-Neptune conjunction in the 12th house, and Sun in late Aquarius conjunct Uranus in early Pisces, along with Mercury and Moon in Pisces in the 1st house (Chart 16). At age 6–7 Ramakrishna experienced his first ecstatic state, became completely detached from worldly matters, and began exhibiting behaviors that others viewed as abnormal, peculiar, or crazy. This occurred when transiting Jupiter and Neptune were conjunct at 20 degrees Aquarius, near his ascendant, and when Jupiter conjoined natal Sun and Uranus (strange behavior). At age 9 he began to lose himself in meditation and worship of the Goddess Kali; transiting Saturn was in his 12th house, conjunct natal Mars and Neptune. Between 1856–1859 he passed through a period of "divine madness" in which he experienced a feverish longing for union with God, felt intense physical heat and pain, and passed into a spiritually intoxicated condition. Transiting Pluto was square to natal Neptune; he frequently entered states of *samadhi*, complete inner absorption in God consciousness. Simultaneously, transiting Saturn opposed Mars-Neptune from the 6th house and he began practicing *sadhanas* (spiritual disciplines) from many different traditions.

Ramakrishna's spiritual awakening occurred over the course of many years of deep meditation, prayer, and devotion — while transiting Pluto squared natal Mars-Neptune; transiting Neptune (in Aries) sextiled Mars-Neptune; and progressed Venus squared natal and progressed Neptune (awakening of *bhakti*, divine love). While Saturn transited through his 7th house, Ramakrishna formed relationships with two teachers, Brahmani and Totapuri, who were the only people who understood his unusual condition and could guide him. Under Totapuri's tutelage he was able to reach the highest pinnacles of mystical experience, remaining in *samadhi* continuously for six months — while transiting Jupiter in Sagittarius was conjunct his midheaven, square natal Sun-Uranus. His final enlightenment occurred during his Saturn return and while transiting Uranus was conjunct natal Jupiter; both Uranus and Saturn were activating his natal Grand Trine of Jupiter-Saturn-Uranus. Ramakrishna's path was to completely surrender or dissolve his personal ego in the ocean of divine consciousness. He was one of those rare beings who fully embodied the ideal of egolessness and surrender to God.

This chapter has examined twelve phases or facets of the spiritual journey. By reflecting on the twelve yogas of the zodiac, the case examples, and the major themes of your own birth chart, you should be able to gain a clearer sense of what spiritual paths or practices might be most suitable for you. Remember that your chart may indicate the need to pursue any combination or all of these pathways, rather than one exclusively. Let the symbols of your birthmap help you envision and define the nature of your unique evolutionary road. The biographies in Part III of this book give abundant illustrations of the principles discussed in this chapter. Now let us turn our attention to some theoretical material that will deepen your appreciation of how astrology can illuminate the spiritual path.

Gordon Michael Scallion
September 26, 1942
9:01 PM EWT
Hartford, Connecticut

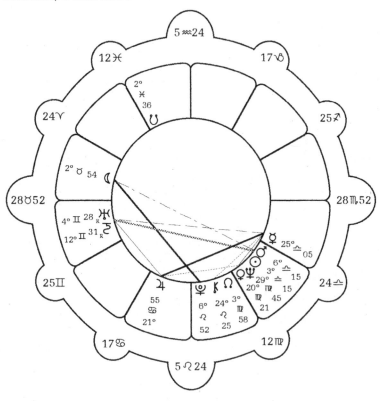

Source: From him

Chart 1

Dane Rudhyar
March 23, 1895
12:42 AM
Paris, France

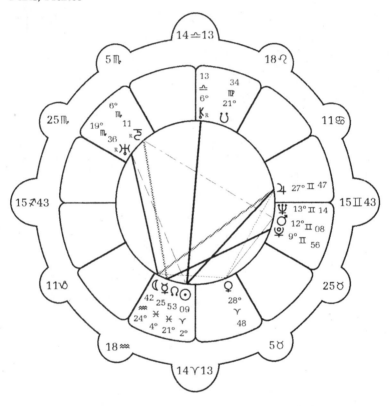

Source: *The Circle Book of Charts*

Chart 2

John Lennon
October 9, 1940
6:30 PM GDT
Manchester, England

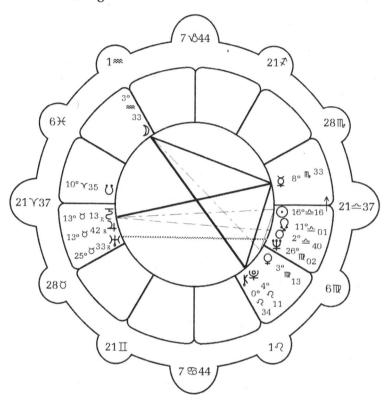

Source: Lois Rodden, *American Book of Charts*

Chart 3

Yogi Amrit Desai
October 16, 1932
6:20 AM
Gujarat, India

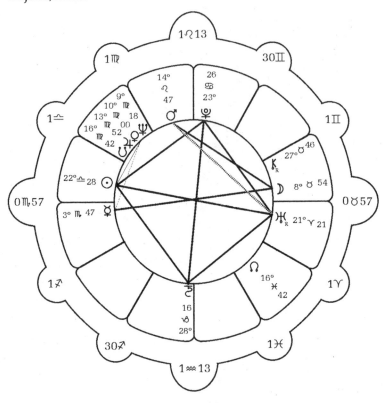

Source: Speculative birth time based on
report of ashram resident

Chart 4

Hazrat Inayat Khan
July 5, 1882
11:35 PM
Baroda (Gujarat), India

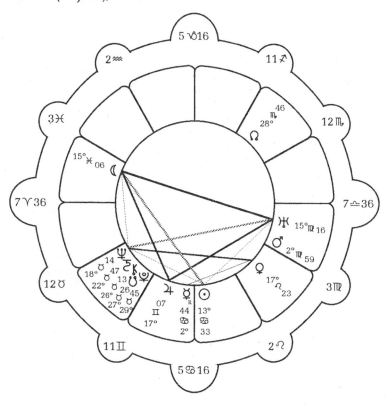

Source: Family Records

Chart 5

Wendell Berry
August 5, 1934
11:33 PM
New Castle, Kentucky

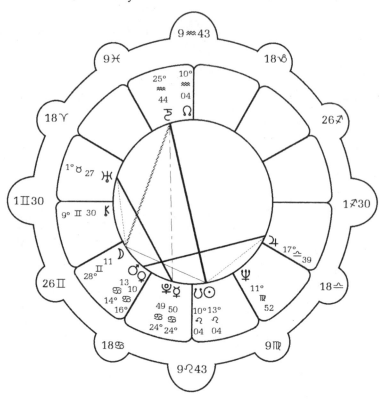

Source: Michel and Francoise Gauquelin,
The Gauquelin Book of American Charts

Chart 6

Liv Ullman
December 16, 1938
7:20 PM JST
Tokyo, Japan

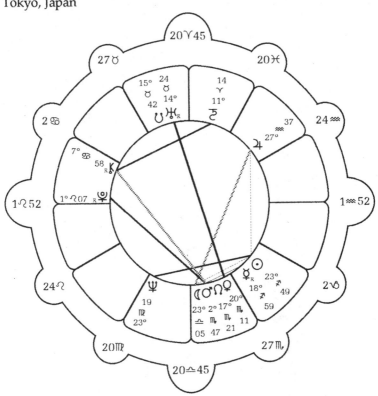

Source: Lois Rodden, *Profiles of Women*

Chart 7

Carl Jung
July 26, 1875
7:00 PM
Kesswil, Switzerland

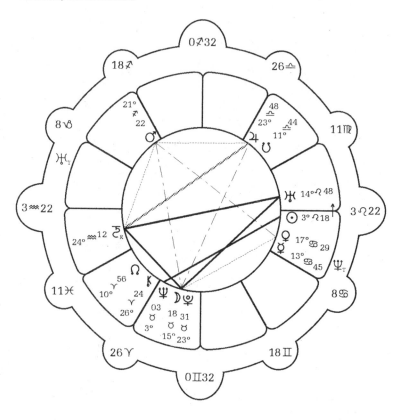

Source: Rectified Birth Time
(Disputed Birth Time)

Chart 8

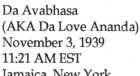

Da Avabhasa
(AKA Da Love Ananda)
November 3, 1939
11:21 AM EST
Jamaica, New York

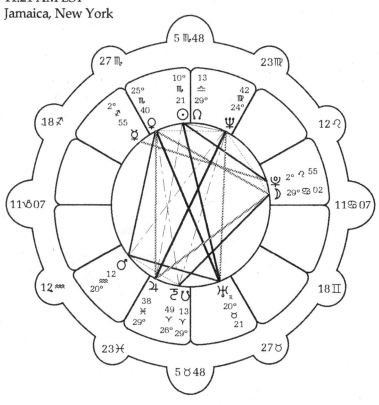

Source: Da Avabhasa, *The Knee of Listening*

Chart 9

Elisabeth Kubler-Ross
July 8, 1926
10:45 PM MET
Zurich, Switzerland

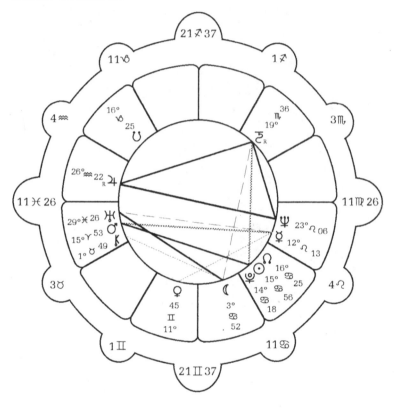

Source: Lois Rodden, *Profiles of Women*

Chart 10

Stanislav Grof
July 1, 1931
6:50 PM
Prague, Czechoslovakia

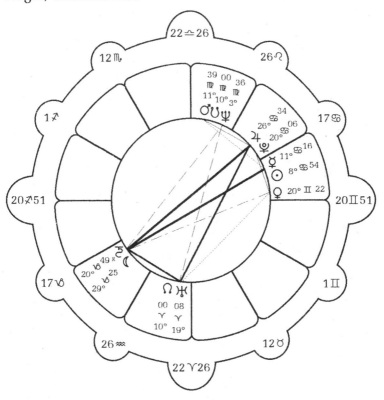

Source: Report from personal friend of Grof

Chart 11

Ramana Maharshi
December 30, 1879
1:00 AM LMT
Tirucculi, India

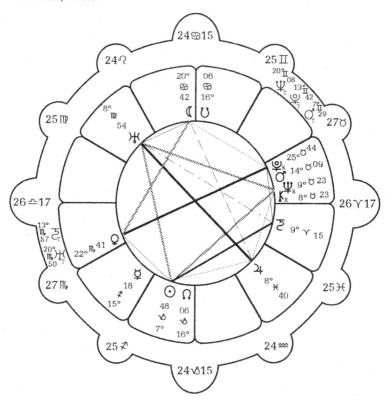

Source: B.V. Raman, *Notable Horoscopes*

Chart 12

Stanley Krippner
October 4, 1932
7:00 PM
Fort Atkinson, Wisconsin

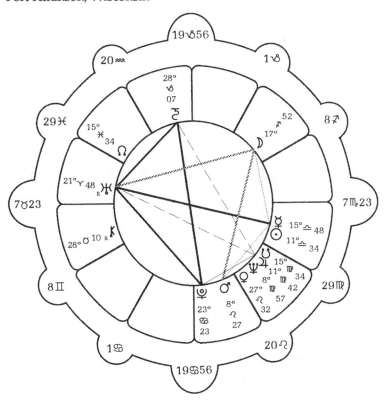

Source: From him

Chart 13

Sri Aurobindo
August 15, 1872
5:00 AM LMT
Calcutta, India

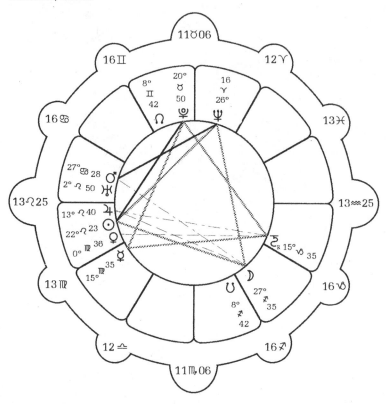

Source: Lois Rodden, *Astrodata III*

Chart 14

Clara Barton
December 25, 1821
11:40 AM EST
Oxford, Massachussetts

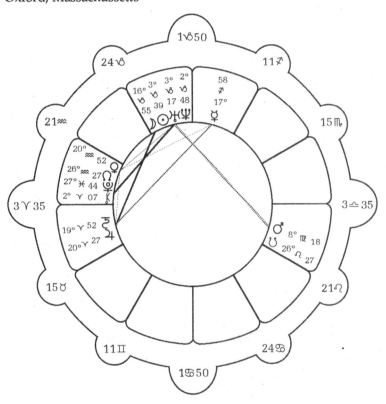

Source: Lois Rodden, *Profiles of Women*

Chart 15

Sri Ramakrishna
February 18, 1836
6:23 AM LMT
Karmarpukar, India

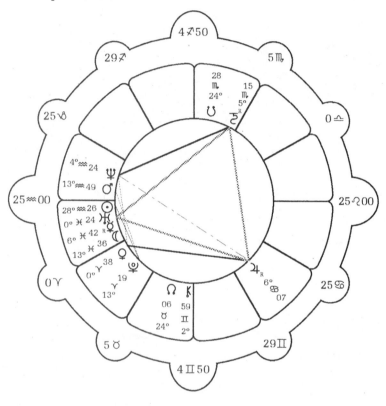

Source: Swami Saradananda,
Ramakrishna, The Great Master

Chart 16

PART II

Transpersonal Astrology and the Path of Transformation

"When I speak of a transpersonal individual. . . [I am speaking] of an individual person who has. . . taken steps on the path of radical and total transformation. The transpersonal way refers to this path which symbolizes a long and arduous process that can take a variety of forms, yet which has a definite, nearly universal structure — just as the embryonic development of a future human being, within the mother's womb, takes place according to a series of clearly marked phases. This process of rebirth is difficult and often requires intense phases of catharsis because of the inertia of the biological past and the socio-cultural and individual karma that must be overcome. All individuals whose minds have opened themselves to the messages or visions that the soul reveals in symbolic forms, and who have accepted the challenge of total transformation, have to undergo such a process of rebirth. "

(Rudhyar, 1980, pp. 112–113)

CHAPTER 3

From Predictive to Humanistic Astrology

Astrology changes as humankind and our contexts of interpretation change. In agricultural societies, astrology was used to determine the times of planting and harvesting of crops. In the eras of great Kings, it was used to foretell the political fortunes of monarchs. In our own, psychologically-oriented era, astrology is increasingly used as a means for self-reflection and psychological awareness. And, as I am trying to demonstrate in this book, it may now be used to understand and navigate complex processes of spiritual metamorphosis. This utilization of astrology as a means of spiritual guidance is known as transpersonal astrology. Although it has precedents in other cultures like India, where a spiritual approach to astrology was developed to a high degree of refinement, this is a relatively new approach that found its clearest expression in the writings of Dane Rudhyar.

In the next several chapters I examine the humanistic and transpersonal astrology described by Rudhyar, and add some thoughts of my own that were inspired by reflecting on his philosophy. Two case examples illustrate the distinctive nature of humanistic and transpersonal chart interpretation. I discuss Rudhyar's ideas in some depth, for I believe his writings provide the most coherent and solid foundation upon which to build an understanding of transpersonal astrology. I also supplement the discussion of Rudhyar with some exploration of concepts from the Indian yogic tradition of Kashmir Shaivism.

The Four Levels of Astrological Interpretation

Dane Rudhyar was the originator of humanistic astrology, which emphasizes a positive, growth-oriented understanding of planetary symbolism and cycles. In his view, astrology is a symbolic language that is not to be used primarily for fortune-telling but rather as a tool to guide and facilitate the transformation of human consciousness. Rudhyar's approach to astrology has been described in many of his books (see bibliography), and by Rael (1983) and Ruperti (1978).

Rudhyar (1980) believed that the symbolic language of astrology is open-ended and can be interpreted on four basic levels: biological, socio-cultural, individual, and transpersonal. At the biological level, astrology, in the form of Medical Astrology, can help resolve difficulties in the development of a healthy physical organism, the foundation for all further stages of human evolution. Applied at this level, astrology has also traditionally been used for weather prediction and coordination of agricultural planting and harvesting.

At the socio-cultural level, astrology can enable an individual to find the most suitable vocation (Vocational Astrology), and to resolve problems of social adjustment and interpersonal relationships. The socio-cultural level of astrology also encompasses the study of Mundane Astrology, which examines social issues, political trends, and historical cycles.

The individual, or humanistic, level of interpretation refers to psychologically-oriented astrology that enables a person to understand and actualize their potentials and inner dynamics. This type of astrology is particularly important because the process of becoming an individual is often laden with struggle, disorientation, and moral crisis caused by choices, interests, and activities that bring one into conflict with social demands for conformity. To break free of social conditioning and become the authentic person one potentially is requires the assistance of a form of astrology that illuminates the challenges of individuation.

Finally, transpersonal astrology provides insight into the process of self-transcendence and spiritual awakening. In Rudhyar's (1979) view, becoming a relatively free and autonomous individual is only a transitional stage in human development, one that is fraught with isolation and desperate attempts to satisfy personal desires. He envisions transpersonal astrology as a means of understanding the dramatic "reorientation of consciousness" that enables one to transcend the state of a power-hungry, "money-conditioned individual" and to become a compassionate, self-consecrated servant of humanity-as-a-whole.

Event-Centered Astrology and the Attitude of Dread Toward the Planets

Astrology practiced solely at the biological and socio-cultural levels is predominantly predictive or "event-centered." This is the level at which many people approach astrology, seeking to unlock the mysteries of the future. Generally, astrological clients and students are eager to know, "Where is my life headed? What will happen when Saturn crosses my midheaven? When will I get married? What is going to happen with my health? Will my career be successful?" These are important questions, and astrology may shed much light on them. Used wisely, astrological techniques like transits, solar arc directions, and solar and lunar returns can undoubtedly be used to make reasonably accurate predictions that can be of great value (see Tyl, 1991). Nevertheless, a predominantly predictive approach to astrology is often associated with a fatalistic attitude that can have very negative consequences and that can obscure other profound, contructive insights that the stellar art can disclose.

This view found its most blatant expression in the views of the Gnostics, mystically oriented sects that flourished in the centuries before and after the beginning of the Christian era. The Gnostics' world view was radically dualistic: they believed that God was transcendent, completely separate from the cosmos, and viewed the material world as a realm of darkness created by a second, evil God called the Demiurge (Jonas, 1958, p. 250). Like the dualistic Samkya philosophy of ancient India, the Gnostics believed that a total repudiation of the physical, material world was required in order to achieve spiritual freedom and return to God. The Gnostics were great mystics, yet their spirituality was extreme. Rather than viewing incarnation and embodiment as sacred, they sought to free themselves from the bondage of matter and time — which included the realm of the planets. To the Gnostics,

> The universe, the domain of the archons [cosmic rulers] is like a vast prison whose innermost dungeon is the earth, the scene of man's life. Around and above it the cosmic spheres are ranged like concentric. . . shells. Most frequently these are the seven spheres of the planets surrounded by the eighth, that of the fixed stars. . . . The religious significance of this cosmic architecture lies in the idea that everything which intervenes between here and the beyond serves to separate man from God, not merely through spatial distance but through active demonic force. (Jonas pp. 42–43)

From this perspective, the planets were considered malevolent beings that imprisoned human beings and actively sought to separate them from their creator. The Gnostics' view of astrology was thus colored by their anguished sense of exile from God, their fatalism, and their desire for liberation from the world. From the gnostic, anti-cosmic perspective, the celestial bodies became objects of hate, contempt, and fear. For they were viewed now as the causes of bondage to an oppressive cosmic fate (*hiemarmene*), the cosmic prison of the Demiurge God. Because the celestial bodies were thought to dispense this hiemarmene — the inexorable law of the universe — the stars and planets became associated with tyranny, rather than divine providence (Jonas, p. 253).

The view that the planets were gods that controlled the destinies of human beings was prevalent in many ancient cultural traditions. And, since the planets were often considered malevolent, astrology was often approached with a certain amount of dread. For example, among the Jewish nation, in India, and in part of the Mediteranean region (during the troubled times of the Roman Empire), this fearful attitude toward the celestial bodies led to development of magical practices, such as use of talismans, gemstones, and mantras. These were intended to ward off and counteract the "evil" influences of certain planetary positions and influences, such as for protection from the damaging effects of a Saturn transit.

Many people today still study astrology with an attitude of dread, viewing their birth charts as a curse that they are stuck with and some even resorting to these kinds of magical practices. I do not rule out the possibility that they may indeed have some efficacy. However, if we wish to utilize astrology as a viable tool for human transformation in the contemporary world it may be advisable to consider alternatives to the view of the world as a "vast prison" ruled over by planetary forces that determine our fate and separate us from the Creator. This begins with an approach to astrology that views the planets as symbols of the complex but inteligent pattern of evolution in which we are all participants. From such a perspective, we try to view even the seemingly most "malefic" planetary placement or combination as having a specific purpose or intention with which we may, indeed should, cooperate. That is not to say that there are no difficult natal aspects or transits. Transits of the trans-Saturnian planets, for example, are rarely easy processes. Nevertheless, it is possible to view such periods as meaningful phases of an ordered process of change. Approached in this way, astrology can become not a symbol of human bondage and imprisonment but an ally in the process of human liberation.

Humanistic Astrology

Rudhyar (1976a, 1980) contrasts the traditional, "event-centered," predictive, "astrology of information" with a humanistic or "person-centered" astrology, which he also calls "the astrology of meaning." At the person-centered or individual level of interpretation, astrology can help us develop awareness of our identity and emotional dynamics, and illuminate our struggles to emerge from the collective as unique and self-defining persons. Practiced at this level, Rudhyar says, astrology can be considered a form of *karma yoga*, which can reveal the kinds of experiences and actions (karma) necessary to actualize our "dharma," our "truth-of-being." Rudhyar (1976a) described the humanistic, person-centered approach to astrology as follows:

> [T]he basic purpose of studying a birth-chart and discussing it with the person to whom it refers is to help this person become more positively, more meaningfully, more creatively, more totally what he potentially is. . . . [Astrology] is a method of "self-actualization"... and. . . a kind of yoga — a yoga with one's destiny. . . . The birth chart is an archetypal form, and through the study of progressions

and transits we can foresee its evolution, that is, the process according to which what is potential at birth becomes actualized through life-events. . . . The fundamental concept of which astrology is based is that everything that is "born". . . at a particular time and point of space is organized according to a particular seed-pattern or archetype symbolized by its birth chart. This seed-pattern defines what that organism. . . SHOULD be if it fulfills its function in the universal scheme of things, or one might say according to God's Plan. . . . [A]strology does not tell us what will happen, but what would happen should the person act consciously and earnestly according to the celestial instructions represented in code by the birth chart. (pp. 78, 81, 95, 100, 102)

Meditation on the astrological seed pattern allows us to discern images of the individual's unique life-project. Thus, at this level we study the birth chart in order to understand the complex challenges that enable the person to proceed consciously toward his or her own form of fulfillment and self-actualization. Rudhyar's writings suggest that although predictive techniques can be quite effective and helpful, the real significance of astrology is that it enables us to reflect on the *meaning* or the *hidden intention* of what is occurring in our lives. Thus, the aim of humanistic astrology is not to predict what will happen, but rather to guide action and to give meaning to events. The same celestial symbolism that might indicate a particular future life development can also reveal steps that could be taken now to make that possibility become an actuality. Instead of being approached as fortune-telling, astrology becomes a means of interpreting the data of past, present, and projected future life experiences within a framework that gives them coherence and purpose, and that provides the basis for appropriate choices and actions.

Approached from a humanistic perspective, astrology helps us discern the thematic contours of a given time period, not the exact experiential content. Astrology enables us to recognize how each moment of our lives is part of larger cyclic processes that bestow significance upon each isolated event. This awareness allows us to "harvest meanings" from our infinitely varied experiences. Rudhyar (1980) writes,

Life, when lived in terms of meaning and purpose, is. . . to be considered a ritual, or, in more modern terms, a structured process whose every phase is filled with significance. (p. 39)

Humanistic astrology can help us understand where we stand in the ritual of existence by illuminating the hidden structure and significance of events. Implicit in this approach to astrology, and to life, is the understanding that meaning is not inherent in experience but must instead be constructed through an interpretive discipline like astrology that enables us to transform our lives into self-created works of art. This process is founded on the insight that the core of personal healing and growth is the reinterpretation of one's biographical narrative or "life-text," and the choices based upon that reinterpretation.

An Example of Humanistic Chart Interpretation

Take for example, a woman named "Jane" with a natal square of Venus and Saturn, with a history of difficult relationships with men, including a two-year marriage in her mid twenties that ended in divorce. In astrological lore Saturn has customarily been called a malefic planet, and the square of Venus and Saturn has a reputation for being particularly pernicious. Thus, a traditional, event-centered astrologer might pronounce that Jane was fated to be unhappy, unsuccessful, or disappointed in love and relationships, perhaps because of her own inability to express affection.

But such was not in fact the case. Through work with a humanistic astrologer and therapist, Jane was able to discern a creative purpose at work behind her past struggles in relationships. Instead of viewing them as signs of a pre-determined fate that she was helpless to change, she chose to perceive these experiences as initial lessons in a process of growth and maturation that would be a major focus for this lifetime. This process challenged Jane to develop greater confidence in her capacity for sustained, loving intimacy, and an appreciation for her need to feel that her partner is stable, trustworthy, loyal, and committed to her.

As she approached her Saturn return, Jane examined many of her fears about relationships, particularly the fear of rejection, and clarified the precise nature of the kind of relationship she wanted. After dating a number of people, she met a man who was financially secure, emotionally steady and reliable, and interested in a committed relationship. They were married during her Saturn return, and, at the time of this writing, have been together for over a decade.

There were two major factors that contributed to Jane's constructive utilization of astrology. First, she developed a positive attitude toward the planet Saturn, the architect of all enduring accomplishments in life. While at times it may be associated with problems, difficulties, and obstructions in various areas of life, it acts to bring about a more serious, and realistic attitude so that through hard work and sustained efforts we can gain mastery, stability, and confidence in those areas — in Jane's case, the area of relationship and marriage.

Secondly, Jane learned to re-interpret her prior difficulties in the light of astrological symbolism. When past events (including failures) are situated within the context of planetary cycles these experiences are revealed to be significant and purposeful, making life a never-ending ritual of unfolding meanings. Practiced at the humanistic, person-centered level, astrology becomes a way of consciously defining and actualizing, step by step, the opus of one's life.

Eonic Consciousness and Life Interpretation

The major tool in this reinterpretation of our personal biographies is what Rudhyar (1973) calls "eonic consciousness," the awareness of "the cycle in its essential unity." (p. 378)

> He who does not really "transcend" time, but rather includes in his greatly extended perceptions the whole of the cycle of his living as a person. . . has developed eonic consciousness. He understands the meanings of and the unfolding interconnections between all the phases of his evolution as a center of consciousness and of power. (p. 378)

Note that Rudhyar is not propounding the transcendence of time and history, a path of release into eternal Spirit or a realm of Emptiness devoid of material form or limitations. For in his view,

> An eternity is a complete cycle of time. The consciousness which can perceive things in their eternal nature is one which sees every happening as definitely related to a particular phase of some more or less vast cycle of existence. (p. 384)

This is a fundamentally different attitude from those of transcendentalist philosophies, such as Vedanta and Gnosticism, which view the world of time and manifest form as a prison or an illusion (see Deutsch, 1969, and Jonas, 1958). Such doctrines do not provide a basis for understanding or responding to the pressures of personal and historical upheaval, except to extol a quest for detachment, renunciation, and inward deliverance. From such a perspective, temporal events have no inherent significance, except insofar as they refer to an atemporal state of salvation or liberation.

In contrast, a humanistic approach to astrology teaches us to sanctify our earthly lives, not by extricating ourselves from temporal events and concerns, but by interpreting events within the context of greater wholes of time and being. Astrological study allows our consciousness to expand to simultaneously encompass the beginning, middle, and end of an entire personal, cultural, or historical cycle. The goal is not to escape from the prison of time, but rather to embrace and draw "transfactual" significance from the very conditions of human experience and our embeddedness in history. With this type of awareness we can then also begin to transform those conditions. Thus, while astrology enables us to reflect upon events from a cyclic perspective that in a sense allows us to transcend time, it also teaches us to live consciously and effectively *within* the realm of time. It is for this reason that I began this book with the statement, "Astrology is the Yoga of Time." These ideas are in accord with one of the basic tenets of Western religions, namely that a spiritual intelligence enacts its relationship to humanity *through,* not despite, the events of time and creation. They also satisfy our longing for a "salvation" that is realized within, rather than outside of, history.

In humanistic astrology, the individual person becomes the focus of attention, in much the way that various gods have captivated the attention and elicited the devotion of human beings throughout history. Rather than contemplating, visualizing, or praying to a deity, as modern students of astrology we contemplate the emergent face of our own unfolding identity as reflected in the birthmap mandala. We then attempt to shape ourselves into the envisioned image through choice, effort, and focused will.

In the process of meditating upon our astrological birth charts, we become our own deities. Discovering the meaning of the symbolic patterns that informed our births, we discern our unique creation myths. By then enacting these myths, our lives become theogonies, performances through which the deities create themselves. In this way, the human and divine planes begin to interpenetrate, the aim of all sacred traditions. Approached from the humanistic perspective, astrology is not merely a means of getting one step ahead of destiny through predictive techniques, but a means of guiding the process of conscious self-creation.

CHAPTER 4

The Transpersonal Level of Chart Interpretation

At the humanistic level of astrological interpretation, one is concerned with becoming an individualized person, breaking free when necessary from the binding forces of culture and the social order. In the 1970s, however, Rudhyar began to explicitly state that astrology in its highest "transpersonal" form, could be utilized not just to aid individuals in emergence from the collective as unique and distinct, but also to guide their metamorphosis into a more-than-personal condition — a condition of awakenened consciousness and compassionate service. Thus, transpersonal astrology is a means of understanding the process of spiritual metamorphosis that Rudhyar calls "the transpersonal way."

The transpersonal way is a process of gradual emergence from the womb of culture and egoic concerns, and the passage into a "transindividual" state of being. This metamorphosis can be conceived of as a reorientation, a turning of the center of consciousness from the ego to a transcendent or more encompassing reality or principle such as God, the Great Spirit, or universal Love.

Traditionally, this kind of crisis in consciousness was brought about through initiations in mystery schools. Today, however, the initiatory process most often operates outside the protective enclosure of the Temple or Ashram, and the success of the project requires clear understanding of its structure and phases.

Astrology is a valuable means of understanding and *guiding oneself* through the process leading to a condition beyond that of mere culture-bound personhood or egoic individuality. It was with reference to this guiding function that Rudhyar (1968) once referred to astrology as a form of "threshold knowledge," knowledge that enables individuals to step over a threshold (p. 21). Reflection on the birth pattern is a process of "self-education," a contemporary path of "chela-ship" (i.e. discipleship) that enables us to facilitate our own self-initiation into the transpersonal life (Rudhyar, 1976b, p. 102).

At the transpersonal level, the whole context of interpretation of astrological factors and biographical material changes. For each event is now referred not to the necessity to establish a distinctive and optimally functioning ego, but to the opening of the ego to the existence, will, or activity of a greater whole — whether this is conceptualized as God/Goddess, Spirit, humanity, the planetary organism, or a state of expanded consciousness. The transpersonal astrologer uses planetary symbols to help the client envision a self-transcending or transindividual state of being, and to interpret each event and each astrological aspect "as an opportunity for transformation on the way to the 'star'" (Rudhyar, 1980, p. 118). The ultimate concern of this process of metamorphosis is *not* individual well-being, but rather the influence of transpersponal forces (symbolized by Uranus, Neptune, and Pluto) that often radically disrupt the security of our personal lives. These transpersonal forces guide us through rites of passage intended to bring about our gradual self-consecration, and the discovery and performance of our individual purpose and function within humanity's evolution. From this frame of reference, the crises, transitions, and various seasons of our lives take on a very different significance. Rudhyar writes,

> a transpersonal astrological and psychological interpretation. . . can help the client gradually to re-interpret all the events of his or her past. By giving a new and transformative purpose to past events — especially past traumas, frustration, and psychic injuries — the past is actually changed. It is transpersonalized. Every tragic occurrence

may be consciously understood as a necessary step in the process that may eventually lead to the transindividual state. (pp. 118–119)

Transpersonal astrology enables us to understand the structure and stages of the process of spiritual awakening, in the context of which even the most difficult experiences can be interpreted as significant phases. A serious illness or injury, for example, can be seen as the occasion for learning the principles of physical and emotional healing that subsequently can become the basis of service to others. Similarly, "a repetitive pattern of frustrating or tragic interpersonal relationships" (Rudhyar, 1980, p. 151) may be viewed as purposeful experiences that can make possible the awakening of a non-clinging, more inclusive type of love.

> In transpersonal living, an individual should not be concerned with "success" and especially with what from the socio-cultural point of view would be called a constructive achievement. . . . An individual on the transpersonal path should realize in what way a present occurrence is an *effect* of the past, and at the same time, understand the *purpose* of the event in generating power to move ahead in the process of transformation. . . . [T]he real issue is whether [one remains] as unaware as before of the *inherent transformative purpose* of the events, or whether the individual will be able to meet these happenings as tools for the cutting and grinding of the coarse and dull stone of personality into a clear and translucent jewel. (Rudhyar, 1980, pp. 151–152)

Operating from the transpersonal level of interpretation, we learn to relinquish concern with success or failure, a major concern of predictive astrology. Thus, if we see what a traditional astrologer might call a malefic or "evil" planetary influence we may view it in a very different light. Rather than becoming resigned to, or afraid of, some great calamity or disappointment, we consider and courageously meet all experiences as necessary phases of our process of spiritual growth. It is precisely this attention to the inherent transformative purpose of life events that distinguishes transpersonal astrology from other approaches.

An Example of Transpersonal Metamorphosis

To illustrate these principles, let us look at an example. "Pam" is a woman in her 40s with an Aquarius Ascendant and a natal conjunction of Sun and Jupiter in the 10th house in Sagittarius, trine to Pluto, Mars, and Saturn in Leo in her 7th house (Chart 17). During the transits of Saturn and Uranus through Sagittarius and her 10th house she enjoyed a period of notable achievement as a university professor. However, over a two year period she passed through an intense series of outer planet transits: transiting Saturn and Uranus conjunct Venus, opposite her natal Moon; transiting Saturn and Neptune passed into her 12th house, and squared natal Neptune; transiting Pluto was nearing conjunction with natal Chiron in her 9th house, and beginning a long square to natal Pluto-Saturn-Mars in the 7th; and transiting Chiron entered her 6th house.

At this time, Pam was experiencing a period of inward and outward dissolution, chaos, and disorientation that was so severe that she had to give up her academic position. With transiting Pluto conjunct her natal Chiron (planet of the wounded healer and of healing crises in general) while transiting Chiron was in her 6th house, she was in the midst of a major health crisis, including a serious stomach ulcer (the sign Cancer, placed on her 6th house cusp, rules the stomach). Although she tried many forms of treatment, nothing seemed to alleviate her symptoms. She was particularly troubled by feelings of helplessness, confusion, and failure because of her inability to work.

With transiting Saturn and Uranus conjunct Venus, and Pluto square natal Pluto in the 7th house, marital tensions were prominent. Both she and her husband had recently had affairs and the bitter reality of their crumbling marriage was becoming vividly evident. She was also becoming aware that she was a survivor of incest.

Pam was enraged about her downwardly spiraling situation, which felt totally beyond her control. In addition, the spiritual practices she had pursued for many years did not provide any illumination of what she was experiencing at this time. She felt that her entire life was falling apart and came to consult with me in a state of profound anxiety and fear.

There are many ways in which an astrological counselor (or psychotherapist utilizing astrology) could approach such a situation. For example, a medical astrologer, focusing upon the biological level, might try to determine the nature of her illness from the birth chart and even suggest appropriate forms of treatment. Because Cancer is on her 6th house cusp, the physical illness might be viewed as a manifestation of deeply rooted emotional conflicts that have been "eating away at her" and that need resolution. Another astrologer

"Pam"
November 29, 1947
11:10 AM PST
Los Angeles, California

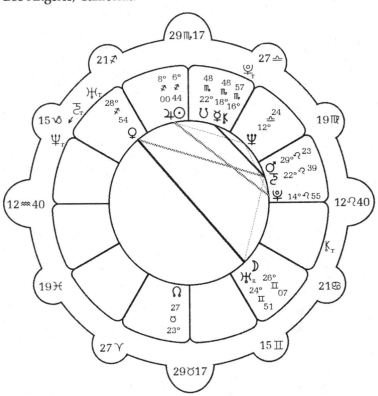

Chart 17

might view this situation as primarily a problem of socio-cultural adjustment and recommend ways of changing her attitude, or her vocation, that might enable her to adapt better to the demands of work and career. Similarly, a person-centered interpretation might emphasize the fact that Pam's natal Sun and Jupiter in her 10th house make an active and successful professional life absolutely necessary for her fulfillment as an individual — making such a period of crisis and uncertainty an unwelcome intrusion upon, or deviation from, her process of self-actualization. However, while each of these interpretations may have some validity, they do not address the potential underlying purpose of this tumultuous period of Pam's life within the context of a process of spiritual awakening. For this we have to turn to a transpersonal perspective, one that includes awareness of the other levels of interpretation and their goals, but goes beyond them by shedding light on the inherent transformational intention or goal that may be embedded in such a crisis.

Saturnian Stability and Preparation for Metamorphosis

Transpersonal chart interpretation is frequently quite delicate, due to the conflicting requirements of socio-cultural functioning, fulfillment as an individual, and the influence of spiritual forces that may feel disruptive or invasive. Individuals drawn toward the path of transformation must carefully consider whether or not they are adequately meeting the responsibilities of earthly life, symbolized by Saturn. At certain times — especially during periods of transits or progressions involving Saturn — it is necessary to temporarily suspend pursuit of higher states of consciousness in order to strengthen the ego in preparation for transpersonal metamorphosis. To receive and contain spiritual energies one needs a strong vessel, forged by the tests of Saturn, which promotes a mature, realistic, and pragmatic intelligence, and the capacity for focused, disciplined effort. It is important to become a person, firmly grounded and functional on biological, socio-cultural, and individual levels before transpersonal growth can proceed in an optimal manner.

However, in the case of someone like Pam, the situation is more complex. She clearly has profound psychological and emotional issues at the personal, egoic level (most centrally those related to her memories of incest) that need to be examined and resolved, perhaps in the context of psychotherapy. These matters are not, in themselves, transpersonal concerns. Yet here egoic stability is not the only factor to consider, for she has already fulfilled an important social role and achieved a high degree of professional stature. We will soon see that what makes her case stand out as an example of a transpersonal metamorphosis rather than just a personal crisis is her conscious decision (guided by astrological symbolism) to transmute her confrontation with painful personal issues into an opportunity to evolve toward a higher mode of existence — one informed by an entirely new set of priorities and commitments.

The Outer Planets and Rites of Passage

Transpersonal astrology can help us to undertand the competing needs and developmental strivings of an individual like Pam making the transition between "personhood" (socio-cultural success and self-actualization) and "seedhood" (self-transcendence, transpersonal creativity and service). For example, during transits involving the outer planets one may become more receptive to mystical and transpersonal dimensions of life, but one may also act in ways that others would consider irresponsible or unrealistic. From an astrological perspective, these developments can be viewed as necessary stages of severance and deconditioning that are prerequisites for deeper transformation. Astrology thus illuminates the dynamic tension often experienced between social adjustment, personal fulfillment, and spiritual awakening.

To grow spiritually one must be prepared at certain times to undergo processes that destabilize the ego and create considerable discomfort. These are the rites of passage precipitated by Uranus, Neptune, and Pluto, the agents of transpersonal evolution. Note that all three trans-saturnian planets were active by transit at the time of Pam's spiritual crisis, not uncommon during periods of profound personal upheaval.

To guide oneself or another person through such periods requires a clear understanding of the specific, transformative purpose of these three planets. In Rudhyar's (1975) words,

As an individual begins to experience his attunement to the spirit, he always has to face a crucial choice: to be a Sun, while dreaming of identification with the Supreme Spirit or, as a star among companion stars, to dedicate to the whole community whatever spiritual inflow has sought in him a focal point and channel for expression. . . . There are three fundamental kinds of test, . . . three levels at which the decision has to be made during the process of transformation of the individual. . . which can be referred to the specific character of the three trans-saturnian planets, Uranus, Neptune, and Pluto. . . . [These symbolize] the hunger for spiritual experiences, the desire for display of miraculous powers surrounding one with transcendent glamor, and the deep yearning for self-glorification and power over other human beings. (pp. 169–170)

URANUS

Transits or progressions involving Uranus precipitate processes of *severance* from rigid cultural conditioning and beliefs. Uranus impels a person to break free of the limitations bred by unquestioning allegiance to family and nation. This may mean either an external act of rebellion or a more internal shift of commitments and priorities. A fundamental lesson of Uranus is that the attainment of a transpersonal state of existence may require risking societal disapproval and stigmatization for unconventional pursuits, ideologies, or lifestyles. Traveling on the frontiers of the transpersonal way often requires taking the courageous step beyond the boundaries of culturally sanctioned beliefs and values. It was in this sense that Rudhyar often posed the question, "Which do you want, security or transformation?" We will see several vivid illustrations of the crisis of severance in Part III. In Pam's case the crisis of severance took the form of her decision to resign from her university teaching job, a position that provided a great deal of stability in her life, a stability that many people would envy.

Nevertheless, when transiting Uranus opposed her Moon, Pam grew restless for a change of direction and for freedom from her habituated patterns of activity. While it is true that she was not able to fulfill her professional responsibilities during this time, she became increasingly aware of a dissatisfaction that she had been feeling (and suppressing) with her comfortable and circumscribed social role and lifestyle. She was finally able to admit that she had secretly wanted to make a career change for a long time but had been afraid of what others might think. The transit of Uranus ripped her free from her bondage to propriety and to the inevitable judgements of parents, friends, and colleagues that she knew would meet her decision to quit her job.

Similarly, Pam felt that her values regarding marriage were being called deeply into question. While Saturn and Uranus transited over natal Venus, she and her husband began attending meetings of a group promoting "polyfidelity", and group marriage (Venus in 11th), and she began opening herself to new relationships outside her own marriage. This was a major shock to her prior sensibilities and to many values she had internalized from her family and religious upbringing. Ultimately she decided that she preferred a monogamous lifestyle, but she felt that this period of experimentation had been a valuable one. Frightened as she was at times by the whirlwind of change she was experiencing, she also reported a sense of exhiliration that she felt came from living at the edge of freedom and uncertainty.

NEPTUNE

On the path of transformation we often feel poised on the edge of two worlds — the world of our culture, and a transcultural, transphysical realm, intuited, but not directly seen. Protracted periods of disorientation and confusion are almost inevitable, and are symbolized astrologically by transits or progressions involving Neptune. During such a period, vividly typified by Pam's spiritual emergency, we must consciously open our awareness to a wider sphere of existence and consciousness, and allow ourselves to become more and more permeable to its subtle, transforming influence. At times, Neptune may permit deepened access to other states of consciousness, visions, profoundly meaningful dreams, deep meditative states, mystical experiences or illuminations of the presence of God/Goddess (see Grof, 1992, for descriptions of the varieties of transpersonal states). At such a time our consciousness is not focused on the material world, the saturnian realm of forms, structures, and earthly responsibilities; and we may feel a powerful pull inward, often calling for periods of solitude, retreat, or meditation. Neptune also makes the imagination highly active, yielding visions or dreams that may seem unrealistic or unattainable at the time but that may ultimately prove to be significant forms of spiritual inspiration.

For example, between 1903 and 1909 Hazrat Inayat Khan experienced an extended transit of Neptune over his nadir and natal Sun (Chart 5). Inayat Khan had already achieved notoriety in his career as a performing musician (Venus in Leo in the 5th). However, during this transit, he began to meditate more deeply, became fascinated with Persian mystical poetry, and dreamed of uplifting Indian music and culture. He experienced states of rapture while singing and playing the *veena* and felt that music and religious feeling were one and the same (natal Venus square Neptune). He realized that he did not want worldly success, but rather to help humanity and to experience God through music. He began to have unexpected experiences in meditation, for example visions of bright lights, and voices giving him direct spiritual guidance. Inayat Khan found a spiritual master who taught him physical exercises for purification, meditation practices, and Sufi doctrine. He also began to experience telepathic communication with his teacher and with others. During this period he attained the highest stages of mystical realization. And his idealistic vision of uplifting humanity through music, poetry, and contemplation of God became the inspiration for his later work in bringing the Sufi message to the West.

It must be stressed, however, that although such experiences of Neptune's influence can transform our vision of life and sense of individual identity, we may also confront a sense of having totally lost our bearings. As we have seen, this was Pam's condition during the transit of Saturn and Neptune to her natal Neptune. Rudhyar (1980) has described the whole initiatory process as

> an unfamiliar mountainous path whose end always seems to recede beyond the horizon. . . . On that path of radical transformation, faith is required — a faith requiring humility, as well as the courage which can only be born of an inner realization of the irrevocable character of a decision whose source is more than purely mental. . . (p. 113)

The recognition of "the irrevocable character of a decision whose source is more than purely mental" brings us to a threshold. This moment of irrevocable decision is the point of no return, beyond which we cease to look backward in longing toward safer paths, and we fully accept that the centripetal forces of the ego are to be reoriented. Only at this point can we be said to be firmly established on the transpersonal way.

PLUTO

The crossing of this threshold often occurs during the tests associated with Pluto. Pluto, by transit, progression, or natal contact, often precipitates periods of emotional crisis, often accompanied by feelings of isolation, exile, or finality. Pluto reveals the dark side of human nature that is deeply lodged in the collective unconscious of humanity: our tendencies to be manipulative, mistrustful, abusive, hostile, and resentful, our capacity for evil, hate, and bigotry. Plutonian periods are often harsh confrontations with the naked truth of such characteristics in ourselves or others. Under optimal conditions, this may eventually lead to purgation, re-centering, transformation of our use of personal power, and a greater capacity to express our essential nature. These are also periods in which our singleness of purpose and commitment to service are tested:

> The aspirant to rebirth in spirit cannot become a safe and valuable member of a galactic type of community if there exists in him the slightest desire for acting as a Sun to a group of dark planets. This is the Plutonian test of total denudation, . . . of absolute humility. Only if the Plutonian catharsis is successfully met can an individual be trusted to be a true "companion." (Rudhyar, 1975, p. 170)

Note that the purification of our use of personal power does not mean that we lose the capacity to act in a purposeful, focused, and individualized manner. Rather it means that we become able to look beyond our own needs and desires and to act without pride and self-glorification. Pluto's goal is to bring about a reorientation of action and intention, from the individual, the personal will, to the higher Will, the intention of God or Spirit. But in actuality this frequently requires a form of painful "surgery" in which events confront us with our misuses of power, our distorted ambitions, our need to control or mistreat others, and our destructive, ruthless tendencies. From the ashes of such periods, a new dedication of one's individuality to purity in action may begin to arise. In the next chapter we will note how Pam experienced such a plutonian purification.

As we undergo the process of transformation we are asked to move outside the rings of Saturn (our secure "home base") and travel to the stations represented by Uranus, Neptune, and Pluto, where new freedom and new levels of awareness become possible. While at first it is difficult to explore these unfamiliar outposts without terror, we can gradually learn to step through the portals of fear and venture forth into the open space of expanded consciousness. At times our consciousness expands into awareness of the Divine, the realms of light revealed and symbolized by Neptune. At other times our growth in consciousness means a new awareness of the Demonic, the underworld realms of pain, darkness, ignorance, and evil that Pluto can uncover. In either case, our limited perspective is shattered. Awe and humility begin to dawn. We will never be the same.

The purpose of transpersonal astrology is to help us walk with balance as we venture forth into new worlds, new visions, new ways of being. Approached wisely, astrology can free us from the confusion associated with this process by illuminating its structure and its potential outcome. Celestial studies teach us to remain centered as we experience profound transformations, and to make periodic incursions back within the boundaries of Saturn to stabilize ourselves and to ground the energies of Spirit. True spirituaity does not mean escape from this plane of existence, as some ancient yogis and mystics contended. As Sri Aurobindo taught, the Universal Spirit is an evolutionary force that is seeking to bring about a renewal and divinization of Matter, Creation, planet Earth — where it may more fully manifest its infinite radiance and splendor. The instrument of Spirit is the transpersonal individual, an incarnate human being, with eyes open to suffering, who has been purified sufficiently that he or she becomes a vehicle through whom God or the greater whole can act. The birth chart vividly portrays the initiations leading to this condition. These issues will be examined further in the next chapter, where I introduce some additional concepts that will deepen our understanding of Pam's transformation.

CHAPTER 5

The Six Shaktis

To guide an individual like Pam, it is often helpful to draw upon the insights and teachings of religious, philosophical, or mystical traditions to supplement or inform our use of the birthmap. There are many maps of the process of spiritual awakening that may be suitable for this purpose, such as the Ox-herding pictures of Zen Buddhism; Christian, Jewish, or Islamic descriptions of the stages of contemplative prayer and meditation; the yogic model of *kundalini* awakening and the opening of the seven *chakras*; or Ken Wilber's (1980) spectrum psychology theory.

This chapter will describe another model that I utilized to assist Pam in concert with her birth chart, a model based on what Rudhyar (1973) called "the six *shaktis*." According to Rudhyar, the path of transformation may be conceptualized as a process of gaining successive mastery of six shaktis, six faculties that enable a person to respond as a stable center of consciousness, able to use power purposefully and in alignment with a spiritual or transpersonal purpose (pp. 300, 310). The brief discussion of the six shaktis in his book, *An Astrological Mandala*, is highly evocative. However, Rudhyar does not seem to have fully known the origins of these concepts, and his understanding was based solely on the writings of an early twentieth century Indian philosopher named Subba Row. In fact, the six shaktis are central concepts of the ancient Indian philosophy of Kashmir Shaivism, a highly sophisticated, ancient system of yoga. In what follows, I combine the basic principles of Kashmir Shaivism with Rudhyar's perspective to define a context for guiding an individual through a spiritual emergence crisis using transpersonal chart interpretation. The ideas I present here are intended to suggest *one way* of applying astrology at the transpersonal level, drawing on the doctrines of a great sacred tradition. Nevertheless, other approaches may also be valid, for example models based on Tibetan Buddhist doctrines, Sufism, Theosophy, or any other coherent theory or map of spiritual awakening applied to chart interpretation. I invite readers to consider how they might apply other teachings that they find compelling to the practice of transpersonal astrology.

Before examining Rudhyar's perspective on the six shaktis and my own understanding of their application, it might be useful to briefly describe Kashmir Shaivism, a philosophy developed by lineages of yogic adepts or *siddhas* in Kashmir and Northern India between about the second and eleventh centuries, C.E. (see Muller-Ortega, 1989). Kashmir Shaivism is based on the idea that the Supreme Source of all that is, called "Shiva," exists in a condition of eternal, self-existent consciousness, bliss, and quiescence. Shiva, for his own sport and enjoyment, chooses to manifest countless forms and universes through the agency of his creative aspect, known as "Shakti." Initially, a subtle vibration or ripple appears in the divine stillness, and this gives rise to subsidiary powers (shaktis) and the stages of material evolution — through the process known as *spanda,* or expansion. This initial movement within the divine Being is known as *para shakti*. Para shakti brings about the concealment of Shiva's eternal presence in the realms of visible manifestation. However, Shiva remains eternally present; and through the para shakti's capacity for "bestowal of grace," the concealed energy of supreme Consciousness (Shiva) ultimately reawakens, destroying the limitations and obscurations that had eclipsed Shiva's self-awareness.

Paradoxically, para shakti both evolves material universes and makes possible Shiva's eventual reawakening as infinite consciousness and eternal presence. Para shakti operates through the mediation of five derivative shaktis: *maitrika shakti*, the power of letters and language, which give rise to myriad forms and objects; *ichcha shakti*, the power of the creative will through which creation occurs and through which consciousness is ultimately reestablished in its own condition of perfection, bliss, and stillness; *jnana shakti*, the power of understanding through which objects are grasped, and through which consciousness eventually detaches itself from identification with objects of perception and becomes aware of itself *as awareness*; and *kriya shakti*, the power of manifestation of forms, which makes use of the creative will of *ichcha shakti*. Finally, the concealed power of Shiva or Consciousness is revealed to the individual through the unfolding of the coiled energy of the *kundalini shakti*.

My own understanding, which blends the traditional meanings (see Muktananda, 1980) of these terms with the interpretations given by Rudhyar (1973, pp. 300–310), is that para shakti represents the primordial movement of the supreme Spirit, which brings about profound physical and emotional cleansings and renewal. Jnana shakti is the power of knowledge, cyclic wisdom, and individualized consciousness. Ichcha shakti is the power of desire and focused will. Maitrika shakti is the power of language to facilitate communication, creative self-expression, or spiritual liberation through the subtle aspect of language known as *mantra*. Kriya shakti is the capacity to act in accordance with imagined goals or visualized images. And kundalini shakti is the power of spiritual expansion and the coordination of individual activity with a transpersonal Will. In the remainder of this chapter I will explain how important facets of Pam's transformation can be understood as manifestations of these six shaktis.

Para Shakti: Physical and Emotional Purification

The transformational process often begins with a profound personal crisis and purification brought about by para shakti, the supreme life-force. Para shakti may awaken as a result of *shaktipat* initiation by an awakened spiritual master (see Chapter 9), or it may awaken spontaneously in an individual who is ardently seeking God or has awakened to the possibility of achieving an expanded state of consciousness. In either case, *para-shakti-pata*, the descent of the power of the divine, initiates a purification of the physical, emotional, mental, and various subtle bodies that may be of varying degrees of intensity. Through these processes, the individual is prepared to become an individualized yet radiant and unimpeded vehicle for expression of the will of the Supreme.

As one begins to awaken spiritually one may need to cleanse the physical body and liberate it from obstructions through exercise, dietary changes, or practices designed to increase strength, flexibility, and alignment. This does not mean that one must adhere to any particular practice or discipline or have extraordinary athletic capacities; but it does imply the importance of establishing an appropriate relationship with the physical body so that it becomes an open channel for the free flow of the supreme life force. By mastering the *prana* and quieting or strengthening the vital force, the body is prepared to contain the eventual unfolding of the kundalini shakti, the power of expansion of consciousness. One may also experience the activity of para shakti in the form of *kriyas*, spontaneous movements of the physical or subtle bodies that bring about deep cleansing and inner balancing.

Pam, for example, needed to improve her physical condition before exploration of spiritual dimensions could truly be fruitful. Just as she was unable to maintain sufficient energy to work, she was also unable to contain any spiritual energy. To the contrary, the more she invoked such forces through intense chanting or trying to channel her spiritual guides, the more her emotional conflicts, her sense of helplessness, and her rage seemed to be energized. Pam moved in the direction of greater physical health by practicing hatha yoga, moderate fasting, and eating a more balanced diet (transiting Chiron in 6th). She also began to experience a tangible spiritual presence that she felt was seeking to mold her physical body into a more sensitive, resilient, refined instrument of infinite Consciousness (transiting Saturn-Neptune square Neptune). While Pam had not formally received *shaktipat* initiation from an enlightened guru, she felt that her own efforts were eliciting a descent of grace that was accelerating her evolution.

The process of awakening may also catalyze a purification of the "emotional body." An airing of the unconscious may occur, allowing one to heal the wounds of the past, and affording greater freedom from negative emotional states and mental attitudes. I have found that this process is often associated with transits or progressions contacting the natal Moon (the planet of emotional memory), or involving planets situated in the 4th, 8th, or 12th houses. In Pam's case, the surfacing of emotional wounds appeared to be precipitated by the transit of Uranus to her natal Moon. Moreover, Saturn and Neptune squared natal Neptune, intensifying her longing for liberation from the limitations of the material world, her feelings of helplessness and martyrdom, and her preoccupation with dreams, fantasies, and memories. The combined transits of Uranus to her natal Moon, Saturn-Neptune to natal Neptune, and of Pluto to natal Pluto brought about a surfacing of painful memories of childhood sexual abuse that seemed to be the ultimate source of many of her emotional conflicts — and which made her current struggles with her husband all the more difficult to endure. Much of her spiritual and psychological work at this time revolved around fully venting the rage and terror associated with these memories.

In addition, Saturn (along with Neptune) was transiting through the 12th house, a transit that often brings into vivid focus the unresolved issues of one's entire life to that point. This was traditionally considered the house of "endings," "karma," and "confinement." The period of Saturn's transit through the 12th house is often experienced as a dissolution of the person's established identity and a closing of accounts with the past. This may take the form of an eruption of unconscious memories and feelings, and the crystalization of one's central conflicts, dilemmas, and unfulfilled aspirations. Previously submerged material often surfaces from both the individual's biography and from more subtle sources such as past lives or the archetypal realm of the collective unconscious. The eruption of this material may be somewhat overwhelming, leading to the kind of panic and psychological paralysis that we see in Pam.

Ultimately, however, such a period can illuminate the subtle karmic forces that have shaped the person's life-experience. It can also yield profound insights into the tasks that still need to be accomplished during the upcoming cycle in order to fulfill the purpose of this incarnation. A transpersonalization of personal identity and life-history can occur in such a crisis, enabling one to live a "symbolic life," viewing one's experience as mythic or archetypal. Pam bravely faced many internal images depicting scenes of violence, abuse, and bondage that emerged through dreams, fantasies, and memories of what she believed to be past lives. While she was terrified and shaken to her depths by these images, she gradually began to discern how her entire life and identity had been shaped, and dominated, by the highly charged emotional material that they contained. In the midst of this engulfing personal crisis, Pam felt the intervention and guidance of a mysterious but tangible spiritual force that seemed to intend that she experience a profound transformation.

Jnana Shakti: The Power of Knowledge and Eonic Wisdom

According to Rudhyar, the second faculty that is crucial in the transformational process is mastery of jnana shakti, the power of mind and knowledge. In Kashmir Shaivism, jnana shakti refers to the power of consciousness to apprehend its own nature. At a more basic level, it refers to cognitive abilities such as perception, memory, anticipation, and rational thought, or higher mental faculties such as telepathy, precognition, clairvoyance, and telekinesis. From Rudhyar's perspective, jnana shakti suggests the capacity for individualized understanding and interpretation of life-experience. This implies a process of deconditioning from some of the dominant beliefs and values of one's society, and the formation of one's own cognitive or conceptual framework. Wisdom (*jnana*) also implies development of "the mind of wholeness" and "eonic consciousness," the ability to perceive every event as a purposeful and meaningful phase of a cycle.

I utilized Pam's birth chart to help her understand the nature and purpose of this period of profound upheaval within the totality of her life-cycle and evolutionary development. This enabled her to gradually detach herself from deeply internalized inner voices, for example those echoing her father's condemnation of her current period of interior search as immature and irresponsible. This process involved a close examination of her parental introjects and other negative patterns of thought and the deliberate construction of more positive thoughts (popularly known as "affirmations"). Pam came to understand that one period of her life had to end before a new period could begin. Her identity, her role, her *consciousness* as a professor had not been one that allowed full awakening of her creative and spiritual potentials. One evolutionary cycle had completed itself and a new cycle of activity was about to begin, one that might enable her to bring about a fuller expression of her capacities. During one session, Pam's anxiety began to lift and her face radiated peace as she came to recognize that this chaotic period was indeed a meaningful phase of her process of transformation.

Ichcha Shakti: The Power of the Will

Utilization of *ichcha shakti*, gives one the power of focused use of will and consciousness. Ichcha, a term deriving from the Sanskrit verb form *ichchh*, which means to wish or desire, also implies the capacity to mold one's experience and one's reality through the power of intention. Many spiritual seekers use traditional mystical doctrines encouraging surrender or submission to God's will as an excuse for passivity, and lack of energy, motivation, and focused effort. However, an alternative view is that the personal will may be aligned with a greater divine or transpersonal will and then directed purposefully. In this manner, the personal will becomes a vehicle through which the divine intention is actualized.

Pam reached a crucial threshold when she recognized that she was not helpless, that her will and actions could be powerful forces in molding the course of her life. Connecting with the efficacy of her will enabled her to slowly craft herself into the image of her personal ideals. Moreover, after receiving instruction in meditation from a wise Tibetan teacher, she was able to use the focused power of will to establish herself in expanded states of consciousness — fulfilling the evolutionary growth potential of Saturn and Neptune's transit through the 12th house, square natal Neptune.

Maitrika Shakti, and the Modes of Creative Activity

According to Kashmir Shaivism (and Hindu Tantric philosophy in general), creation occurs through the power of sound, an initial vibration that arises within the eternal silence of Shiva. This initial movement of the creative force known as Shakti gradually evolves into letters and words that both reflect and help give rise to innumerable material forms. The creative power of language is known as *maitrika shakti* and is associated with the growth of complexity of the world of forms. It is also the basis of *mantra yoga*, the use of sound vibrations endowed with the power of maitrika shakti to induce deep states of meditation (see Dyczkowski, 1987).

However, maitrika shakti may be utilized not only to move inward toward God but also to actively participate in the continuing creative outpouring and evolution of Spirit. An individual in transformation may wish to wield maitrika shakti, the power of letters and speech, through a variety of artistic or literary pursuits. In these ways spiritual insights can be expressed and exert a resonant and transformative impact on others or the world. To experience peace of mind through practices such as meditation is an important aspect of the path of awakening, yet it is not an end in itself. For transpersonal growth also involves metamorphosis on the plane of action. One of the foundations of Rudhyar's philosophy is that spirituality is more than just a quest for altered states of consciousness and personal, inward enlightenment. To Rudhyar, the spiritual path is a dynamic life of *transpersonal activity* in which heightened states of awareness are expressed through well-executed, creative acts.

Rudhyar (1977) distinguished a number of levels of creative activity according to the purpose for which they are intended: glorification of cultural symbols and institutions ("aethetic art"), personal expression ("romantic art"), rebellion or protest ("catabolic art"), or revelation of new possibilities for the future of a collectivity ("hierophanic art"). In Rudhyar's view, periods of historical crisis such as our own call forth responses of hierophanic creativity, which he describes as a "conscious release of power" impelled by transpersonal forces. Hierophanic art or creativity expresses new myths, new visions of the future, and new understandings of individual and social upheavals. It is the revelation of sacred power through artistic and literary forms. A hierophanic artist is thus a person who expresses symbols, imagery, and ideas deriving from inspired states of consciousness and revealing original artistic, scientific, moral, and interpersonal responses to historical crisis.[2]

The creative process became a central part of Pam's transformation. In her youth, Pam had been a promising poet, and recalled having a special gift for writing sonnets (Moon-Uranus in Gemini in the 5th house: unique literary creativity). However, as a teenager she became impatient with conventional literary forms and became a somewhat wild, bohemian poet for several years, writing formless, experimental poems and angry feminist and anti-war polemics that she read in cafes and at political rallies. Having lived out in these ways the aesthetic, romantic, and catabolic levels of artistic expression, Pam grew weary of the whole project of being a poet and returned to graduate school for her doctorate. Now Pam felt her long submerged creativity beginning to come alive once

---

[2] See *Culture, Crisis, and Creativity: The Prophetic Vision of Dane Rudhyar*, by Greg Bogart, available from Dawn Mountain Press.

again (transiting Uranus opposite Moon in 5th house). Tentative first attempts gave way to tempestuous gusts of rhythmic poetry describing her soul's torture, testing, and renewal, her death and rebirth (transiting Pluto square natal Pluto). They are particularly powerful communications of the subjective experience of incest (Pluto) and the slow process of emotional, psychological, and spiritual healing. She also movingly relates her personal experience to humanity's abuse of Planet Earth. The poems, in my opinion, are of more than personal significance, speaking to the pain and the hunger for redemption that nearly all of us experience. They are scintillating, hierophanic creations.

Around the same time, while transiting Uranus was conjunct Venus (planet of art and beauty), Pam also began spontaneously painting mandalas depicting the turbulent qualities of her inner world and her intuitions of the renewal that she viewed as the goal of her present condition. These paintings helped Pam to appreciate the depth and beauty of her own psychic upheaval and to trust in its ultimate resolution. Both her paintings and her poems enabled her to mythologize her personal history and to ritualize this period of transition, thereby transforming it into a sacred event. She also found a way of communicating her experience to others and to inspire them to take steps toward their own metamorphosis. Her pain and her hope have become windows through which the pain and hope of all beings who suffer may be perceived. The paintings also contain images that refer to contemporary social issues, the need for inter-racial and inter-cultural tolerance, and the hope for a new era of world peace and unity (Venus in 11th house). Finally, these creative activities (Venus opposite Moon in 5th) allowed many images to arise from her unconscious and her imagination that played a central role in her transformation, especially images of her potential future identity in a role of service and dedication to others (natal Sun sextile Neptune).

Kriya Shakti: Action Transformed Through Visualization

Fueled by the power of the focused will, mental images can exert a major influence on the process of transformation. According to Rudhyar, *kriya shakti* enables a person to pass through a reorientation of consciousness based on a clearly visualized image or archetype to which he or she becomes committed with a deep "feeling-urge." The capacity to influence personal reality through conscious use of mental images has been known and utilized for millennia. Ancient shamans used images perceived in altered states of consciousness to bring about healing of individuals and communities (Achterberg, 1985; Eliade, 1964), and many spiritual traditions emphasize visualization practices. Gawain (1978) has outlined "four basic steps for effective creative visualization":

> 1. Set your goal. . . . 2. Create a clear idea or picture. . . of the object or situation exactly as you want it. You should think of it in the present tense as already existing the way you want it to be. . . . 3. Focus on it often. . . . 4. Give it positive energy. . . . Think about [your goal] in a positive, encouraging way. Make strong, positive statements to yourself that it exists, that it has come or is now coming to you. See yourself receiving or achieving it (pp. 29–30).

An important dimension of transpersonal metamorphosis is the capacity to envision the next stage of personal or collective evolution and to allow this ideal to become "an irrefutable reality for the consciousness and a steady, indestructible commitment" (Rudhyar, 1973, p. 308). Thus, even while Pam was flooded with painful, previously unconscious material, she began to envision a transformed identity that she considered the end state of her metamorphosis. She viewed her voyage into the raging storms of the psyche as a rite of passage that would enable her to teach others in a much more wise and subtle manner than that for which her previous schooling had prepared her. Pam dedicated herself to becoming the embodiment of this ideal, the teacher who speaks with the illumination of one who has confronted the depths of the human soul.

According to Rudhyar, an important stage of the path of transformation is reached when, having overcome the inertia of one's biological and culture-bound nature, the clinging, centripetal forces of the ego begin to be repolarized. As we saw earlier, this involves the purification of intention and use of power associated with Pluto, and the awakening of compassion, associated with Neptune. Thus, Pam began to recognize some of her major limitations as a person and as a teacher: her anger, arrogance, condescension, and sense of superiority; her mistrustfulness, and her tendency to manipulate others through her sexual attractiveness and powerful, persuasive intellect. She began to feel a deep remorse for all actions she had taken in her life that had been injurious to others (Pluto square natal

Pluto in 7th). Simultaneously, a feeling of universal concern, compassion, and desire to serve others began to arise within her. As this new intention strengthened, she was able to meditate more deeply and began to feel an almost ecstatic inner peace (Saturn-Neptune in 12th square natal Neptune). She asked friends to forgive her for past actions and made known her willingness to support them in their own transitions and transformations. She continued to fight with her husband, then forgave him and began to acknowledge her own mistakes and imperfections.

The erudite professor now volunteers at a soup kitchen for homeless people and works with battered women and abused children. She is immersed in studies of mythology, art, and anthropology, and hopes to teach again one day, in a completely new field. While Pam is still in transition and in pain, she has been transformed in a short period of time from a self-absorbed, materialistic, and almost entirely intellectual person into one filled with wonder and a clear awareness of a spiritual presence active in her life, motivated more by compassion and the desire to use her skills to serve others.

Kundalini Shakti, Self-Consecration, and Transpersonal Activity

An important element in such an internal transformation is what Rudhyar calls "self-consecration to the whole." Self-consecration opens the individual to a larger field of existence, which often makes itself known in the form of *kundalini shakti*. Kundalini, sometimes called the "serpent power," refers to a powerful energy that may be experienced emerging from a dormant state and rising up from the base of the spine toward the top of the head — often catalyzing powerful physical movements and streams of energy in the *chakras* (major energy centers) that remove blockages in the physical and subtle bodies. Kundalini has been extensively described in the yogic traditions of India and Tibet, and in Taoist mysticism. There are allusions to it in European alchemy, accounts of Christian and Sufi contemplatives, among !Kung tribesmen, and in descriptions of shamanic experience (Sannella, 1987, pp. 37–56).

Sannella hypothesizes that kundalini is the manifestation of a physiological mechanism leading to a series of identifiable psycho-physical symptoms:

> Such physical sensations as itching, fluttering, tingling, intense heat
> and cold, photisms (perceptions of inner lights) and the perception
> of primary sounds, as well as the occurrence of spasms and
> contortions, seem to be "archetypal" features of the process. . . . It is
> this universality that leads me to postulate that all psychospiritual
> practices activate the same basic process, and this process has a
> definite physiological basis. (p.24)

Sannella contends that kundalini awakening results from activation
of a specific current of energy in the brain that gives rise to these
symptoms. But he also notes that the physiological mechanism by
which it operates does not explain "the meaningfulness of the
kundalini experience itself," particularly its emotional components,
which can range from confusion and depression to ecstasy and
"superlucidity" (p. 24).

Scott (1983) attempted to explain the deeper significance of
kundalini, describing it as a "cosmic force" that "guides evolution
from within as well as from above" (p. 77). She notes "kundalini's
connection with terrestrial currents," viewing it as the microcosmic
aspect of the same energy that flows through the geomagnetically
sensitive "ley lines" along the earth's surface (p. 108). She calls
kundalini "a force in nature which can connive at the evolution of the
ego and then, in due time, facilitate its transcendence" (p. 109).

In addition to the physiological and evolutionary significance
that Sannella and Scott attribute to this mysterious phenomena, the
subjective experience of kundalini suggests to me yet another level of
meaning: Experiences of kundalini are often accompanied by a
strong feeling of "otherness," the sense of confronting an
autonomous power with a will and intention of its own — a spiritual
force (akin to what the Sufis call "the spirit of guidance") that is
actively seeking to bring about a reorganization of the personality.
Thus, kundalini awakening can be considered the manifestation of a
transpersonal intelligence. Once a human being has made an internal
shift beyond egoic motivations and begins to awaken compassion
and the desire to serve in whatever way is possible and appropriate,
then a spiritual force may come to meet that individual and guide his
or her actions. This spiritual power, which in some cases manifests as
the serpent power, often seems to have a specific intention for the
individual. Rudhyar (1973, pp. 308–309) hinted at this understanding
of kundalini when he referred to it as a principle of *coordination* that
brings about a universalization of the individual. I believe that the

dramatic, sometimes violent experiences often associated with kundalini awakening can be viewed as symptoms or reflections of a more subtle process — a process through which the will and actions of the individual are reoriented to come into alignment with the will of a greater whole: God, Gaia, or humanity.

Rudhyar often described this spiritual intelligence as one that embodies the unified will of humanity-as-a-whole. He called this unified will of humanity "the Pleroma," a non-physical community of beings that have achieved a consciousness of unanimity and dedication to humanity, the planet Earth, and ultimately a greater galactic community. Others have called it "the Hierarchy" or "the White Brotherhood." Experiences of kundalini may be viewed as the intervention of this spiritual power of the whole, the Pleroma, as it attempts to come into relation to an adequately prepared individual, to become embodied through that person, and to become the new "guiding field" of the personality. This does not mean that a transpersonal individual becomes possessed by another entity like a passive medium but rather that he or she becomes the conscious, responsible agent (or "avatar") of a transpersonal purpose with which he or she becomes identified:

> When the individualized "mind of wholeness" apprehends the archetype which is his or her guiding field and begins to resonate to the spiritual Quality of his or her innermost beingness, then individual freedom can only mean choosing the best way to actualize this archetype. In this sense, the truly "liberated" person is consciously and willingly determined by his or her archetype. Freedom and determinism merge. (Rudhyar, 1982, p. 33)

Pam's meditations began to be filled with awareness of an all-pervasive spiritual presence, which she often experienced as the activity of kundalini energy dancing inside her body and manifesting in all directions as the universe. She had passed through a profound physical, emotional, and interpersonal crisis and purification, expanded her understanding, strengthened her will, awakened her creative capacities, and aligned her life and actions with visualized ideals. Now she was surrendering, moment by moment, to the will of God. She was becoming, in Rudhyar's terms, a "self-consecrated individual," willingly determined by her archetype and the embodiment of spiritual qualities such as service, faith, equanimity, visionary inspiration, and dynamic creativity. She increasingly experienced her life as a process of merging into the Absolute and standing in the world as an instrument, agent, and messenger of the Light.

From Karma to Dharma

Rudhyar often stated (1973, 1976) that the universe calls forth the birth of each person for a reason, as an answer to a need of humanity. In the practice of transpersonal chart interpretation one attempts to intuit the collective need to which an individual's birth was a potential response and an image of this person's role within the greater tribal, national, planetary, or galactic whole. Thus, one goal of transpersonal astrology is to evoke images of the potential role or function for which the individual could be utilized as an instrument, once he or she has become committed and ready for transpersonal activity. Informed in this manner with an image of one's *dharma* or fundamental life task, the transpersonal individual attempts to gradually merge his or her will with the unified mind and will of humanity-as-a-whole, thereby becoming an agent through whom this greater whole can act:

> The human receiver acts as a focalizing agent for the need of his people and his culture. Though he or she may be unaware of it, the entire inner being of such an agent takes the form of a "prayer" of the Pleroma — the greater planetary whole operating at a higher level of the hierarchy of being. . . . The transpersonal action or communication answers not only a personal need, but, even more, the need of the community" (Rudhyar, 1983, p. 227).

Study of the birth chart reveals an image of the purpose for which the individual's birth was called forth. It also illuminates the nature and timing of crises, which are both the means of neutralizing personal karma and the occasion for transmuting that karma into dharma — a sacred performance of the task or purpose with which each person was invested at birth (Rudhyar, 1980, p. 131). The next section of this book examines the lives of several individuals who transmuted karma into dharma — who transcended cultural conditioning and responded in an effective manner to collective needs and the dictates of Spirit.

To sum up, Rudhyar views the transpersonal life as a life of hierophanic creative acts inspired by a more-than-personal purpose, acts that may also inspire understanding, vision, and courage in others. Astrology, approached from the transpersonal perspective, can help an individual on the transpersonal way to proceed safely and wisely through the ordeals of physical, emotional, mental and supramental preparation for this kind of self-consecrated, transpersonal activity. Whereas the purpose of astrology at the person-centered or humanistic level is to seek greater fulfillment as an individual, the goal of transpersonal astrology is to transcend personal problems by referring them to a new purpose: the opening to an infusion or descent of spiritual, supramental forces that inspire transpersonal creativity. Transpersonal astrology can be a clear, individualized guide through the stages of this great spiritual adventure.

PART III

Astrological Biographies of Spiritual Teachers

The following chapters consist of a series of astrological biographies of well known spiritual teachers of the 20th century. They are intended to demonstrate astrology in action through detailed chart interpretations. They also provide examples of the kinds of tests one is likely to face on the path of transformation.

These biographical studies vary considerably in their length and degree of detail. For example, the chapter on Rajneesh focuses on one brief but significant period of his life, while the analysis of Tagore's birth chart is more comprehensive. Although the Tagore chapter is somewhat lengthy, this study allows us to explore the unfolding of an extraordinary, multi-faceted life exemplifying the principles of transpersonal activity.

A few words are necessary about my approach to chart interpretation. In these studies I stay close to the basics of astrology. I make occasional references to midpoints and to interplanetary cycles, for example the transiting conjunction, squares, and opposition of Jupiter and Saturn. However, I do not discuss "minor" aspects (such as the quintile, septile, or novile), or the asteroids. Nor do I refer to the New Moon Before Birth, harmonics, solar arc directions, Uranian methods, or heliocentric charts. Some student's of Rudhyar's work may find it surprising that my interpretations are not based predominantly on techniques that he emphasized, such as the use of

Sabian Symbols and the Progressed Lunation Cycle. I also do not examine elemental emphasis or triplicities because I personally do not find these useful.

Our understanding of these charts could undoubtedly be enhanced through utilization of any of these methods and perspectives. However I have intentionally chosen not to do so. For I believe that in our eagerness to learn and utilize as many techniques as possible, many students of astrology are unable to give coherent interpretations of the most basic factors in a birth chart. Therefore I deliberately focus on the fundamentals of astrology: the signs, house placements, dispositorships, and major aspects of natal planets, transits, and secondary progressions. These studies demonstrate how much depth and richness of understanding is available when we simply dwell with basic horoscope symbols fully, and interpret them within the context of the transformational process.

Of course, as each astrologer follows an idiosyncratic method of interpreting a birth chart, I emphasize certain features of these charts and have inevitably omitted features that other astrologers might find important. No astrologer can interpret *all* of the information contained in any horoscope. Rather than focusing on those details I have neglected to mention in my delineations, I hope you will be inspired to fill in any gaps and develop your own understanding of each chart presented. And by all means, look up the Sabian Symbols for the Sun, Moon, and other important degrees of each chart, study midpoints, harmonic charts, and Solar Returns, or use whatever other method works for you that supplements my analysis. Above all, savor the beauty of the connections we will observe between biographical events and planetary symbolism. Watch astrology come alive.

Finally, while one may feel humbled when studying the biographies of great individuals, it is important not to judge oneself harshly in comparison to them. The key is to learn from their stories and then to live one's own life fully. In my opinion, you, the reader, are not in any way inferior to any of the individuals we are about to examine . Not everyone is called to the paths that people like Ram Dass, Tagore, or Eliade followed. However, they might be filled with amazement at some of the skills, understandings, and spiritual qualities that *you* have developed and some of the tests that you have passed through. Each of these individuals had a particular *dharma* or path to Wholeness. Studying their lives will help you find your own.

CHAPTER 6
An Astrological Biography of Meher Baba

This chapter examines the life of Meher Baba, one of the great spiritual leaders of modern India, in relation to his birth chart. I have consulted Hopkinson and Hopkinson (1982) for biographical information.

Meher Baba was born with a prominent Pluto-Neptune conjunction in the 5th house. Also, the Aquarius ascendant and Venus in Aquarius are square to Uranus on the midheaven, which suggests both that he might project himself as a being of love, and that he might be unusual and eccentric in some ways. In fact, Meher Baba did many things that surprised, baffled, and shocked people. He also had a revolutionary quality that fits the Uranus-Aquarius emphasis. This was mainly expressed through a kind of social work project to which he became committed, as we will see later. While he was mostly a mystical, neptunian visionary, Uranus also gave him a commitment to social betterment. Clearly, with the ascendant ruler Uranus elevated, culminating in the chart, one would expect this chart to be that of someone quite unique, and someone known for unpredictability or for shaking things up in his environment. Later we will note several examples of Meher Baba's tendency to suddenly and radically change everything in his life.

With Uranus squaring Venus in Aquarius he was not drawn toward an ordinary social life. Venus retrograde often symbolizes an interiorization of social energies. It doesn't mean that the person doesn't get along well with others; but it suggests that one's fundamental orientation with respect to Venus — the life of the senses and of close personal relations with others — somehow goes against the conventional grain. A person with Venus retrograde has to define a unique set of values or needs with respect to social interaction and personal tastes. In keeping with his Uranus square Venus, Meher Baba never married, or had any interest in what most people would consider normal social relationships. There was an air of freedom and detachment in all of his relations; he loved very freely, but in an impersonal kind of way.

Now note his Sun in Pisces in the 2nd house, square to its ruler, Neptune, which is conjunct Pluto. Also, Mars is in the 12th house, the most interior zone of the chart, the area associated with Pisces, and which is generically governed by Neptune. The Sun in Pisces in the 2nd house might be the symbol of someone who would feel called to some practical expression of his compassion. He might take on responsibility for alleviating other people's suffering through very concrete, material forms of service. It might also symbolize an attitude of surrender or trust with regard to money. With the Sun square Neptune-Pluto in the 5th house, he might also project himself as an embodiment of God, a mystic, a seer, a sage, or a holy man. As we will see, Meher Baba openly proclaimed that he was the Avatar of the age, the "Godman."

The Sun's square to Pluto and Neptune is a major aspect that needs further examination. Any close aspect of the Sun is significant, but one must take notice even more so in a case like this where the Sun is aspecting its own ruler, Neptune. Here there is going to be an identification with the circuit of energies symbolized by the conjunction of Pluto and Neptune, which coincided historically with major breakthroughs in electronics, quantum physics, x-rays, new communication technologies, psychoanalysis, and most importantly, the growth of an international, global kind of awareness. The Pluto-Neptune conjunction represented a trend toward a more inclusive social vision with which Meher Baba became personally connected because these planets closely squared his natal Sun. (One can read

Meher Baba
February 25, 1894
4:35 AM
Bombay, India

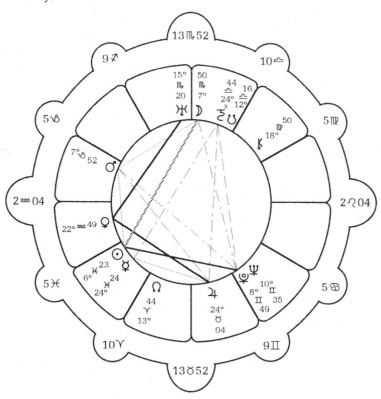

Source: Lois Rodden, *American Book of Charts*

Chart 18

more about this conjunction in Rudhyar, 1969, Arroyo and Greene, 1983, and Baigent, Campion, and Harvey, 1984.) In chart interpretation, it is very important to understand the relationship of the individual to collective, historical trends that are symbolized by the positions of the outer planets. It is no accident that this man was born on a day when the Sun was strongly aspecting the Pluto-Neptune conjunction. It suggests that he was meant to embody in his own life some of the new values and new visions, symbolized by Pluto-Neptune, that were beginning to emerge collectively.

The symbolism of Sun square Neptune-Pluto suggests a powerful idealism and a total dedication to higher ideals such as service and the relief of suffering. Pluto conjunct Neptune could unleash a tremendous compassion, a deep devotion to the betterment of the greater whole, or in Aurobindo's terms, utter "self-consecration." Having a Pisces Sun while Pluto is conjunct Neptune implies the potential for self-surrender, self-sacrifice, complete awakening of visionary capacities, profound mystical experience and expansion of consciousness.

With Pluto-Neptune square his Pisces Sun, Meher Baba had a tremendous urge toward self-renewal, to undergo a profound transformation of awareness. This aspect might generate a strong charismatic energy that could be utilized, not for selfish ends, but for service (Neptune), through a refinement and complete transformation of his use of power (Pluto). Pluto, a symbol of concentrated power and intensity, was conjunct Neptune, which is always dedicated to the most expansive frame of reference possible — the good of all humanity and of all beings. With his Sun in Pisces square Pluto and Neptune, this was the chart of someone with the potential to become an illumined mystic, a servant of humanity, a spiritually awakened person, a man of great power and influence. It could also mean that this person's consciousness was in some way going to be overwhelmed or flooded by a higher force or presence, perhaps leading to dissolution of ego boundaries, a spiritual death and rebirth. Meher Baba was to live out all these themes in a most dramatic manner.

In addition to having Sun in Pisces squaring Neptune, Meher Baba also had natal Mars in the 12th house, the house of transcendence through introspection, meditation, solitude, retreat, or monasticism. In the 12th house self-transcendence is also possible through altruistic activity, which, as we will see later, was very important to Meher Baba. With Mars in the 12th house, he applied a lot of energy toward solitude and meditation; Mars was not expressed outwardly in the form of sexuality, and his vital energy was applied solely to the quest for the higher life, a higher state of existence. This is one possible expression of a 12th house placement of Mars.

Mars was square to the Moon's nodal axis and sextile to both the Sun and Moon; in fact Mars is exactly conjunct the Sun-Moon midpoint. In addition, the Moon is in Scorpio. The strength of Mars in the chart and the Scorpio Moon may symbolize the fact that he had great power and charisma. Scorpio can signify a sexual kind of energy, but it can also be *shakti*, the force of *kundalini*, and a magnetism that draws people to you and impacts them.

Natal Mercury in Pisces might suggest that he would speak softly or sensitively. Eventually Meher Baba took a vow of silence for many years. He relinquished the function of speech, dissolved it, let it go, and communicated through a mysterious, subtle inner language. He may have felt that by shutting off his words, his transforming influence might be more effectively received by others. His manner of communicating went beyond actual spoken language or words, which fits the symbolism of Mercury in Pisces perfectly.

A Sudden Awakening

In 1911, Meher Baba began college. It is said that he had many friends and that he was known for his love of poetry, especially the writings of Hafiz, a renowned Sufi devotional poet, a great mystic. At that time, transiting Saturn was conjunct natal Jupiter and square natal Venus, which fits both his social popularity and his love of poetry. Jupiter can evoke literary interests, which in this case involved love poetry. His Venus was expressed less through personal love than through love of God.

In May 1913, he met a woman named Hazrat Babajan, an elderly and extremely unusual guru, who lived by herself underneath a tree. A lot of people apparently thought that she was crazy, while many other people revered her as a mystic of the highest order. As transiting Uranus began to cross his ascendant, Meher Baba met her, and she kissed him on the forehead. This was the beginning of a long relationship with this woman, who was to be one of his two main teachers. She had a tremendous impact on him, and after meeting her his whole life changed. He began to lose interest in everything except God, and he became deeply drawn into the spiritual life. In January 1914, she blessed him and he experienced electric shocks moving through his body, a sign of *kundalini* awakening. He soon entered a state of trance and complete disinterest from the world for nine months. My understanding is that he did not eat at all during this period. I don't know whether or not other people fed him, as was the case with Ramana Maharshi and Ramakrishna, both of whom were kept alive for months by devotees. But Meher Baba had no impulse at all to eat. He was gone, zapped, completely "out there." Several transits occurring at that time suggest that a profound reorientation of consciousness was occurring. Transiting Saturn was conjunct his natal Pluto-Neptune: his potential for an awakened state was tapped, and he experienced a profound explosion of higher consciousness. His ego-centered awareness was washed away, and he was absorbed in the Light. He was not of this world during this period.

In addition, Uranus was square his Moon as well as conjunct his ascendant. The square to his Scorpio Moon in the 9th house suggests the sudden, penetrating, electrifying contact with this female guru, who was also like a mother to him. With transiting Uranus on his ascendant, he was acting quite strangely from the viewpoint of observers. His parents thought that he had gone mad because he was acting in what seemed to be an irresponsible manner (Uranus), not working, just sitting in *samadhi* all the time. Transiting Neptune was forming a square to natal Saturn, which can symbolize loss of control, loss of focus, loss of identity, dissolution of ego boundaries, and acting in what appears to be a delusional fashion. In fact, he was having a genuine, illuminative mystical experience, quite in keeping with the influence of Neptune. Throughout 1914, Pluto was sesquiquadrate to his natal Uranus in the 10th house, so he suddenly developed a reputation as a somewhat unusual, strange person. Clearly he did not seem suited for a conventional profession or career. Medical treatment had no effect on his condition, and it was said that he suffered acutely at this time.

Saturn was also sesquiquadrate to natal Uranus, and transiting Uranus passed over his ascendant for the final time. The coordinated activity of transiting Saturn, Uranus, Neptune, and Pluto had combined to bring about a complete change in his personality, his state of consciousness, his life-orientation, and his position in the world. Such is the nature of those crisis periods when major transits of the outer planets coincide. On the outside, it may appear that the stability and integrity of the individual's life have been disturbed and that great personal losses have been incurred. Nevertheless, all of this is secondary to a deeper process occurring beneath the surface, the process of transformation described in all spiritual and religious traditions.

In December 1915, he visited another great sage named Upasni Maharaj, who greeted him by flinging a stone at his forehead. It is curious that the woman had kissed his forehead and that Upasni threw a stone at his forehead. Perhaps that was a manifestation of the square between natal Mars (which rules the head) and the Moon's Nodes. He began to visit Upasni, as well as Hazrat Babajan, and in 1916 he began to take some odd jobs. He was 22 years old and was starting to work a little bit, presumably getting out of his state of *samadhi*, and trying to figure out what to do.

He would work, sit with Hazrat Babajan and visit a temple called "The Tower of Silence." At this time, transiting Uranus was conjunct natal Venus. Appropriately enough, his main relationship was with this odd woman, who was considered an outcast. Apparently she refused to move from underneath her tree and her devotees built a whole ashram right around where she sat. For him to have an unusual relationship with an eccentric, older woman was in accordance with his natal Venus in Aquarius square Uranus, then being activated by transiting Uranus. During this period of close contact with this spiritual teacher, transiting Neptune was conjunct his descendant. This fits not just with his having a personal relationship with someone who was a mystic, but also a personal relationship with God.

In *Memories, Dreams, and Reflections,* Jung described his confrontation with the collective unconscious, in which he was flooded with prophetic dreams and symbolic material. This occurred while transiting Neptune was conjunct Jung's descendant (and near his natal Sun) (Chart 8). Similarly, Meher Baba was coming into a close alignment with God, or a higher force or presence that had been awakened in him by the blessing of Hazrat Babajan.

A Transmission of Power

In July 1921, he went to spend six months with Upasni Maharaj, undergoing training with this great sage. Upasni Maharaj proclaimed Meher Baba a Satguru and an Avatar (a guru with a special mission to assist humanity's evolution during a particular historical period) at the age of 27. At that time, transiting Neptune was square Uranus, transiting Uranus was conjunct his natal Sun and square to Pluto-Neptune, and there was a Jupiter-Saturn conjunction in his 8th house, opposite natal Mercury. According to Alexander Ruperti (1978), the Jupiter-Saturn conjunction concerns the formation of a new sense of "social destiny." Meher Baba's social destiny for the entire twenty-year period of that Jupiter-Saturn cycle appeared to center around receiving spiritual energy from his teacher and having a great impact on others. This point deserves further explanation.

The 8th house refers to those circumstances in which two persons meet deeply and intimately through a close business association, sexual relationship, or, in this case, the profound mutual commitment of guru and disciple. Through the contact of their respective boundaries, a spark ignites that can transform both individuals involved. Traditionally this process was conceived of in terms of the somewhat confusing notion of "occult power"; whereas it can be more easily understood in terms of the conflicts of will and the purification of interpersonal motives — to control, dominate, or manipulate — that emerge whenever two people attempt to fuse their wills and energies for a common purpose.

The transiting Jupiter-Saturn conjunction in Meher Baba's 8th house may be a symbol of his being "called" both to receive and to give to others the transmission of spiritual energy that is often spoken of as *shaktipat*. He was to have a transforming influence on others through the inner power that he had generated and with which he had been invested by his teacher. Upasni was not just proclaiming him a teacher; he was also passing on to him the power of his lineage. The 8th house is concerned with making relationships productive through a merging of wills and energies. Here it is experienced as a transmission of energy, consciousness, and authority from one awakened soul to another, the kindling of the flame of the heart. Upasni Maharaj set Meher Baba on fire and then said, in effect, "Go! You are now a live fire in your own right."

During a significant 8th house transit, we might experience a similar kindling through a deep sexual relationship. Or we might have a total transformation of our attitude or orientation by being committed to a business partnership in which our tendencies toward dominance or manipulation are made known and purified. There are a myriad of ways of experiencing this, but clearly power is generated in the 8th house through interpersonal transaction. And one never knows how it will be experienced unless one knows the level of consciousness at which the person is operating. Here it is operating at quite an evolved level.

Note that, because Uranus is both his ascendant ruler and placed near his midheaven in the 10th house, the transit of Uranus to his natal Sun had particular importance. Meher Baba was blessed with this sanctification of identity, this spiritual investiture, this confirmation that he was indeed out-of-the-ordinary, an extraordinary person with a unique mission and path and destiny. All of this was proclaimed and acknowledged by Upasni Maharaj. Moreover, as often occurs during Uranus transits, this event happened suddenly, unexpectedly, and was relatively unprecedented. It is not typical to be proclaimed a living Avatar by a great guru. As it contacted his Sun, Uranus also activated the Pluto-Neptune conjunction, so his identity as a great mystic, saint, and spiritual teacher was awakened and confirmed.

Austerities

Subsequently, in 1922, Meher Baba spent five months in retreat, living in a hut. He soon began to gather disciples around him, and in May 1922 he moved to Bombay to found an ashram. He underwent a very rigorous discipline and also imposed it on his followers. Transiting Pluto was sesquiquadrate Venus, signifying the way Meher Baba was beginning to have a magnetic influence on others and draw people to him after the announcement of his avatorhood by Upasni. In May 1922 there was a Full Moon right across his midheaven-nadir axis. This kind of transit can have an effect on a person's public standing or bring about some kind of notoriety, if there are other major transits operating at the same time. Transits occur in a hierarchy. A Full Moon across your midheaven might not mean much unless other major developmental processes are underway (outer planet transits) for which the Full Moon acts as a trigger. That is how it operated here. The Full Moon changed his position in the world and allowed him to come more into public view. It also saw him establishing a new foundation or base (4th house/nadir) for his work.

Let us look at the rigorous discipline for a moment. It seems that to fulfill his potential for evolution into a higher state of consciousness Meher Baba had to strip himself completely bare. With natal Neptune-Pluto square the Sun, it was not difficult for him to relinquish worldly attachments, to eat very little, and to meditate a great deal. What might seem like a strenuous discipline to someone else may have been just the natural orientation of his being, to flow inward and upward toward the Source. He simply did not want to be encumbered by worldly activities or by food. The Sun square Neptune-Pluto made him feel drawn toward solitude and retreat, to spending long periods like this alone in a hut.

In March 1923, he embarked upon a period of much traveling and austerities for himself and his followers. Transiting Jupiter was conjunct the midheaven, while transiting Pluto was conjunct his 6th house cusp and opposite natal Mars in the 12th. This was the beginning of a long period of spiritual practices, fasting, little sleep, and intense meditation. The 6th house is a realm of self-purification through discipline, through following practices of any kind. Transiting Pluto opposite Mars in the 12th symbolizes his drive to forcefully apply himself to the inner quest. Because Pluto was on the 6th house cusp, he began to do this by changing his habits and his diet. He also began to lead others along a similar path, right into the heart of spiritual life and the inner kingdom through these kinds of disciplines.

In March 1924, Meher Baba founded his second ashram in Meherabad. He ate once every week or two and lived the rest of the time on liquids. This was during his Saturn return. Appropriately enough, with Saturn in the 9th house (education), he created a new teaching institution that solidified his stature as a teacher. He wasn't that much different from the rest of us during his Saturn return: he felt compelled to create some kind of form or structure, like this new ashram. He also became aware of social realities in a new way and began to get involved with community service and education projects. This also occurred while transiting Jupiter was in his 11th house, the house of response to social-historical conditions.

Silence

On July 10, 1925, Meher Baba went into silence, giving no indication that this silence would, in fact, last for the rest of his life. Uranus was conjunct natal Mercury, and Meher Baba became known for his odd habit of not speaking. It is important to note that natal Mercury is in a "Yod" or Finger of God pattern with Saturn and Jupiter, perhaps suggesting a desire to communicate his wisdom through restraint of speech. Under the transit of Uranus to Mercury, Meher Baba did something one would not expect from a great spiritual master who is supposed to give discourses and teach people. He stopped talking and began to write on a little blackboard. He would put his hands to his lips as if to say, "Shh. Listen to the inner truth."

Another surprising event occurred on October 26, 1925 when he announced the closing of the ashram. Transiting Mars was on his nadir that day and transiting Saturn was conjunct natal Uranus. Thus he changed things dramatically and acted unpredictably in public, baffling everyone. He created a big upheaval around him and no one could figure out what he was doing.

Saturn was conjunct his midheaven in late 1925 and into 1926. On his birthday in February 1926, twenty thousand people came for his *darshan* (literally to have a look at him). His reputation as a great spiritual Master was really evident at this point. He was proclaimed the Avatar in 1921. But in 1926, he was getting public recognition of this, and his reputation became firmly established while transiting Saturn was conjunct the midheaven. At the same time, transiting Neptune was opposite natal Venus, which may have elicited from him a great outpouring of generosity and the kind of universal, boundless, and unconditional love for which he was often noted. In addition, at this time Meher Baba's progressed Sun had moved from the natal square to Pluto-Neptune to a sextile to those same planets which would last from 1926 until 1929. This symbolizes the culmination of his spiritual awakening and expansion of consciousness, sometime during that period.

In 1930, he became ill while transiting Saturn was conjunct Mars in his 12th house. Then in 1931, he embarked upon several years of travel in the West, where he met many people and mingled with the masses. Transiting Neptune was opposite natal Sun, square natal Pluto-Neptune, perhaps signifying the widening of his circle of influence as a spiritual Master, and being surrounded by an aura of holiness and mystery. This transit might also have symbolized his magical, liberating influence on others.

Serving the Masts

In 1935 and 1936, Saturn was conjunct Meher Baba's natal Sun, a very important transit that corresponded to the beginning of his work in India with the "*masts*." The masts are a class of socially marginal outcasts who seem a little crazy, but whom he viewed as extremely evolved beings. They're distinguished from the *sadhus*, the wandering mendicants and yogis, because they're fairly dissociated and withdrawn. Western psychologists might diagnose these people as schizoidal or schizophrenic. Masts are unable to communicate with others for the most part. Some of them are catatonic. They were considered insane, cast out of ordinary social affairs, and no one paid much attention to them. Most of them would wander around aimlessly, like some of the street people in American cities today. However in India they were also known as "God-intoxicated mad-men" (and probably mad-women, too). There were tens of thousands of these people in India at that time.

In 1936, with Saturn conjunct his 2nd house Sun, Meher Baba began to feel a commitment to working with and serving these people. The theme of self-sacrifice and dedication to the welfare of others mentioned earlier was beginning to be evident as Meher Baba now embododied some of the qualities often associated with Pisces, Neptune, and the 12th house. He was not just preaching the importance of service; he went out and did it in a very practical way. He spent years and years serving the masts, washing them, feeding them, communicating with them silently, honoring them, and giving them money. As transiting Saturn activated his Pisces Sun square Pluto-Neptune, all of his personal resources were directed toward service and healing. He became selfless.

The New Life

In 1949, an incredible series of events unfolded. First, Meher Baba went into what was called "The Great Seclusion," in which he gave away everything he owned. Then on October 16, 1949, he proclaimed "The New Life." This was perhaps the most astonishing event in his life. Meher Baba had thousands of followers and a huge ashram. No one had the slightest inkling of what was about to happen. He announced the closing of the ashram (again!) and the entire operation was to be shut down immediately. Everything was to be given away to the poor. Everyone would have to leave. Then he said, in effect: "Those of you who are my real disciples will henceforth enter the New Life with me. This means that we will wander together as companions, depending only on God for our every need, for our food and our shelter. We will own nothing, and we will travel without knowing where we are going or where we will stay." Here we see his 2nd house Sun in Pisces manifesting. He gave everyone about one day to decide whether or not they would leave the world with him. Within a few days, his thousands of followers had been reduced to about twenty people. He was challenging his followers to make a profound commitment that would enable them to transform their lives. He was asking for complete surrender and renunciation without desire.

He and these twenty or so followers began to wander around with no possessions, begging for food. They underwent great sufferings, poverty, and deprivations. During this time, he did not allow others to view him as the Guru, but rather insisted upon being treated as "a companion" among his companions. He did not allow others to show him signs of respect, and he washed and served the poorest of the poor. The group members loved and served one another, living in a state of "complete hopelessness and helplessness." This is what he taught them. This hopelessness and helplessness relates directly back to the symbolism of Pluto-Neptune square Sun in Pisces: letting go completely, dying for no reason. Meher Baba taught them to practice *manonash*, which has been translated as "the annihilation of the mind into love." It was said that the ordeals that New Life participants underwent were not tests, but were the ends in themselves. This way of complete surrender, service, dependency on God, the Great Spirit, this *was* the New Life.

All of this happened while Saturn was just past the square to natal Pluto-Neptune and opposite natal Sun, again bringing into focus the themes of selflessness, god-consciousness, and self-consecration. Transiting Pluto was square natal Uranus and Meher Baba's midheaven: he was completely disrupting the lives of many people, as well as having a profound impact on them. He was also undergoing a death and rebirth himself, and he was emerging in a completely new role. Transiting Uranus was also opposite natal Mars in the 12th house, so again we see a sudden intensity of yearning for God, renunciation, the inner life, and complete surrender. Transiting Uranus in the 6th house led him to teach a new spiritual discipline: *manonash*, the annihilation of the mind into love, a 6th house discipline undertaken to achieve 12th house goals.

During that time, transiting Uranus was also conjunct the Venus-Uranus midpoint, especially significant since the planets are square to each other natally. This might symbolize the "companionship" and group living of the New Life (see The Yoga of Sangha in Chapter 2). That transit activated his unconventional kind of love for his circle of companions, his community of love, an apt expression of Venus in Aquarius. Thus, when Uranus — an important planet in his natal chart, and one associated with so many unpredictable actions in his life — transited his 12th house Mars, he did this totally outrageous, shocking thing, which took everyone by surprise and shook up the lives of all of his followers.

Skipping ahead to 1951, Meher Baba went into seclusion again while transiting Neptune was sesquiquadrate his Sun. On May 24, 1952, he had a car accident. Transiting Saturn was on his 6th house cusp, opposite Mars, a transit that manifested as a car crash and an injury (Mars), hospitalization (12th house), and health issues (6th house). Neptune was still sesquiquadrate his natal Sun, which suggests themes of being convalescent, weak, and unable to move.

The Avatar

In September 1953, during his second Saturn return, Meher Baba proclaimed himself the Avatar of the modern era. With natal Saturn in his 9th house, he felt compelled at this time to announce to others his stature as a teacher, with confidence and authority. This is just after the time when Jupiter was conjunct natal Pluto-Neptune. Interestingly, the notable event did not occur until after the exact aspect of Jupiter was over. One possible explanation of this is that his own sense of divinity or avatarhood was reconfirmed to him during the exact transit of Jupiter over Pluto-Neptune and that only subsequently did he announce this publicly. Clearly the Jupiter transit seems to have reawakened a deep sense of his destiny, and caused him to proclaim more openly his avatarhood and his commitment to service of the masts, and ultimately all of humanity. According to Rudhyar, avataric beings are ones who reveal to others a new, emergent spiritual quality that becomes the model for action in a future cycle of a culture. Thus, I think Meher Baba's avatarhood can best be understood in terms of his demonstration of the spiritual quality of compassionate service.

Meher Baba had another car accident in December of 1956, after which he imposed a new suffering on himself by refusing medical treatment. Transiting Saturn was square his Pisces Sun, so he became a suffering servant or savior, and he underwent a form of self-imposed martyrdom. At this time, he also demanded total love, obedience, and acceptance of himself as the Avatar from his followers. His demand that others acknowledge his divinity and his identity as a great spiritual Master corresponded to Saturn's transit square the natal Sun and opposite Pluto-Neptune. In addition, Uranus was conjunct the descendant and square his Moon. He was acting in an unusual way, changing his relationships with others (no longer just acting like a "companion"), demanding that others recognize his spiritual authority (Uranus in the 10th house) and his uniqueness. This may seem a little arrogant, but this too was a perfect manifestation of the qualities of Uranus.

In May and June of 1960, he gave *darshan* to ten thousand people per day while Uranus squared his midheaven. Transiting Neptune was conjunct his Moon, and he no doubt had a euphoric, uplifting, magical sway over the masses. He may have been in a "mystic mood," a mood of compassion and generosity of spirit. This transit symbolized a magical air in the life, an expanded emotional outpouring, and warm nurturance of others.

In 1961–1963, Meher Baba passed through a period of seclusion, solitude, disinterest in the world, and inner silence. He also underwent a great deal of physical suffering. Transiting Saturn was in his 12th house, an apt symbol for such a period of retreat, withdrawal, and inner detachment. Pluto was opposite natal Sun and square Pluto-Neptune, bringing out even more deeply his state of god-intoxication. This could be the essence of his life's work: to achieve and maintain this total absorption in the Source, to rest in that state where awareness of the self has passed away and only the fullness of God remains.

When transits activated Meher Baba's natal Sun square Pluto-Neptune, he either went through some deep spiritual awakening, took on austerities to deepen his god-consciousness, or proclaimed and demonstrated his avatarhood to others. Similarly, when transits contact important areas of one's own chart, central life-themes and facets of the personality will come to the fore again and again.

In 1969, Meher Baba's last major *darshans* were planned. Transiting Saturn was conjunct natal Venus, and he urged many people to visit him on a certain day that he promised would be an important occasion. Tens of thousands of people arrived, and that was the day he left his body.

CHAPTER 7
An Astrological Biography of Bhagwan Rajneesh (Osho)

In this chapter, we will examine the birth chart of Bhagwan Rajneesh, a controversial spiritual teacher who inspired devotion from some quarters and animosity from others. To gain some understanding of his birth pattern we will focus on one critical period of his life, November 1985, when Rajneesh was suddenly expelled from the United States after pleading guilty to federal immigration law violations. As you may know, in the aftermath of that deportation, the community of Rajneeshpuram in Antelope, Oregon disbanded. I was saddened by the demise of that community and by Rajneesh's death, for while I took exception to some of his actions and ideas, I was sympathetic to aspects of his teaching and to the unique spiritual and cultural experiment that his communities represented.

Rajneesh's natal Sun is in Sagittarius on the descendant, in a Grand Trine with Uranus and Jupiter. The Sun trine Jupiter symbolizes his deep understanding of philosophical issues and the fact that he was a great teacher. Before he became a guru, Rajneesh was a philosophy professor at the University of Jabalpur in India.

The connections of Uranus with Sun and Jupiter symbolize the genius and originality of his philosophy and teachings, and his unusual vision of the future and of a new way of life. Also note the T-Square between Moon-Saturn in the 8th house, Uranus in the 11th house and Pluto in the 2nd house. Attempting an initial synthesis of the planets and houses involved, we might speculate that this pattern would symbolize important issues regarding finances and concentrations of wealth (Pluto in the 2nd house), feelings stirred by working relationships with others (Moon-Saturn in the 8th house), and his involvement in groups, communities, and living experiments (Uranus in 11th house).

This combination also seems to indicate the fact that Rajneesh was an extremely radical figure, an iconoclast, a breaker of traditions. With Uranus at the apex of his T-Square and square Saturn and Moon, Rajneesh often questioned and opposed authority and tradition. He was famous for outraging devout Hindus. The priests and established institutional, religious people in India disliked him because he challenged their authority, criticizing the anti-life and anti-sexual attitudes implicit in the teachings of most religions and spiritual teachers. He was a profoundly rebellious person with a passion for questioning old doctrines and attempting to create new ones, and with a penchant for confronting taboos and inhibitions. For example, he challenged the repression of both aggressive and sexual impulses, and his communities are famous for the space they give for the free expression of these energies. He also reinterpreted the teachings of world religions and articulated the nature of the spiritual path in a highly innovative way. Rajneesh was a truly revolutionary figure.

He also had problems because of his tendency to confront authority, symbolized by the Uranus square Saturn. This became particularly obvious with the establishment of the Rajneeshpuram community. Uranus is an extremely strong planet in his chart, being trine to the Sun and Jupiter and also being the focus point for the dynamic tension of the Saturn-Pluto opposition. One of the other main themes in his life was that he always wanted to build a community (Uranus in the 11th). He inspired his followers to try to create a new world from the bottom up at Rajneeshpuram. But his unwillingness to operate within the bounds of propriety backfired in Oregon. The neighbors of the community were very saturnian, traditional people, many of them "born again" and not very receptive

Bhagwan Rajneesh (Osho)
December 11, 1931
5:13 PM
Gadawara, India

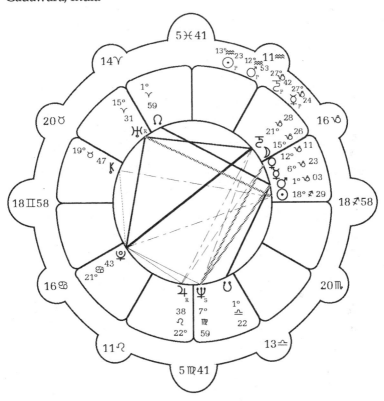

Source: Ashram Resident

Chart 19

to New Age ideals or lifestyles. They felt that they were treated with disdain and disrespect by the members of the Rajneesh community and they responded in kind. These neighbors were upset by the sudden influx of thousands of unusual, uranian, orange-clad people to their vicinity. And they were put off by Rajneesh's brash, confrontational style, especially as this was communicated by Anand Sheela, Rajneesh's lieutenant. Just as had occurred in India a few years earlier, the local people exerted great pressure on Rajneesh to leave Oregon.

At the time Rajneeshpuram was founded, in 1981 and 1982, Saturn was transiting through Libra along with Pluto. Saturn was opposite Rajneesh's natal Uranus and square both Pluto and natal Saturn. Thus Saturn was forming a Grand Cross with his natal T-Square, a very important transit. During this time, all of the possibilities implicit in his T-Square came to fruition. The founding of the community was a major event in his life, and fulfilled his innate need to generate wealth through soliciting financial contributions and the freely donated labor of others (Moon-Saturn in the 8th house) in order to sustain the growth of a unique, progressive, politically controversial, New Age community (Uranus in 11th house). However, the actual experience at Rajneeshpuram was very turbulent, and there were tremendous tensions involved in constructing that community. Many of the community's neighbors mistrusted Rajneesh and his followers, and the antagonistic feelings were mutual.

Rajneesh had a Moon-Venus conjunction, trine Neptune, which gave him a capacity for compassion, warmth, and lovingness. The Mercury-Venus conjunction is the symbol of his melodious speaking style, as well as his skill in writing. But Rajneesh also had a strong Mars-Mercury conjunction in Capricorn, which gave him an acerbic tongue, sarcasm, a critical way of speaking, as well as a quick mind. He was very funny and often criticized other gurus in a vitriolic manner.

Also note that Saturn is in its own sign, ruling the 8th house of his chart, and it is dispositor of Moon, Venus, Mercury, and Mars. This might indicate that he would be an authoritative person, someone for whom it would be important to organize and direct things, to have a certain degree of control, and to provide leadership, especially in his 8th house working partnerships. He would want to know what was going on.

However, in 1984 and 1985, Neptune entered Capricorn and started transiting back and forth over Rajneesh's natal Mars. For a couple of years it appears that someone deceived him, particularly with respect to the movement's financial holdings and dealings (Moon and Saturn in the 8th house). In 1985, Uranus was also crossing repeatedly over his Sun and descendant. In keeping with the symbolism of this transit, there were unexpected changes in his personal relationships and some of his followers rebelled against him, all of which took him largely by surprise.

The most important event occurred when his secretary, Anand Sheela, the director of the community, his mouthpiece — one of the closest people in the world to him — betrayed him. If Rajneesh had been married, one might have expected some restructuring of his primary relationship, a breakup, or a divorce. In a sense that is exactly what happened. Rajneesh and Sheela got "divorced" from each other. She embezzled a bunch of his money, fled the country, and denounced Rajneesh. This was very shocking and disruptive, especially since with his Sagittarius Sun in the 7th house he had dedicated much of his teaching to demonstrating his wisdom about relationships.

With Neptune crossing over natal Mars things got out of control. Perhaps he trusted other people too much, giving other people too much authority for the dissemination of his work and the administration of the community, instead of exercising it himself. When Neptune came along, Sheela appears to have used her authority in a deceitful manner. The disagreement between them involving the movement's financial holdings was murky and shrouded in lies.

Having two simultaneous transits of trans-saturnian planets was enough to precipitate a major life crisis for Rajneesh. Thus, you can get some perspective on the deep changes that you yourself may have gone through, or may be going through now during similar periods of multiple transits. Nevertheless, these changes will always be in accordance with the precise symbolism of your birth chart. That is why it is so important to understand the language of astrology clearly and precisely.

One would expect that, with all the negative press and publicity that Rajneesh received at this time, there would have been some kind of important 10th house activity. Note that it was indeed Neptune, ruler of the 10th house, which was associated with these difficult events as it passed over Mars. With this transit, he experienced the dissolution of his community, his financial stability, and some of his magical, charismatic aura. He lost much of his credibility in the eyes of the public. The community in Oregon disappeared practically overnight, eroded by Neptune like a sandcastle by the shore.

In the year or so before these events, Pluto was semi-square his Sun and conjunct his Vertex[3]. There may have been many power struggles between Rajneesh and Sheela, as well as with his other associates. During the time of these Pluto transits, Rajneesh was faced with all sorts of animosities, as well as issues about control and the utilization of his power and charisma.

An interesting point about Rajneesh's chart is that with natal Pluto in the 2nd house, he was quite fascinated by (some might say "obsessed with") possessions, wealth, Rolex watches, and expensive cars. Another reason why Rajneesh could never be a total ascetic, a celibate, or a renunciate, and why he initially became famous as the "sex guru," is his natal Venus-Mars and Venus-Moon conjunctions. The conjunctions of Venus-Mars (wide in orb though it may be) and Moon-Venus make sensuality, love, and sexuality an important part of his path and of his teachings. In keeping with the Capricorn placement of these planets, he taught Tantra, which is, as he would say, a total letting-go, but which also involves a certain degree of control — a saturnian structuring of sexual energy intended to lead to the neptunian goal of enlightenment. Note that he also has Venus-Neptune and Mars-Neptune contacts, indicating his concern with the transformation of sexual love into a sacred, ecstatic experience.

Looking briefly at Rajneesh's progressed chart, two major aspects had formed during the turbulent period when his community disbanded and he was deported. First, ascendant ruler Mercury was exactly conjunct progressed Saturn. This correlates with the fact that he had been silent for several years, disciplining his tongue, refraining from speaking. However, the progressed conjunction of Mercury and Saturn also heralded a dramatic change in Rajneesh's mode of thinking. Imagine the circumstances: things were falling apart all around him. Perhaps he suddenly had to sober up and think realistically about the fact that he had to sell

---

[3] The Vertex is an angle in the birth chart that is considered as sensitive as the ascendant, descendant, midheaven, or nadir. It is formed by the intersection of the Great Circle known as the Prime Vertical with the plane of the Ecliptic, which is formed by the earth's passage around the Sun.

everything, leave the country, and pay the $500,000 fine that was levied against him. He had to think seriously about the misappropriation of funds and the criminal actions that some of his followers allegedly carried out — for example, attempting to poison the patrons of a restaurant or trying to illegally affect the outcome of a local election. Much of this may have happened without his awareness or consent. Now, however, he was faced with a set of very limiting, confining circumstances, and he had to make concrete decisions about where to go from there. This could not have been an easy time. But in a sense, this could be viewed as the beginning of a new evolutionary cycle for Rajneesh. For although he was an ecstatic mystic, during this progressed Mercury-Saturn conjunction he now had to deal with planning and decision-making, because most of the people he had depended upon in the past were gone.

This example has taught me to take more seriously the traditional astrological lore about the strength of the ascendant ruler. Here the progressed conjunction of Rajneesh's ascendant ruler, Mercury, with Saturn created a major change in his life, one requiring a more realistic and clear-minded perspective.

In addition, Rajneesh's progressed Sun was conjunct Mars in the 9th house at the time of these events. This might relate to his numerous moves from country to country after he was deported from the United States (9th house: foreign travel). Several other countries denied him asylum and pressured him to leave. The aspect was separating in 1985, so it had been developing for several years before his deportation. Note that Mars ruled his 6th house natally: Rajneesh was having a lot of health problems, and was in a wheelchair with back problems when he was deported. Moreover, transiting Saturn was in the 6th house at the same time. Saturn in the 6th plus the Sun-Mars conjunction corresponded to considerable strain and difficulty he experienced regarding his health.

The progressed Sun-Mars conjunction also symbolizes the general climate of hostility in Rajneesh's world at that time. During this progressed aspect, things are generally not so calm, smooth, or loving in a person's life. One becomes more aggressive, volatile, impatient, and irritable, and is faced with confrontive circumstances that evoke anger. Rajneesh was quite familiar with all of these feelings, amd encouraged his students to express their aggression in encounter groups. He didn't believe in trying to transcend aggression and taught people to go deeply into anger and follow it to its source. The progressed Sun conjunct progressed Mars (which also ruled his 11th house) symbolized the unleashing of his own anger as a result of the problems and misunderstandings that arose within his community. The progressed Sun-Mars conjunction was an "incendiary" aspect, symbolizing the various forms of hostility, friction, and battles that seemed to follow Rajneesh at every turn.

Between 1988 and the time of Rajneesh's death in 1990, Saturn, Uranus, and Neptune were all in Capricorn, transiting over his Capricorn planets. Because of the 8th house placement of these planets, he may have had much to learn about working together with others to rebuild his community in India after his expulsion from the U.S. Rajneesh also had very complex financial dealings and in all likelihood had to deal with creditors and to seek out new sources of loans in order to revive his spiritual community, perhaps courting people of social position to help bankroll his operations (8th house: money received from others). He may have also had to learn to manage the resources solicited from others in a more disciplined way. And, in keeping with the traditional connection of the 8th house with death, when transiting Saturn came into conjunction with his 8th house natal Moon and the midpoints of Moon-Saturn and Moon-Pluto in early 1990, Rajneesh's health deteriorated until his death from a heart attack on January 19.

CHAPTER 8

An Astrological Biography of Mircea Eliade

Mircea Eliade was one of the spiritual and intellectual geniuses of this century, whose accomplishments in the fields of religion and philosophy rank among those of Jung, Rudhyar, and Aurobindo. In addition to being probably the greatest historian of religions of this century, he was also a prolific novelist. His books on yoga, shamanism, alchemy, and myth are among the most insightful and exhaustive scholarly studies of these subjects available. I think you will also find that he lived a most fascinating life. In this chapter I will examine some of the events of his first twenty six years described in volume one of his *Autobiography* (Harper & Row, 1981). His birth data was published in a recent biography (Ricketts, 1988).

Introduction

Eliade was born in Bucharest, Romania with Venus rising in Aquarius conjunct Chiron. Although it was two degrees above the ascendant, I interpret Venus as being placed in the 1st house. He was considered an attractive person, much sought after by others, yet he also suffered very painful wounding social experiences, especially with women (Venus conjunct Chiron). As we will see later, Eliade's love life was quite colorful, unconventional, and unpredictable.

Like Meher Baba, Eliade had Sun in Pisces in the 2nd house. However, Eliade's path was not to renounce physical attachments as Meher Baba did, but rather to earn his livelihood (2nd house) through involvement in the field of religious and mythic studies. With a conjunction of Sun and Saturn, Eliade was extremely focused on professional achievements. By the age of thirty and his Saturn return, Eliade had written and published fifteen books, and had achieved widespread recognition in Europe as one of the foremost authorities in the study of myth, religion, and philosophy. The Sun-Saturn combination in Pisces symbolizes Eliade's capacity to give methodical and disciplined exposition of profound mystical and religious doctrines, to expound them and explain their deeper meaning. He studied all facets of world religions, utilizing a variety of historical, thematic, and cross-cultural methodologies. With Sun-Saturn in the 2nd along with Mercury, he supported himself as a professor of religions and solidly established himself as an eminent researcher and professor in this field.

With Sun-Saturn square Pluto in Gemini in the 5th house, the richness of his inner life often sought literary expression not only in scholarly writings, but also in the form of novels that seemed to erupt periodically from his deepest inner regions. However, his professional responsibilities as a scholar and professor of religions often interfered with the flow of his literary creativity (Sun-Saturn square Pluto). Nevertheless, he was ultimately able to pursue both endeavors, and both of them were expressions of his piscean attunement to the worlds of myth, dreams, symbols, and religious mysteries.

Eliade spent most of his life reading and writing, and engaged in an active intellectual life. This is symbolized in his chart by the placement of Mercury, the planet of writing and communication, in the 2nd house closely square to Jupiter, Neptune and Uranus. Jupiter gave his writings a depth of philosophical understanding, Neptune attuned his thinking to religious concerns, and Uranus gave his ideas and writing style great originality.

Eliade's natal conjunction of Jupiter and Neptune (ruler of his Pisces Sun) symbolizes his interest in comprehending (Jupiter)

Mircea Eliade
March 13, 1907
5:00 AM
Bucharest, Romania

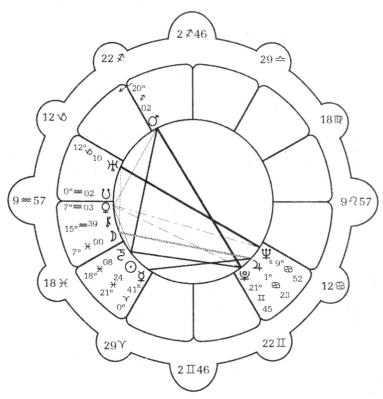

Source: M. Ricketts, *Mircea Eliade: The Romanian Roots*

Chart 20

spiritual or metaphysical (Neptune) truths and doctrines. Throughout his life, Eliade was focused on the Quest, the search for higher knowledge, liberatory wisdom, spiritual awakening, and direct spiritual experience. And because these planets were placed in his 5th house, he was a somewhat charismatic person, although he may also have been somewhat puzzling to those who did not understand his mysterious and seemingly other-worldly interests. Jupiter-Neptune in his 5th house suggests that he was a mystic, one who sought to understand the mysteries of existence, to experience expanded states of awareness, and to give expression to some esoteric or sacred form of knowledge. As Jupiter also ruled his Sagitarrius midheaven, the conjunction of Jupiter and Neptune may also mean that he felt a natural identification with the archetype of the spiritual teacher or pandit. He was not exactly a guru, but he did act in the world as a kind of spiritual teacher or wise man.

There is a very revealing section in his autobiography where he says that he was often to subject to fluctuations between an exalted opinion of himself and a megalomaniacal sense of failure. On the one hand he was full of a sense of his importance and great wisdom, and identified with the image of the Sage possessed of all-encompassing knowledge. He had, in other words, a prophetic kind of calling, and a sometimes inflated, unrealistic self-image. On the other hand, he had equally unrealistic feelings of worthlessness and insignificance. These fluctuations in his self-image seem to be an apt expression of Jupiter-Neptune in the 5th house. For while Jupiter could expand Neptune's tendency to make an individual feel special, expansive, or uniquely illumined, it might also augment Neptune's tendency to erode or weaken the stability of a person's confidence in his or her creative gifts. This combination suggests that one might feel a strong desire to express oneself in an inspired, almost incantatory manner using mythic, symbolic, or archetypal motifs. Eliade spent much of his time totally absorbed in writing either novels or books about myth, religion, and mysticism, and often seemed to others as if he were lost in another world altogether. Eliade ultimately utilized this combination of energies very productively, transforming his personal experience into expressions of religious, symbolic, and mythic themes through both his scholarship and his literary efforts.

Early Years

In his autobiography Eliade states that from his youth he was engaged in prolific reading and writing. He read all the great novelists, poets, and philosophers of Europe during his teens and early twenties. He especially loved Dante, Goethe, Kant, and East European folk literature. He explored his cultural heritage and made it a part of himself. He was in love with learning, including natural sciences, anthropology, botany, and hermeneutics — the study of interpretation of religious and literary texts.

Eliade also reports that he suffered from severe myopia as a youth, was extremely shy and very awkward with girls, and that he frequently experienced extremely melancholy moods. All of these traits seem to relate directly to his Sun-Saturn conjunction: feeling shy, sad, socially inept, and very serious. With these two planets in Pisces he was quite withdrawn, absorbed in the private world of his studies. He was a sensitive young man, totally focused on his inner world of fantasy, fiction, imagination, mythology, religion, and philosophy.

An interesting detail of his life is that from his mid teens he began to systematically deprive himself of sleep. He would periodically set his alarm back a few minutes earlier and slept progressively less and less so that he could read through most of the night. Eventually he slept no more than four hours per night. This was an intense, saturnian discipline. Appropriately enough for someone with Saturn in Pisces, it was an effort to structure and gain mastery over *sleep*.

Eliade had tremendous will power (Mars square Sun-Saturn) and his intellect was insatiable. He began to write and publish articles in his teens. At the age of 12 he suddenly started to do well in school and to collect information on all kinds of subjects, like plant morphology, entomology, evolution, chemistry, physics, the Orient, occult sciences, and philosophy. In the spring of 1921, he wrote and published his first article on entomology in "The Newspaper of Popular Sciences." Subsequently he entered a contest the publication was sponsoring, submitting a story called "How I found the Philosopher's Stone," about a chemist who falls asleep in his laboratory and has a dream about a chemist who shows him the philosopher's stone. This is quite fascinating because at the time he had not even heard of alchemy. However, later on he became fascinated by this subject and wrote many books about the alchemical symbols and practices of many cultures, the most famous of which is called *The Forge and the Crucible.* Eliade's story won first prize in the contest and was published in the fall of 1921. He won some money and was asked to contribute regular articles to the magazine. For some time he wrote articles about entomology, until his interests began to change. He was just fourteen years old at this time.

At the time of this event, there was a progressed Mercury-Saturn conjunction, signifying a period of serious study of mysterious, esoteric subjects (Mercury-Saturn in Pisces). In addition, transiting Neptune was conjunct his descendant and transiting Pluto was conjunct natal Neptune, an apt set of transits for having a dream revealing deep religious and symbolic insight. From his very depths, Eliade was discovering new vision. Moreover, Jupiter and Saturn reached conjunction in his 8th house at that time, directly opposite his natal Sun-Saturn. This set in motion a commitment to a life project that involved revealing to others the long-hidden meaning of the mysteries of alchemy — an 8th house process involving magic, power, and transformation.

Voyage to India

At some point during his teens he became obsessed with India. This was back in the 1920s before the fascination with oriental cultures and religions was popular among westerners. Eliade began to read all the early studies of Indian mythology and philosophy that were beginning to be written by scholars like Max Muller and also started to study Indian languages. Around 1925, when Eliade was 18, his progressed Sun was square Neptune and progressed Neptune. This progressed aspect was within orb for most of the time he was in college; thus the whole period was tinged with the undercurrents of this aspect. The progressed Sun square Neptune represents a time when a person can experience a dramatic opening to another level of perception, to another world, a world of mystery, magic, mysticism, Spirit. It can symbolize a developing concern with spiritual, religious, or metaphysical doctrines and truths. Now Eliade was becoming a seeker of enlightenment and sacred knowledge and began to be absorbed in his studies of religion, mysticism, and mythology, all subjects ruled by Neptune.

Neptune is not of this world. It is the function of expansion, which can liberate us and lead us toward moksa or nirvana. These subjects became his passion during this period, during which he was internally aligning with Neptune. This progressed Sun square to Neptune symbolized a powerful spiritual awakening during this period of his life.

Eliade's exploration of the wisdom of the East began at the time of the progressed Full Moon at 7 Aries/Libra 58, which closely squared natal Neptune. Thus he experienced a period of interior realization of the purpose and direction of his life, focusing upon the path of spirituality, sacred knowledge, and liberation. The progressed Moon aspecting the long Sun-Neptune aspect acted as a trigger that brought all of these developments into vivid focus. The inner tide of his life was culminating, leading him to realization of the importance of religious studies and the spiritual quest.

Before too long he had exhausted all of the resources available to him in Romania for continuing his studies of Indian languages, philosophy, and culture. Then he got the idea of writing a letter to a "maharajah" whom he had heard was a philanthropist who had helped other scholars pursue their work. He asked for assistance in coming to India to study philosophy and Sanskrit. To his great surprise, the maharajah wrote back offering him a scholarship and introductions to some prominent people. He also received a scholarship from the government of Romania.

This was the beginning of one of the most important phases of Eliade's life, his sojourn in India, which lasted three years and changed his life forever. He set sail on November 28, 1928. Nowadays such journeys are not such a big deal. We simply get on an airplane and fly to India for a few months to study with our favorite guru, then fly back. In the 1920s, however, it was unheard of for a young man in Romania to leave home and go to live in the Far East. This is in keeping with the fact that at this time Eliade's progressed Sun was at 12 Aries 55, square to natal and progressed Uranus, a major aspect. This progression symbolizes Eliade's growing defiance of social convention and the opinions of others. Because Uranus was ruler of the ascendant and Venus and placed in the natal 12th house, the progressed Sun's contact to Uranus would cause him to seek freedom from social norms and expectations with respect to his personal identity (ascendant), his unusual spiritual quest (Uranus in 12th house), and (as we will soon see) romantic relationships (Venus). This progressed aspect coincided with a choice that was considered shocking, irresponsible, unprecedented, unusual, and downright weird according to the standards of his time, but a choice that was necessary for his individuation. By leaving Romania to go to India, Eliade was seeking the freedom to discover himself and to develop his unique perspective on religion, spirituality, and Yoga.

Here we see a beautiful illustration of what Rudhyar would call a test of "severance." According to Rudhyar, those who wish to go beyond the condition of a merely culture-defined and culture-bound person must undergo a severance of some sort from their culture of origin, inwardly if not outwardly. Eliade's fundamental commitment to a radical life-project emphasizing spiritual growth and religious studies came into focus during the period while progressed Sun was square first to Neptune and then to Uranus. Simultaneously, transiting Uranus was in Aries, squaring his natal opposition of Uranus and Neptune, between 1929 and 1931, corresponding exactly to the period of Eliade's extended sojourn in India. This transit would signify the pressure to pursue unusual religious and spiritual interests, as well as the potential for Eliade to have significant personal experience of yogic practices and altered states of consciousness.

Progressed Mercury was at 19 Pisces 04, near natal Sun-Saturn, an appropriate symbol for a period in which Eliade was about to undertake a prodigious scholarly endeavor requiring incredibly strenuous and focused mental effort, described below. This progressed aspect of Mercury was a significant factor that lasted for many years. Moreover, the progressed ascendant was at 18 Pisces 15, exactly conjunct natal Saturn, another symbol of defining individual purpose in terms of a strenuous project of study of religious and mythic texts.

On the day he left Romania for India, transiting Mars was conjunct his Jupiter-Neptune, so he may have been in an ecstatic, euphoric mood, in a state of great excitement about his wondrous journey to this mysterious, magical country. Transiting Jupiter was square his nodal axis and Venus, and transiting Saturn was conjunct his Mars in Sagittarius, both symbolic of the fact that he was traveling across the world, one of the ultimate sagittarian experiences. The progressed Moon was at 19 Sagitarrius 10, also in his 10th house conjunct natal Mars, another appropriate symbol for embarking on a period of study and travel in a foreign culture. Transiting Saturn was also square natal Sun-Saturn and opposite Pluto. The activation of his natal T-square involving Sun, Saturn, Mars, and Pluto corresponds to a period in which he was ready to learn and to become a great writer and scholar.

In addition, transiting Uranus was conjunct Mercury at this time. This was an unconventional kind of voyage involving unusual kinds of learning and study. He was definitely considered quite strange for going on this voyage, as his friends and family did not understand what he was doing. Uranus was also square natal Jupiter, which gave the trip the quality of *foreign* travel as well as the emphasis on reading (Mercury) philosophical material (Jupiter). Uranus awakening his natal Mercury square Jupiter led to new kinds of reading and learning during this period.

When Eliade arrived in India he settled in at the home of the teacher whom the maharajah had arranged for him to meet. This teacher was Surendranath Dasgupta, the most famous, esteemed scholar of religion and philosophy in modern India. He was a great pundit, author of the classic five volume history of Indian philosophy. He was an imposing figure, an intellectual giant. Eliade began a program of study with him that involved twelve to sixteen hours a day of learning Sanskrit and translating primary sources from the Hindu and Buddhist scriptures. Practically all he did was read and study Sanskrit. This fits well with progressed Mercury stationary direct, conjunct natal Sun-Saturn. During this period, Eliade became mentally sharp, focused, disciplined, and productive, bringing out many of the best potential qualities of his Sun-Saturn conjunction. He was engaged in reading, learning, foreign languages, and translating, all focused on the piscean realms of Indian religion, philosophy, and mythology — an enormous task.

Then came a dramatic but tragic development. In 1929, Eliade fell in love with Dasgupta's daughter, Maitreyi, who was apparently both brilliant and quite beautiful, a poetess. They were attracted to each other but were rarely allowed to be alone. But at one point they were assigned the task of working on the index for Dasgupta's *History of Indian Philosophy*. As Eliade recounts the story, "One day our hands met over the little box of cards and we could not unclasp them" (p. 185).

On September 18, however, Maitreyi sent Eliade a note saying that her father had found out about their love and that she had confessed everything to him. The following day Dasgupta kicked Eliade out of his house and banished him forever. Think of what a blow this must have been, to be rejected by his guru and mentor! Apparently this was a pretty serious matter and Dasgupta took it as a matter of honor to punish Eliade for acting inappropriately.

At this time, there was a progressed trine between Venus and Jupiter, signifying a profound experience of falling in love. However, transiting Uranus was square natal Neptune, perhaps symbolizing an unexpected lapse in his judgement, and the secretive, hidden quality of their love for each other. He was filled with romantic longing, but it was for the most part covert, surreptitious, and involved a certain amount of idealization of this young woman — who later became the focus of one of Eliade's most famous novels, *Maitreyi*. The relationship between them was also socially unacceptable, at least to Dasgupta, whether it was because of the differences in their nationality and cultural background, or because Eliade did not court her in a discrete, "proper" manner. Uranus square Neptune may also symbolize a feeling of confusion Eliade may have felt, precipitated by his banishment from Dasgupta's home. He probably didn't know what had hit him. During Uranus square to Neptune, this romance ended up a complete mess, a true calamity for the young scholar and would-be lover.

A Tantric Interlude

Eliade's love life was always a bit complicated, and the unsuccessful affair just described was followed by another remarkable episode. As I mentioned earlier, Eliade's connections with women were often unconventional, suddenly changeable, and subject to a certain amount of social disapproval.

After Eliade left Dasgupta's home in Calcutta, he traveled to Hardwar and Rishikesh in the Himalayas, seeking a hermitage where he could dedicate himself to yoga practices. He met Swami Shivananda and stayed in his ashram for some time. Then around Christmas of 1929, a woman named Jenny arrived from South Africa to visit the ashram. Jenny seemed quite dedicated to the disciplined yogic lifestyle being practiced in the ashram, and often came to Eliade seeking spiritual guidance.

At one point, Shivananda left town for a while and Jenny came to see Eliade. They got involved in a discussion of Tantric Yoga, about which Eliade had been reading. He tried to avoid the subject, but she was insistent on finding out whatever he knew. Soon they began their own explorations of these practices, particularly the rites of sexual yoga. This was strictly forbidden according to yogic tradition, for a guru was thought to be necessary to pursue these practices safely and fruitfully. Nevertheless for several months he visited her frequently and they would make love through most of the night. Eliade wrote:

> From then on I came late, after midnight, and returned to my kuitar an hour before dawn. I succeeded in preserving my lucidity and my self-control, not only in the "preliminary rituals," but also in all that followed. Jenny was astonished, but I sensed that I was on the road to becoming another man. Sometimes I only slept two or three hours a night, yet I was never tired. I worked all the time, and I worked better than ever before. I understood then the basis of all that vainglorious beatitude that some ascetics, masters of Hatha-yoga proclaim. I understood, too, the reason why certain yogis considered themselves to be like the gods, if not even superior to them, and why they talk about the transmutation and even the immortality of the body (p. 198)

Then the following incident occurred. Eliade lived in a hut next to another hut inhabited by a "naga," an ascetic with matted hair.

> Upon returning to my hut one morning in March, I found my naga neighbor waiting for me in the doorway. "I know where you've been," he said as soon as we had entered the kuitar. "I believe you could be compared with Maha Bhairava! But do you have enough virya (energy) to proceed on this path? People of today are impure and weak. Very soon you will feel a strong fever in the crown of your head. You will know then that you do not have much time. It is better that you stop before this happens."
> He had spoken as clearly as he could, using whole clauses of Sanskrit so that I could understand him. I understood him.
> "But what if I find a Guru?" I asked.
> "You already have a Guru," he said smiling. Then he saluted me, bringing his palms together in front of his face and returned to his hut (pp. 198–199).

In January 1930, when Eliade began his relationship with Jenny, there was a transiting Saturn-Mars-Venus conjunction between two and five degrees of Capricorn, near the cusp of his 12th house, and opposite his natal Jupiter-Neptune — symbolizing a secret (12th house) love affair and a sexual relationship (Venus-Mars) oriented toward mystical experiences and altered states of consciousness. Moreover, progressed Venus and Jupiter were still in an exact trine and progressed Mars was opposite natal Jupiter, symbolizing Eliade's experience of adventure, strength, and sexual prowess. This intense relationship, although it only lasted a short time, was a major event in Eliade's life; for this represented his most profound and direct personal experience of the ancient yogic and specifically Tantric teachings of which he had, up to this point, only been a scholar.

Soon Eliade left the ashram and continued to travel throughout India gathering material for his doctoral thesis. He began to feel that he had been mistaken in attempting to renounce his own cultural heritage and retire to the life of an ascetic yogi:

> What I had tried to do — renounce my Western culture and seek a "home" or a "world" in an exotic spiritual universe — was equivalent in a sense to a premature renunciation of all my creative potentialities. I could not have been creative except by remaining in my world — which in the first place was the world of Romanian [sic] language and culture. And I had no right to renounce it until I had done my duty to it; that is, until I had exhausted my creative potential. . . . To believe that I could, at twenty-three, sacrifice history and culture for "the Absolute" was further proof that I had not understood India. My vocation was culture, not sainthood. I ought to have known that I had no right to "skip steps" and renounce cultural creativity except in the case of a special vocation — which I did not have. But of course I understood all this only later (p. 200).

Return to Romania

Eliade's extensive travels and studies were cut short suddenly by the notice that he was being recalled to Romania for military service. On Christmas Eve 1931 he arrived back in Romania after three years abroad. Let's think carefully for a moment about what had just happened to him. While transiting Uranus was square natal Uranus and Neptune, Eliade went on this incredible journey to the exotic land of India to study esoteric, mystical subjects.

The influence of the trans-saturnian planets like Neptune and Uranus can draw some people more or less permanently beyond the boundaries of Saturn, into a transcendent realm or an unconventional lifestyle. But Eliade had natal Sun conjunct Saturn and in the 2nd house, so his "dharma," his path, was to be a man of prominence and influence *in the world*. Sooner or later, gravity would pull him back to earth, back to his role as an academician, back to what Dane Rudhyar called the level of socio-cultural functioning, signified by Saturn.

On the day Eliade arrived back in Romania (Christmas Eve 1931) there was a Full Moon at 2 Capricorn/Cancer 13, across his natal 6th and 12th houses. Moreover, progressed Venus at 5 Pisces 40 was nearing conjunction to natal Moon, symbolizing a warm return to his family, his friends, and his homeland.

Upon his return home a number of things began to happen. First, he began to enjoy a considerable amount of professional success and notoriety. He wrote and published *Maitreyi*, one of his most important novels. This book won him first prize in a major literary contest, and also caused a scandal; for it was a scarcely veiled description of his love affair with Dasgupta's daughter, written almost directly from his journal notes. This book made him a "famous writer." Transiting Neptune was opposite natal Moon in late 1931 and throughout 1932 when the book — one of his most imaginative, emotional, and inspired works — was conceived and written. Neptune opposite Moon stirred great public controversy. In addition, transiting Pluto had moved from its natal square to the Sun to trine Eliade's natal Sun between 1931 and 1933, corresponding both to a growth in his public influence and prominence in the fields of literary fiction and religious studies (Sun in Pisces), and to his increased income (Sun in 2nd house) upon returning to Romania. In April 1933 he won the literary prize for *Maitreyi*, which appeared in May and made him instantly famous. In June he also received his doctorate. Progressed Mars at 3 Capricorn 01 was opposite progressed Jupiter (3 Capricorn 38), especially important because Jupiter ruled his 10th house (career). Moreover, as progressed Venus reached exact conjunction to the natal Moon, Eliade soon became involved in another romantic adventure, to which we now turn.

Two Women

In the spring of 1932, while transiting Saturn was nearing conjunction to his natal Venus and while transiting Jupiter was conjunct his descendant, he met a woman named Sorana, with whom he soon became involved. She seemed an appropriate partner for him, as she was bright, beautiful, and from a family of high standing. However, Eliade soon became uncomfortable with her. He wrote,

> Sorana Topa was always with us. Accompanying her home, I would have to listen once again to her criticisms of the symposium — her criticisms of me in particular, if I had happened to have spoken that evening. Sometimes her observations were just and invaluable, but at other times they seemed irrelevant and pretentious. On the first of December, 1922, I concluded my military service and received my discharge papers. Now Sorana and I could spend more time together. This concentrated and prolonged intimacy was not always to my liking. For one thing, Sorana's presence was exhausting. With her it was always necessary to be unceasingly intelligent, profound, original — and above all, "spontaneous." Love, for her, was a constant "burning at white heat," as she liked to say (p. 237).

Transiting Saturn was conjunct Venus throughout the year, corresponding to their important but difficult relationship, which was marked by her criticism of him, his annoyance with her, and, perhaps, his desire to free himself from her. Then, around Christmas 1932, he met another woman, named Nina, who captured his interest. This occurred while Saturn was passing for the second time over his natal Venus in Aquarius, the sign of experimentation, non-normative behavior, and the search for freedom. And, in keeping with his aquarian Venus, he was involved with both women for many months. He tried to keep the secret from both of them, but eventually they found out, as did a number of his friends. This, too, became something of a scandal.

Today we may take such arrangements for granted, but in the 1930s they were not so common. This situation caused considerable tension and anxiety for Eliade, for he knew things could not continue as they were; yet he could not decide between Sorana and Nina. The following passage reveals his internal struggle at this time, as well as the meaning which he attributed to this experience:

> I sensed that the trials through which I was passing were pursuing an end that was for the time being indecipherable, but one that I did not despair of deciphering some day. . . . I had to acknowledge that. . . there was something I wanted very much: namely to be able to love — simultaneously and with the same intensity — two women. . . . I tried to make sense out of it by saying that I wanted

to live a paradoxical experience. . . because I wished to attain to another mode of being than the one we are fated to live. . . . Even in adolescence I had tried to suppress normal behavior, had dreamed of radical transmutation of my mode of being. . . . Perhaps my yearning to love two women at the same time was none other than an episode in a long secret history. . . . In my way, I was trying to compensate for my fundamental incapacity of becoming a "saint" by resorting to a paradoxical, non-human experience. . . . (pp. 255–256).

His effort to conduct two relationships at once became part of a larger project of attaining a sacred, non-ordinary mode of existence.

Nina was considered quite unacceptable for a man of Eliade's stature by his friends and his family. They considered her to be beneath him, socially and intellectually. Her first marriage had ended in tragedy and divorce. No one could understand why someone so highly esteemed and successful as Eliade would be attracted to a poor, divorced woman. She was considered completely unworthy, especially when compared with someone like Sorana, who was a woman of high social standing. Yet the fact remained that Sorana aggravated him constantly, and he cared very deeply about Nina. Between April and September, 1933, Eliade was tortured by this dilemma, vacillating between his affections for the two women, trying to deceive them, then filled with shame and remorse as the facts became known to both Nina and Sorana. His guilt was so great that he seriously considered leaving the country forever to escape the situation.

Finally, after agonizing all summer, he broke off his relationship with Sorana and made a commitment to Nina in September 1933. Ultimately he married Nina, much to the consternation of his family. At the time of this crucial decision, progressed Venus was at 7 Pisces 12, opposite the vertex. Transiting Saturn was conjunct natal Venus during this whole episode. Since Venus was in Aquarius, the sign of behavior that is at times shocking to those bound by mainstream social values, it is not surprising that Eliade was drawn to an unusual form of relational experimentation and attracted to a woman of a different social class and background.

Earlier we noted how, in going to India, Eliade made a crucial choice that involved defiance of the wishes of his family and the norms of society for the purpose of establishing a unique and independent identity. While Saturn passed over Venus in Aquarius and stationed exactly conjunct his Aquarius ascendant (in September and October 1933), Eliade was faced with another crucial decision. Eliade's choice to marry Nina was an act of great courage; for he thereby broke free of the binding structure of social convention, following a path that led him, in his own way, toward freedom and the fulfillment of his individual destiny. He married the woman he truly loved, despite the fact that it led to an irrevocable falling-out with his family. Eliade may have felt himself to be something of a pariah or an outcast as a result of his decision. Nevertheless, while Saturn was conjunct his Aquarius ascendant, unconventional behavior would almost of necessity become an essential facet of his identity.

Saturn's passage over Eliade's Aquarian ascendant precipitated another classic process of severance from the rigid cultural conditioning and beliefs of his time. He dared to break away from these, from the limitations bred by unquestioning allegiance to family, nation, or culture. To achieve a higher mode of existence, at times all of us must risk social disapproval or stigmatization for living in an unconventional manner and holding unorthodox beliefs.

Eliade married Nina despite the loss of his close ties with family and many friends. He endured these losses and moved on. Uranus and its home sign Aquarius are concerned with seeking freedom at any cost. During Saturn's transit over his Venus and ascendant, Eliade's choice of a marital partner became an occasion for him to experience freedom to will his own destiny. Thus, this event carries great spiritual significance. It was in the midst of these complex events in his early life that Eliade launched his career as a scholar and writer, ultimately becoming one of the great intellectual figures of the twentieth century.

CHAPTER 9
An Astrological Biography of Swami Muktananda

Swami Muktananda was one of the most outstanding spiritual teachers of our era, a being of power and wisdom who inspired and guided countless seekers, kindling in them the longing for truth and illuminating the path to liberation. Thousands of people experienced dramatic spiritual awakenings through hearing his words, receiving his gaze, his touch, being in his mere presence. Many people reported having the most profound meditations of their lives while in his company. Others said that when sitting in a room with him, they would feel waves of joy, currents of *kundalini* energy in their bodies, or an intense pressure at the top of their heads. To others he demonstrated his awareness of the entire record of their lives, for example knowledge of the full details of the most traumatic events of a person's childhood. Who was this man, and what does his birth chart reveal about his identity and how he became who he was?

Muktananda's Birth Chart

Swami Muktananda was born with a Full Moon straddling the horizon of his birth chart, with the Sun in Taurus on the ascendant, and the Moon in Scorpio on the descendant. Taurus represents the phase of the zodiac that concerns development of an appropriate relationship with the material world, whether this means enjoyment of money and physical comforts or the attitude of detachment from the whole Taurean realm prescribed by many spiritual traditions. Muktananda's Sun in Taurus suggests that there might be an emphasis in the life either on the physical plane, materiality, money, and personal resources, *or* their renunciation. He was born into a well-to-do family, and his father was a wealthy landowner. This fits with his Jupiter in the 4th house, which often indicates that the native comes from a family of prominence, noble standing, and means. However, from a young age, Muktananda gravitated toward the monastic path, which encourages the renunciation of wealth and possessions, the control of the senses, the withdrawal of awareness inward away from objects that cause craving. If he had not become a renunciate, Muktananda would have inherited a great deal of land from his father.

He possessed many of the qualities typically associated with Taurus: stubbornness, determination, perseverance, a hard-working attitude, practicality. He loved nature, and was a master gardener and cook. His physical appearance and mode of self-presentation was also in keeping with his Sun and ascendant in Taurus. His physique was "bullish:" he was short, stocky, and muscular. He practiced hatha yoga for years, and developed a powerful physical body. And later in life, after he had established a large organization, he was quite involved in its administration and financial decision making. He was very concerned with the concrete methods that would lead either to material success or to spiritual realization. He approached the spiritual quest quite pragmatically, trying every available method to alter his consciousness and to find a path to liberation.

The Sun and Moon in his chart were in their strongest configuration, the opposition. Thus, the Scorpio Moon was reflecting the Sun fully. Scorpio is the phase of the zodiac that concerns the transmission of energy from one person to another, and the powerful impact that such an interchange has on both persons. In the most

Swami Muktananda
May 16, 1908
5:11 AM IST
Dharmasthala, India

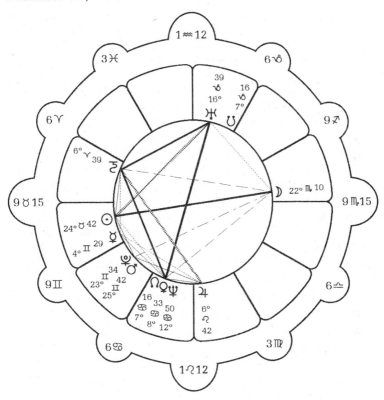

Source: Lois Rodden, *Astrodata III*

Chart 21

mundane sense Scorpio concerns one's use of financial power in business, investment, and partnerships of all kinds. In a deeper sense it concerns the transformation of sexuality, Tantra, generating inner power through yogic means, *shaktipat* — the transmission of power from an illumined guru to a spiritual seeker.

This Full Moon is a key symbol in his chart, signifying one of the most significant themes of his life. The Moon in Scorpio in the 7th house suggests a longing for transformative experience through interactions with others, for a powerful interpersonal transmission of energy. It implies a need to be deeply affected by some significant other person in his life (Scorpio Moon in the 7th house), but also to powerfully impact or transform others. In fact, much of Muktananda's life was spent searching for a teacher who would transmit the liberating divine force to him that would awaken the dormant kundalini energy, which yogis believe dwells coiled up at the base of our spines. The most important phase of his long spiritual journey was catalyzed by a significant relationship with a spiritual teacher who awakened kundalini through shaktipat, speeding up his evolution greatly. Subsequently Muktananda himself became the holder of a vast wealth of spiritual energy or *shakti*, which he transmitted to others, and which profoundly shook up everyone he met. Practically everyone he encountered after his enlightenment had some experience of the tremendous spiritual force he embodied. His powerful impact on others can be directly correlated with the symbolism of the Scorpio Moon in the 7th house. He spent years searching for the gaze of the Master that would transform him. And from his storehouse of knowledge and spiritual power, he bestowed that same gaze on others and had an explosive, liberating, and catalytic effect on many, many people.

Venus, ruler of his Taurus Sun and ascendant, is conjunct the north node and Neptune, symbolizing an inclination toward an unconditional, all-encompassing divine spiritual love, a love of God (*bhakti*). Muktananda was drawn from his early youth to devotional music, plays, and chanting and enjoyed these throughout his life.

Note also that Venus rules the 6th house, the house in which we pursue self-improvement and purification through methods, techniques, apprenticeship, or discipleship. Muktananda ultimately discovered that for him the most important facet of the spiritual path was discipleship. After years of striving, he concluded that self-effort in spiritual practice must be accompanied by a receptivity to a higher force perceived as grace and power. In his own case, that force was received through spiritual apprenticeship, through following the teachings and being in the presence of his guru, Bhagwan Nityananda. He used to say over and over again, "I attained nothing on the path until I became a disciple." All of this refers back to the fact that the dispositor of his Sun and ascendant is also dispositor of the 6th house. With Venus conjunct Neptune, Muktananda's 6th house apprenticeship was with a highly evolved, remarkable, God-conscious, and completely ecstatic being: Nityananda.

Uranus is the most elevated planet in the chart and is in a T-Square, opposite Venus-Neptune and square Saturn in the 12th house. Uranus is in the 9th house, traditionally the house of the guru. Thus we might expect Muktananda's teacher to be somewhat unusual. In fact, Nityananda was a very unpredictable character who hardly spoke and walked around practically naked. But there is more to this. In the 9th house, we define a belief system, a cosmology or doctrine that gives meaning to life. It isn't the house of the overwhelming unitive spiritual experience that mystics often speak of, the experience of unmediated contact with the Real, which is associated more with the 12th house. The 9th house is more concerned with the doctrines that would enable an individual to give meaning to such an experience. With Uranus there, we would expect that Muktananda's spiritual perspective was in some way radical or distinctive. He was a follower of Kashmir Shaivism, a philosophy and initiatic tradition that affirms the physical world as an emanation of the divine. Basically, Muktananda was very impatient with philosophies, and was always restless for direct experience of the truths they proclaimed. Also, he passed through periods of rejecting philosophy and religion because they had not led him to any significant spiritual experience. He longed for the pure experience of a higher state of consciousness that is beyond all conceptualization. The placement of Uranus in the 9th house also relates to the fact that he was known to walk all over India (the 9th house rules long distance travel) and often went on pilgrimages to various sacred sites.

Let's look now at the opposition of Uranus to Venus-Neptune. Uranus in the 9th accounts for the restless checking out of various teachers that we'll see later on and his experimentation with many philosophical and religious ideas. Venus and Neptune are placed in the 3rd house, the house of language, words, and the narrative faculty. With Venus and Neptune in the 3rd house square Saturn, Muktananda believed that control of the tongue, of the faculty of speech, was extremely important to spiritual advancement and recommended that seekers remain silent as much as possible, purify their minds and thoughts, avoid small talk, and repeat *mantras* inwardly. With Venus-Neptune in the house of words and speech, he was an enrapturing lecturer, a great expositor of the scriptures and of the spiritual path. He would go into an ecstatic state talking about his love of God, his guru, and the visions and realizations he had perceived in meditation. Also, because in yogic philosophy and science, sound is considered the purest physical manifestation of Spirit, Muktananda's favorite spiritual practice was to chant the various names of God. Thus, his Venus-Neptune in the 3rd house can be said to symbolize his devotional love, and his desire to give voice to it in the form of inspired lectures and chanting.

The Uranus-Neptune opposition is also important. Uranus-Neptune combinations can signify sudden mystical experiences, visions, or expansions of consciousness. As we will see, Muktananda experienced many alterations of consciousness that revolutionized his awareness and that often took him by surprise. Moreover Muktananda broke with the precedent of secrecy in the esoteric traditions by writing a unique book (Uranus in the 9th house), *Play of Consciousness* (1974), openly describing the process of kundalini awakening that he experienced over the course of nine years after receiving shaktipat initiation from Nityananda. This awakening process included periods in which he felt as if he was going crazy, as well as meditation experiences that were mystical, mysterious, numinous, and awe inspiring. Natal Uranus opposite Neptune manifested in the form of unusual kinds of mystical experiences that have not been written about by many other people. He also experienced a series of miraculous events in which spiritual guidance came to him suddenly and from unexpected sources, another manifestation of Uranus in the 9th house.

Notice that the natal Sun is widely trine Uranus and semisquare Venus-Neptune. The latter aspect suggests that Muktananda's spiritual longing and aspiration were a central part of his life-purpose. He was to find a way to utilize the stability and solidity of his Taurean personality to receive and transmit to others the efflorescence of spiritual energy that he received through meditation and devotion. His Sun contacted the Saturn-Neptune midpoint, perhaps symbolizing a transformation in which the subtle spiritualizing influence of Neptune would refine the physical structure (Saturn), creating what the Tibetan Buddhists call the Diamond Body, the body of light and power.

Muktananda's natal Venus was also opposite Uranus. Like Meher Baba, who had Venus square Uranus, he was not interested in marriage and a conventional expression of Venus. His relationships with people for many years were those of a monk and his few close friends. His friends tended to be somewhat strange or unusual people like Zipruanna, a sage who used to sit around on dung heaps, and Hari Giri Baba, a mysterious spiritual teacher who wore five or six layers of clothing, spoke cryptically, and was considered a madman by many people. Also, at times when Muktananda was deeply involved with his meditation practice, he was known to act impetuously, telling people to go away so he could be alone to meditate. He had a very expansive, loving side; but he was also somewhat detached from others.

The fact that his Venus was square Saturn may have also been a symbol of his monastic lifestyle and austere values, and his renunciation of attachments to others. He consciously chose not to expend a great deal of energy relating to people during the period of his sadhana (spiritual discipline). He was very serious about his inner quest (Saturn in the 12th house) and he chose his interpersonal associations carefully. It is possible that he experienced some conflict between the very friendly, congenial, open-hearted nature shown by Venus-Neptune opposite Uranus and the way his 12th house Saturn was calling for solitude and inwardness. A recurring theme in the account of his spiritual awakening is the tension he experienced between letting himself be sociable and outgoing, and keeping his vow to remain in solitude, to meditate.

The Mars-Pluto conjunction might lead us to expect that he would be quite forceful, willful, powerful, magnetic. The native with this aspect might also feel impelled to transmute or sublimate sexual energy in some way. This was, in fact, a major issue in Muktananda's life. With the Sun in Taurus along with Mars-Pluto in the 2nd house, the essence of Muktananda's wealth or personal resources was spiritual energy or shakti. He was a kundalini guru, who taught primarily not through philosophizing and techniques (although he did teach methods and philosophies) but through the energy he transmitted. He was a man of power, a shaman, a magician, who transformed people through contagious influence. With Mars-Pluto in the 2nd house, he was sizzling with shakti, and people who were in the same room with him would often experience intense heat, visions, emotional catharsis, movements of energy through the chakras, as well as feelings of great love.

Natal Saturn is in the 12th house, the domain of solitude, retreat, or, in some cases, monasticism. It is the house associated with the phenomena we most commonly associate with spirituality and mysticism: visions, altered states of consciousness, kundalini awakening, loss of body consciousness, superconscious or transcendent states, meditative and ecstatic experiences. Many of us think of these types of phenomena as the essence of spirituality. However, altered states and mystical experiences are only one facet of the process of transformation.

Here we are looking at the chart of someone whose life involved a major focus on mystical experiences. But this doesn't necessarily mean that they should be the major focus of our own lives, since we each have different life-tasks that are reflected in our birth charts. In my personal contact with him, Swami Muktananda repeatedly discouraged me from being overly preoccupied with dramatic mystical experiences and led me to understand that they would unfold in a natural way after I had completed other kinds of personal development and evolution, especially in the realms of work and relationships. It is important to broaden our conception of spirituality and of the activities conducive to its unfoldment. The key is to understand the symbolism of our unique birth charts clearly and realistically in order to discern what kinds of tasks we are called upon to accomplish in this life. Hazrat Inayat Khan (1978) once said, "The perfect life is following one's own ideal. . . and each one should . . . travel along the path that is suited to his temperament." While it is important to emulate saints and sages, each of us also has to find our own unique path in life. The purpose of this book is to demonstrate how astrology can help us find that path.

With Saturn in the 12th house, Swami Muktananda made a determined effort to experience higher stages of consciousness and the deepest realizations of meditation. But it did not come easily, and there were many obstacles and fears that he had to overcome before his vision fully awakened. The 12th house is the house of what Jung called the "collective unconscious," from which contents emerge that are not merely one's own, and that can overwhelm or disturb the stability of the conscious self. The material that arises here can be terrifying because the entire ancestral memory of the species is contained here, including images of violence, catastrophe, and suffering. As we will see momentarily, in the course of his meditative journey Muktananda passed through a dramatic confrontation with the unconscious in which, during one period, he experienced confusing and terrifying visions. Gradually, however, he became fearlessly stabilized in the inner world of expanded consciousness.

Saturn refers to processes that occur over long periods of time, with determination and patience. So those of you who have been meditating for years in a seemingly futile manner, take heart! Muktananda's enlightenment through yogic meditation did not happen all at once either. Prior to receiving shaktipat, he spent many years trying to alter his consciousness through yogic techniques, penances, fasts, and prayers; and he would have been the first to tell you that not a whole lot happened. He became physically strong; but he had no inner experience of God.

However, when Muktananda finally received initiation from Nityananda, his inner experience began to deepen, and he embarked upon nine years of extremely concentrated, focused saturnian effort in the practice of meditation. His monastic discipline was severe. He followed strict vows and spent most of his time in solitude, staying in his hut in a small village. In *Play of Consciousness*, he repeatedly mentions his need to strictly limit social contact with others, as their presence disturbed his meditation. The only thing that concerned him was to be able to meditate deeply three times a day. He spent all of his time meditating, reading about meditation, and thinking about his meditative experiences. All of this was the manifestation of Saturn in the 12th house. He had to do it, for nothing else mattered to him.

Early Interest in Spiritual Life

Let us examine the details of his life more closely. When he was around 12 or 13 years old, he began to become interested in God and in spirituality. He loved to chant and watch plays depicting religious themes, such as the lives of sages and spiritual masters. This was about 1920–1921. Between 1920 and 1925 transiting Pluto passed over his Venus-Neptune, corresponding to the time when the young seeker began to yearn after God realization. Between 1920–1922, progressed Sun in Gemini sextiled natal and progressed Jupiter, which may have given him a precocious understanding of life's meaning. A progressed New Moon also occurred in 1922. Because the progressed New Moon was sextile to Jupiter, Muktananda became interested in philosophy and in having contact with people of learning and wisdom. This progressed aspect to Jupiter also signified his emerging love of travel and adventure.

A crucial event occurred in 1923. One day while he was near his school, he met a wandering naked *sadhu* (holy man), who walked over to him and patted him on the head. Muktananda was deeply moved by the man's presence; but soon the sadhu walked away and disappeared into the jungle. This encounter made a great impression on Muktananda. Within six months he had left home in search of Truth. He set forth without telling anybody and traveled a thousand miles across India before he wrote a letter home to his parents. Although he had the Sun in Taurus, he preferred a life of poverty to the considerable wealth he would have inherited from his father. Remember that a Taurus emphasis in a chart doesn't necessarily mean the individual will be "materialistic," "sensual," or "avaricious." It does mean that the person must define for himself or herself an appropriate attitude toward the world of money, possessions, and the senses. That attitude can range from enjoyment of and attachment to physical objects and wealth, to their complete renunciation, the latter being the path that Muktananda chose.

In 1923, transiting Jupiter crossed his descendant. In Indian astrology, Jupiter is called "Guru." When it crossed his descendant, he had this significant encounter with a guru, which had a continuing impact upon him. Also, transiting Saturn was passing through his 6th house square to natal Uranus and Neptune; during that time he experienced the kind of sudden awakening of higher consciousness and of love that I spoke of earlier. He was suddenly drawn to a higher mode of existence, and this led to actions that were uranian, rebellious, unconventional: breaking away, running away from home. Thus, when Saturn activated his Venus-Neptune opposite Uranus, he was struck by the longing for divine love and, perhaps, a desire to meet this man again. His encounter with the sadhu had lured him beyond the point where he could stand still and be a conventional youth. He had to get away to seek God.

In the period after he left home, he wandered all over the vast reaches of India. There is a gap in our knowledge of Muktananda's life between the early 1920s when he left home and the mid 1940s. A biography written by Swami Prajnananda mentions some anecdotes about that period but few dates are given. It is known that around 1925, at the age of 17, Muktananda settled in a Vedantic ashram and took *sannyas* initiation, meaning that he became a monk, a Swami, taking vows of poverty, homelessness, and celibacy. He also studied Vedanta philosophy and other scriptures. At this time, transiting Jupiter was in his 9th house conjunct Uranus and opposite Venus-Neptune. Advaita Vedanta is not a conventional worldly philosophy, but rather a system of radical non-dualism which posits that *Brahman* (God, the Absolute) is the only reality; and that the physical world as we perceive it is a deceptive illusion (*maya*) created by our limited perceptual frames. Thus, while Jupiter was in his 9th house, he was studying philosophy and religion. Transiting Saturn was conjunct his descendant at the same time; and he had a very important relationship with his Vedanta teacher, whom he revered greatly until the end of his life. This crucial association with a teacher occurred with transiting Jupiter in the 9th house of the teacher and with transiting Saturn entering the realm of primary relationship, the 7th house.

Transiting Pluto was conjunct natal Neptune and opposite Uranus at this time. His longing for God-consciousness was fully awakened during this transit. The transit of Pluto conjunct Neptune often corresponds to a deepening interest in or commitment to a spiritual path. It became clear to Muktananda during this transit that the spiritual path was the direction for him. He developed a consuming, passionate desire to experience the highest states of consciousness.

Finding the Guru

Between 1923 and 1947, Muktananda wandered all over India. During that time, he met over sixty of India's greatest living spiritual teachers, but he felt that none of them were his Guru. With Uranus in the 9th house, he was restless and did not stay with any one teacher. The fact that he had not met anyone whom he could fully accept as his spiritual master was very discouraging to him. He himself was known by many as a great yogi, very powerful, learned, and wise. He was a practitioner of hatha yoga postures, pranayama (breathing practices), and different sorts of meditation; but as he would often say later on, he had not experienced the higher states of awareness he was seeking. Finally one of his favorite friends and teachers, Zipruanna, advised him to stop wandering around and to go to Bhagwan Nityananda in Ganeshpuri. And, while I do not know if Muktananda knew this or not ahead of time, Nityananda turned out to be the same holy man he had encountered so many years earlier. My understanding is that he had heard stories about Nityananda from others who had met him. Like many spiritual seekers today, he checked out all of the teachers of his era and had his ears open for the latest gossip about every supposedly enlightened person around.

In 1947, at the age of 39, after wandering around India since he was 15, he went to Nityananda. There are different accounts of what happened next. Apparently Nityananda tested Muktananda for several months, giving him a hard time and ignoring him for long periods. It is customary for teachers to test students who approach them for initiation, to check whether the student is a worthy recipient of the teacher's knowledge. They create trials to test the students' one-pointedness, faith, and maturity.

Muktananda was determined to stay, for he perceived the greatness of Nityananda. He visited the guru's ashram often and began to practice a form of meditation described in the Yoga Sutras involving meditation on an enlightened person, worship of the guru. He began to sit in the room with Nityananda, gazing at him, inwardly merging with him, mentally installing Nityananda inside his own body. He became completely absorbed in this practice. Nityananda indicated that this was the correct meditation for him to practice and encouraged him to continue. Gradually Nityananda began to show his favor toward this Swami, whom no one knew and who kept a very low profile.

Shaktipat Initiation

Then an event occurred, described in his book *Play of Consciousness* (Muktananda, 1974, pp. 58 ff.), which I will explore in some detail because of its significance in his life. One evening he stayed late near Nityananda, who did not give his characteristic indication that Muktananda should leave. He sat up all night watching his guru and meditating. At dawn on the fifteenth of August 1947, Nityananda lovingly offered him food, a shawl, and a pair of sandals he had been wearing. He then looked directly into

Muktananda's eyes and the awestruck disciple saw rays of dazzling, radiant, multicolored light emanating from the guru's eyes.

Muktananda was overwhelmed with gratitude for this powerful transmission of spiritual energy. After Muktananda prostrated at his teacher's feet, Nityananda sent him away, telling him to go to a small village named Yeola to practice meditation. While leaving Ganeshpuri, Muktananda entered a profoundly altered state of consciousness, perceiving all things as filled with divine light. He was in an ecstatic, high state.

When he arrived in Yeola, however, problems emerged. He began to experience vague fears, and devotes a chapter of his book to describing what he called "My Confused Condition" (pp. 66 ff.). He did not know why, but he began to grow very anxious, troubled by bad dreams, aches and pains, feeling as if every cell in his body was being pierced with needles. His previous ecstasy vanished and he was filled with fear and remorse. He became filled with a sense of panic, a desire to jump around and scream that he could not explain. "The whole earth was spinning. The sky was twirling and so were the trees" (p. 70). His body was very hot. He became frenzied and feared that he was going completely crazy. He had visions of a universal conflagration, dissolution, and apocalypse, and of strange, terrifying creatures dancing naked with their mouths agape. In his own words, "I was fully conscious, objectively witnessing a state of madness" (pp. 70–71).

This extraordinary account, which I suggest the reader study in its entirety, shows an eruption of the collective unconscious similar to the one Carl Jung described in *Memories, Dreams, and Reflections*. One important phase of the path of transformation is the navigation of such confusing, at times overwhelming upsurges of disturbing imagery and visions — what these days we might call a "spiritual emergency." They are well documented in the literature describing kundalini awakening.

Now let us examine what was going on for Muktananda astrologically during this period when he received this powerful initiation and then experienced these dramatic alterations of consciousness, which encompassed both a unitive, mystical state and a state of temporary madness. In 1946–1947, around the time that Muktananda returned to Nityananda, transiting Jupiter was again conjunct the descendant, the same transit that had occurred during his first meeting with the sadhu as a boy. Jupiter conjunct the descendant brought further development of this important relationship.

Also he had a progressed Venus-Mars conjunction. For most people such a progressed aspect would suggest marriage, sexual desire, or falling in love. However, one must always refer back to the natal chart to understand how an individual will respond to such a progressed combination. Muktananda had natal Venus conjunct Neptune, suggesting a longing for *bhakti*, or divine love. Thus, instead of getting involved in a romantic relationship, Muktananda channeled the energy of Venus-Mars into a devotional relationship focused on the transmission of shakti (spiritual energy) from guru to disciple. A principle similar to (but distinct from) that experienced through sexuality was operative in this transmission: interpenetration, psychic merger, changing of boundaries of both individuals, who are separate and yet deeply connected by a force that changes them forever. This was an unusual way of expressing the energy of the Venus-Mars conjunction and yet it was quite appropriate. Muktananda was totally enraptured with Nityananda and became his devotee.

This progressed Venus-Mars aspect lasted several years and had a lasting impact on Muktananda's whole life. It may also relate to the fact that even though he was a very austere, strict monk, committed to celibacy, he still had to actively struggle with issues related to sexuality. In *Play of Consciousness* he reports that for a brief period he became inflamed with desire, which disturbed his meditation greatly. Only gradually did he learn that this was a manifestation of the piercing of the sexual chakra (energy center) by the kundalini, which was bringing about a transmutation and internalization of sexual energy. The whole episode seems to directly relate to the symbolism of the progressed Venus-Mars conjunction.

Transiting Jupiter was activating the natal Full Moon between January to October 1947. During this time Muktananda formed this strong connection with Nityananda. Transiting Saturn reached the nadir about the time he settled in Ganeshpuri, ceasing his wandering and deciding to stay around for a while and become a disciple of Nityananda. He did not "settle down" in the way some of us might if we had transiting Saturn enter the 4th house and cross over natal Jupiter in the 4th, namely through finding a wonderful home; but he did establish a new residence and begin to organize his life around a particular place and purpose in the context of his deepening commitment to his teacher.

In addition, transiting Uranus was conjunct natal Mars-Pluto between July 1947 and the spring of 1948. Uranus was exactly conjunct Mars on August 15, 1947, the day of his initiation, which he described as "the most remarkable day of my life — the most significant day not only of this lifetime, but of many lifetimes!" (1974, p. 58). Uranus conjunct Mars is a beautiful symbol of this remarkable, sudden, powerful transmission of energy and the awakening that this event catalyzed. His kundalini was *quaking* after Nityananda initiated him, and he began to undergo a series of extraordinary experiences: he had numerous visions, spontaneously assumed difficult yoga postures, and began to roar like a lion or hop around like a frog while he was meditating, to name just a few things. All of these were "kriyas," purificatory movements that happened spontaneously through the intelligence of the awakening kundalini, which is said to remove blockages and impurities as it unfolds. Uranus conjoining natal Mars-Pluto symbolizes the powerfully charged circuit of energy that was suddenly activated within him.

Uranus is known as the Great Awakener, which works suddenly and irrevocably to awaken us to the existence of a greater whole, to new possibilities. Transiting Uranus conjunct natal Mars-Pluto manifested as the awakening of power, shakti. Many of the images Muktananda used seem quite appropriate for this transit: he said his body felt as if it were burning hot, on fire, and as if pins and needles were penetrating every cell. Mircea Eliade mentions in some of his books that one of humankind's primordial religious experiences was the mastery of fire and that shamans are supposed to be masters of fire. Part of the process in becoming a shaman is to experience the body as filled with fire and to allow it to purify and divinize the body. Bodily heat was considered a sign that one had entered a sacred condition.

When Muktananda received shaktipat initiation transiting Neptune was also square natal Venus and his nodal axis, symbolizing an awakening of devotion. This is a very important transit since the two planets are conjunct at birth. Neptune had moved from the natal conjunction to the square to Venus. Generally, transits involving two planets are particularly important if this planetary pair was aspected at birth.

Right after Muktananda received initiation, in the last two weeks of August 1947, transiting Mars was conjunct transiting Neptune, triggering these mysterious, wondrous, altered states of consciousness, but also his "confused condition." During this time there was a sense of his being out of control, which you might expect given that he was experiencing a major Neptune transit. Put together a Neptune transit and transiting Uranus crossing Mars-Pluto and you've got the potential for some wild, mysterious, mystical forces and spiritual energies to become active. The kundalini shakti was moving, and his heart was opening. The activation of natal Mars-Pluto might also relate to the somewhat violent, cataclysmic quality of some of his visions.

In addition, transiting Neptune was opposite natal Saturn, activating the natal T-square and forming a Grand Cross with it, when all of this happened. Neptune contacting Saturn can be very disturbing to one's sense of personal focus and will. Neptune temporarily weakened Muktananda's psychic equilibrium and allowed all of these visions and strange experiences to invade him. Neptune dissolved his previous structure, his normal state of consciousness and sense of identity so that gradually his awareness could be expanded and universalized. Neptune transits often feel like an erosion of structure, which in this case operated to open up Muktananda's consciousness, making him available for deep transformation. And Neptune's disintegrative action was complemented by the internal awakening precipitated by Uranus conjunct Mars-Pluto.

Intensive Meditation

Turning to the nine year period when Muktananda was doing intensive meditation practice and experiencing many visions and transformational events, the progressed Sun was square to Saturn and progressed Saturn. The discipline with which he pursued his 12th house solitude, retreat, monasticism, and meditation practice was intense and utterly unshakable. He devoted himself completely to the quest for enlightenment, meditating three times a day for several hours each time. Meditation was his job, his leisure, his passion. Saturn is traditionally associated with renunciation, and his natal Sun in Taurus semisquare to Saturn signified his renunciation of desire and attachment. With progressed Sun square Saturn (1952–

1955), he was fully focused on strenuous ascetic activity, retreat, and contemplation.

Between 1954 and 1958, progressed Mercury and Neptune were in conjunction, suggesting Muktananda's constant reflection on spiritual truths, scriptures and doctrines. His mind was becoming more subtle and expanded, making his intelligence more refined, allowing spontaneous and direct apprehension of the truths of the scriptures.

Between 1958 and 1960, progressed Sun was conjunct natal and progressed Neptune. Progressed Sun had been crossing over the natal North Node-Venus-Neptune conjunction since 1952, when a Progressed New Moon occurred conjunct his north node, and 1953, when progressed Sun conjoined natal Venus. Thus we can say that throughout this time (1952–1960) his mind and consciousness became filled with love and established in an expanded state. When progressed Sun contacted Neptune, he reached the culmination of his visionary awakening, his pursuit of enlightenment.

He also reached an important conclusion, that the attitude of renunciation of the world that he had maintained for most of his life was no longer appropriate, because he now perceived that the whole world was vibrating with consciousness. His ultimate liberation took the form of the understanding that the world of form is not separate from God, and that true renunciation is renunciation not of objects but of the dualistic attitude, the false separation of self from world. The realization that the world of substance and forms is the embodiment or play of Spirit was the ultimate outcome of the spiritual journey of this man who had started out by turning away from the world. The physical plane, he discovered, is filled with the divine presence. Thus, among the qualities that he was later known for was his great love of food, plants, flowers, and animals, another manifestation of his Taurus Sun.

When the progressed Sun contacts a natal planet, the individual absorbs the essence of that planet. When progressed Sun conjoined Neptune, Muktananda developed an expanded vision, a state of all-inclusive awareness, culminating in his final enlightenment in 1956. He lost awareness of himself, and his boundaries were dissolved in the highest stages of *samadhi* in meditation. In *Play of Consciousness* he describes how he experienced a continuous vision of divine, conscious, blue light throbbing in all directions as bliss (p. 162).

> I was conscious of the world no longer.... Muktananda was bereft of consciousness and memory. The distinction of the 'inner' and 'outer' evaporated. He was no longer aware of himself. (p. 162)

This is the kind of experience that is at least possible, when the progressed Sun aspects Neptune, for a person who is consciously working to expand consciousness and evolve spiritually.

A similar thing happened to Sri Aurobindo, whose natal Sun was trine Neptune (Chart 14). When the progressed Sun moved to the quincuncx to Neptune, Aurobindo was thrown off balance temporarily. He had been a journalist and political activist. However when progressed Sun formed the quincunx to Neptune he began for the first time to develop an interest in spirituality. Soon thereafter he was arrested on charges of sedition and thrown into jail for a year. While in solitary confinement, he experienced profound states of meditation and visions of other worlds. Neptune suddenly wiped out his previous awareness of himself and the world and uplifted his consciousness to a different plane altogether. The mysterious events that occurred at that time seemed to ruin his outer life as a journalist and activist, but ultimately allowed his awareness to move inward and to expand greatly.

Similarly, while progressed Sun was conjunct Neptune, Muktananda completed his spiritual journey and achieved yogic liberation (*moksa*). He understood the universal truths of the world's religious traditions, confirming the findings of the great mystics. He had visions of other planets, of past lives, and of his future. He became enlightened, God-conscious, fully awakened. Such a progression can symbolize becoming highly sensitized, even to the extent that, as in Muktananda's case, it is possible to reach *nirvikalpa samadhi*, the condition of formless, fully expanded consciousness.

Transiting Uranus was also conjunct natal Venus-Neptune in 1950–1952, during which time his state of wisdom and illumination and enlightenment was awakened. This transit was particularly significant since natal Uranus opposed natal Venus-Neptune, and Uranus was now directly activating his potential to experience divine love and altered, mystical states of awareness.

In 1956, transiting Saturn was conjunct the Moon and opposite the Sun. Remember that when the same transit had occurred for the first time thirty years earlier, he stayed in the Vedantic ashram, absorbing spiritual teachings from a great teacher, from whom he also took *sannyas* initiation. The difference with the second transit is that the activation of the natal Full Moon does not correspond simply with a transformational relationship with a guru — which he definitely had with Nityananda — but also with the growth of a personal, devotional relationship with the Supreme Being. Because natal Venus is conjunct Neptune, his primary relationship was always with God. And one of the most interesting parts of his description of his final realization is a section where he recounts the visions he had of numerous deities, beings from other planes of existence. Thus, at this time most of his interaction was with beings in the inner world.

After 1956, it began to be apparent to other people that something profound had happened to him, that he was indeed fully enlightened, and he began to be known and recognized as the chosen disciple of Nityananda — between about 1956 and 1961 when Nityananda died. In 1959, progressed Sun and Venus reached an exact conjunction exactly along the Uranus-Neptune midpoint. His Uranus-Neptune-Venus axis was being activated by the progressed Sun throughout the 1950s, corresponding to the time when his inner journey culminated.

Progressions show processes of slow growth and maturation through which the potentials of the birth chart are actualized. When the progressions make the time ripe, then transits can have maximum impact. Many transits to Muktananda's natal Venus-Neptune during his lifetime symbolized major events in his quest for God, truth, divine love, and higher consciousness. For example, you will recall that he left home as a youth to seek enlightenment when transiting Saturn was square Venus-Neptune. But the process did not reach fruition until his late forties when the Sun progressed from its natal position to the conjunction to Venus-Neptune and opposite Uranus, linking up with the Venus-Neptune-Uranus circuitry of higher consciousness that was latent in his birth chart.

Understanding Muktananda's life astrologically can inspire us to study our own charts carefully, looking for the factors that correspond to our own spiritual longing and aspiration. For example, I have a natal Sun-Neptune square, and some of the most significant transits and progressions that relate to my own interest in, and pursuit of, spiritual awakening are those that contact this aspect. Similarly, somewhere in the chart of each person reading this is a symbol of your interest in astrology, mysticism, spirituality, or the lives of enlightened people. The whole point of studying the chart of someone like this is to begin to reflect upon what *our* birth charts might teach us about our own spiritual paths, and thus to gain some understanding of the rhythm of our own evolution. Hazrat Inayat Khan (1978) said, "For everything there is a time, so there comes a time for the unfoldment of the soul." This ripening of the soul has many phases, including periods of discipline, suffering, joy, testing of our courage and patience, and refinement of our aesthetic and spiritual sensitivity. Astrological study has the power to foster in us the knowledge that we are ripening perfectly, in our own way and in our proper time.

Muktananda's Career as a Guru

During 1958, transiting Saturn was opposite natal Mars-Pluto. At this time Nityananda began to let people know that Muktananda was a teacher in his own right and began sending students to him. Subsequently, in 1961, Nityananda died and public focus began to move toward Muktananda, who was now recognized by others as an illumined being. Before Nityananda died, he told Muktananda to move down the road to Ganeshpuri to a piece of land. Muktananda lived there, planted gardens and orchards, and continued to meditate. A remarkable ashram, the Shree Gurudev Siddha Peeth, now stands there and continues to operate under the direction of Swami Chidvilasananda, current head of the Siddha Yoga lineage.

In 1961 there was a transiting Jupiter-Saturn conjunction which fell exactly on Muktananda's midheaven, coinciding with his rise to public prominence. His spiritual father (10th house) died, and his own stature began to be seen and appreciated. His public identity as a spiritual master began to really grow. As noted earlier, the Jupiter-Saturn cycle concerns the formation of one's sense of "social destiny." In the midheaven and 10th house one's social and spiritual accomplishments begin to be recognized. Thus, having this conjunction fall on his midheaven heralded a twenty-year cycle of public activity, notoriety, and broad social influence. Previously he had lived mostly as a monk in solitude. Now, during the Jupiter-Saturn conjunction on his midheaven, his career as a guru began. Over the next twenty years, he became one of the world's most famous spiritual teachers.

Transiting Uranus was square natal Sun and semisquare Venus-Neptune between August 1960 and May 1962, around the time

Nityananda died. There was a major change in how he projected his identity, and, true to his Taurus Sun, suddenly he had lots of fertile soil in which to plant gardens and orchards. Transiting Neptune was also conjunct his descendant at this time, a transit that was also significant in the lives of Jung and Meher Baba. Neptune signifies surrender, and Muktananda had surrendered his existence to God and to Nityananda, making him ready to assume the role of a guru for others.

In 1962–1963, progressed Mars was conjunct the nadir; Muktananda was busy building up his new ashram, which would later be visited by thousands of seekers from around the world. Around 1964, he had some initial contacts with people from the West. During 1969, while progressed Venus and Mercury were in conjunction, he wrote *Play of Consciousness*, his most important book. The Mercury-Venus combination enabled him to experience a very easy, harmonious, graceful flow of writing. The first major influx of Western disciples occurred between 1968–1970, and he took his first world tour in 1970. Progressed Venus Retrograde went back over its natal position and the North Node in 1970–1971; and he made contacts with many people who became important disciples. Swami Rudrananda (Rudi) invited him to America where he formed many new connections.

In 1970, progressed Mars was conjunct natal Jupiter in the 4th house. Jupiter is the symbol of travel, contact with foreign nations and cultures. He traveled all over the U.S. and wherever he went he was treated like a king. With Jupiter in Leo the 4th house, he enjoyed regal circumstances wherever he went. In fact, he had always had pretty good fortune with finding places to stay even when he was a wandering mendicant. Thus, while during progressed Mars was conjunct Jupiter, he traveled far and wide, came in contact with all sorts of people, cultures, and places of importance, and lectured extensively.

There was one progression that seems to aptly symbolize his growing reputation as a shaktipat guru. Progressed Pluto finally conjoined natal Mars between 1969 and the end of his life. At birth, Pluto was only two degrees away from Mars, but Pluto is a very slow-moving planet by progression. When it came to the conjunction to Mars, his tremendous power began to be fully apparent. He had an overwhelming impact on others, shaking them up, awakening kundalini. All of these phenomena seem to fit with the symbolism of

Pluto and Mars. He initiated many thousands of people into Siddha Yoga — the yoga that unfolds spontaneously as a result of receving the grace of an awakened being, a *siddha*. This path had previously been revealed only to the most prepared, seasoned aspirants on the spiritual path. No one had ever spoken so openly before about the way in which a guru can catalyze in others a spontaneous unfolding of the kundalini through shaktipat initiation. And it was certainly unprecedented to initiate people on such a mass scale as he did.

In 1970, the Jupiter-Saturn cycle, which had begun with the conjunction on his midheaven in 1960, reached a peak moment as these planets came into opposition. At this time, Saturn was conjunct his Sun, and Jupiter was conjunct his Moon, both falling across his natal horizon. These planets activated the heart of his birth chart, and his destiny really began to unfold at that point. He made all kinds of contacts with people and turned on the Western world to a new approach to yoga and meditation. He was trying to transmit to the public the energy with which he had been entrusted by his guru, establishing transformative relationships with many people, thereby fulfilling an essential life-purpose (Saturn conjunct natal Sun, opposite Moon in 7th).

His second world tour began in 1974. Saturn was conjunct Venus-Neptune in his 3rd house, and he traveled a lot, speaking on spiritual topics, and chanting with large crowds. Progressed Mars and Pluto were in semisquare in 1974–1975; these two factors that were conjunct natally were now in another important aspect, corresponding to a potent expression of his spiritual power.

Then in August 1975, he underwent a health crisis, a series of major heart attacks. The doctors didn't know what was happening to him, and many people feared he might die. He sat in his hospital bed, gazed at Nityananda's picture, and chanted. When it was all over, he said it had been a test of his faith in God and the result of some past karma. In July 1975, there was a transiting Full Moon right across his midheaven/nadir, indicating some impending developments that might involve increased public attention. In August, transiting Mars was conjunct the Sun and opposite the Moon, a transit that could precipitate fevers or heart attacks (Sun rules the heart), as well as intensifying whatever other transits were occurring at that time. Most importantly, during the attacks transiting Pluto was conjunct the 6th house cusp, exactly opposite natal Saturn, precipitating a major health crisis, hospitalization, a near-death experience, and a test of faith and surrender (12th house). Because natal Sun and Saturn are semisquare to each other, transiting Pluto was also sesquiquadrate to natal Sun in 1975 and 1976 from the 6th house. In keeping with the symbolism of Pluto, this transit precipitated a major death-rebirth experience.

During the heart attacks there was a very potent aspect pattern between Jupiter, Saturn, Uranus, and Neptune: transiting Jupiter was at 25 degrees of Aries, square Saturn at 26–27 degrees of Cancer; Uranus was at 29 degrees of Libra, square Saturn and opposite Jupiter; and Neptune, at 10 degrees Sagittarius, was in a sesquiquadrate aspect to Saturn and Jupiter, and in a semi-square to Uranus. Having such an intense configuration form while transiting Pluto was opposite natal Saturn indicates the possibility of the kind of crisis that occurred, one that affected the lives of many people who cared about him and feared he would not live through it.

At around the same time as this health crisis, Muktananda established his U.S. residence in Oakland, California. Transiting Saturn was conjunct his nadir in the fall of 1975. He stayed put for a while after these heart attacks and established the SYDA foundation to promote his work.

In 1977 and 1978, his progressed Moon was in its balsamic phase, which usually feels internally like an ending, the closing of a period in one's life. Muktananda went back to India and stayed at home in the ashram for awhile, doing work on the grounds and building a new wing. There was also considerable growth in the Siddha Yoga movement during this time, which corresponded to the progressed Sun reaching the nadir. There was also an initiation of some of his western disciples into *sannyas*, with a series of ancient fire ceremonies called Yajnas. This refers back to the progressed Sun conjunct the nadir, establishing a new foundation which, even though it partly took the form of the expansion of the physical ashram, also concerned establishing a lineage of transmission, preparing a small group of qualified disciples for a deeper level of commitment to the path and of responsibility for the future of the movement. Progressed Moon was conjunct natal Mars-Pluto at the time, an appropriate symbol for the purificatory fire ceremonies that were conducted as part of these initiations.

On the day when he actually did depart from the earth, October 2–3, 1982, there was a Full Moon at 10 degrees of Libra/Aries across his 6th and 12th houses, conjunct natal Saturn and square natal

Venus-Neptune-Uranus. Transiting Mars was exactly conjunct the 8th house cusp and transiting Jupiter was near the descendant in Scorpio. Transiting Neptune was at 24 Sagittarius 28, closely quincunx the natal Sun from the 8th house, while transiting Saturn and Pluto in Libra were also quincunx the natal Sun from the 6th house. Thus, his natal Sun was the focus of a Finger of God pattern involving Saturn, Neptune, and Pluto.

The progressed Moon was in his 4th house, often associated with the end of life, conjunct Jupiter and progressed Mars. He left his body in a state of peace, after saying goodbye in many ways to many people during the preceding days. His sudden passing was mourned by thousands throughout the world.

CHAPTER 10
An Astrological Biography of Sri Kriyananda

Sri Kriyananda (born Donald Walters), founder of the Ananda-Expanding Light Community, was born with the Sun in Taurus, the sign of pragmatic intelligence and constructive, productive activity. The Sun is involved in a Grand Cross with Jupiter in the 9th house, Saturn in the 5th house, and a conjunction of Moon and Neptune in Leo in the 3rd house. With Sun square Jupiter in the 9th house, Kriyananda was interested from his youth in philosophy, religion, and the search for wisdom and truth. In college he was very thoughtful about philosophical matters and eventually wrote a book entitled *Crises in Modern Thought*. Jupiter in the 9th house square the Sun symbolizes a desire to understand the truth of life from a religious or spiritual perspective. The fact that Jupiter is in Aquarius suggests the development of an unusual or innovative world view, deriving new perspectives from foreign cultures, and adhering to beliefs or doctrines that would be considered unusual, shocking, or revolutionary by others.

From a young age, Kriyananda yearned for expansion of consciousness, as symbolized by Sun square Neptune and by the

Moon's conjunction with Neptune in Leo in the 3rd house. The Sun is the point of release for the Jupiter-Neptune opposition, signifying the potential for achieving an expanded state of consciousness. With both Jupiter and Neptune square his Sun, Kriyananda was very sensitive, experienced some dissatisfaction with mundane human life, was a seeker of meaning, and eagerly pursued a spiritual quest for enlightenment and God consciousness.

Moreover, the Sun is placed in the 11th house, the house of groups and communities. In Aquarius and the 11th house, one moves from the 10th house/Capricorn focus on one's own personal achievements to a concern with society as a whole and the future of humanity. In the 10th house you want to achieve things, to become someone, to assume your rightful place in the social hierarchy. But in the 11th house and Aquarius you become concerned with how you fit into the community and how your efforts will contribute to a better future for humanity as a whole. This is the realm of *sangha*, an important facet of spirituality, to belong and to build community with like-minded people. As noted in Chapter 2, if you have a strong 11th house emphasis in your chart natally (or by progression or transit) you may have a strong need to become involved in some kind of group activity or association with others who share common goals and ideals. Kriyananda's natal Sun in the 11th house, square Jupiter in Aquarius, gave him these kinds of concerns. Moreover, with the Sun in Taurus he has been interested since his early 20s in the organization, the practical details, and in particular the *economics* of forming alternative communities,

His Grand Cross includes the opposition of Jupiter-Neptune, two planets very important for anyone on the Path. Jupiter, the ruler of Sagittarius, is concerned with conceptual or philosophical understanding. In contrast, Neptune (the ruler of Pisces) symbolizes the desire to attain higher states of consciousness or nonconceptual, transcendental experiences beyond philosophy, intellect, and doctrine. However, when Jupiter and Neptune work together in a chart as they do here it often indicates the desire to study higher truths, and to learn about religion and spirituality. Such a person approaches the spiritual journey very philosophically, with a richness of understanding and comprehension. Mircea Eliade, the great historian of religions, had the conjunction of these two planets, as do David Spangler, a noted mystic and spiritual teacher, and Stanley Krippner, who has written over five hundred articles and

Sri Kriyananda
May 19, 1926
7:00 AM
Teleajen, Romania

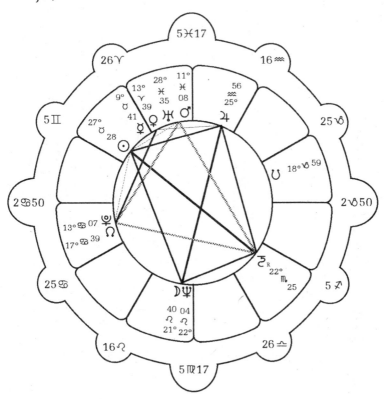

Source: Sri Kriyananda, *The Path:
Autobiography of a Western Yogi*

Chart 22

many volumes on parapsychology, transpersonal psychology, shamanism, and psychic healing (Chart 13). With these two planets opposing each other from the 3rd and 9th houses, Kriyananda has always been interested in learning and reading (3rd house) about religion, yoga, meditation, the lives of saints, spirituality, and eventually became a spiritual teacher himself.

The 3rd and 9th houses are both associated with different aspects of teaching. The 3rd house is the realm of collecting information, data gathering, while in the 9th house we attempt to pull together the information, make sense of it, and derive meaning from it. Both houses are connected to teaching in that in the 9th house you formulate your world view, while if your 3rd house is functioning well, you can verbally communicate your understanding through speaking and writing. Let us also note that both houses are concerned with different aspects of traveling, something Kriyananda has done extensively. The 3rd house is associated with the actual movement from place to place through driving or other means of transportation, while the 9th house is associated with foreign travel and pilgrimage.

Natal Saturn is in the 5th house, the house of pleasures, creativity, enjoyment. With Saturn in the 5th opposite his natal Sun, Kriyananda became a renunciate, restraining (Saturn) the desire for the pleasures that most people seek in life. Moreover, he has always been a very serious and responsible person, able to wield authority and perform a leadership function within a community or group (11th house). Ultimately, with Saturn in the 5th house, Kriyananda also became highly creative, a musician, singer, and poet who has also written about the education of children.

The Jupiter-Saturn square signifies his strong desire for social accomplishment. Even when we're on the spiritual path, most of us have to remain within the Jupiter-Saturn domain of embodied life in time and culture — except in rare cases of renunciates who live in complete retreat, or those such as Ramakrishna, for whom the pull toward the divine Source was overwhelming (Chart 12). When in strong aspect, these two planets suggest a strong desire to be a person of stature in the world. Although Kriyananda possessed a deep devotion to the Lord, he also clearly had a task to accomplish in the world. Kriyananda's chart is remarkable because of the integration that it suggests, and which I believe he has in fact achieved, between spiritual and material accomplishments. He has succesfully grounded his meditative experiences and his quest for spiritual knowledge and awakening (Sun square Jupiter and Neptune) in a very concerete, Taurean way in the formation of the Ananda community.

When Kriyananda was 22, he read Paramahamsa Yogananda's *Autobiography of a Yogi.* He devoured the book quickly and was so taken by its stories of saints and Kriya Yoga (an ancient system of meditation) that he immediately knew what he wanted to do with his life: to find a teacher and follow the spiritual path. Then he did a remarkable and courageous thing: he bought a bus ticket, left everything, traveled across country to California, and knocked on the door of Yogananda's community asking to be admitted. He literally walked into his first meeting with Yogananda and said I want to be your disciple. Yogananda accepted him immediately, which was very unusual and exceptional, as most people had to wait months just for an interview.

Let's look at the transits and progressions for these major events. A new cycle of his life was beginning. This was clearly indicated by the fact that this was the time of a progressed New Moon. The progressed lunation cycle shows the cyclic development of the personality over a thirty-year period. The New Moon is the beginning of a cycle of activity that climaxes about 15 years later at the progressed Full Moon. Kriyananda's progressed New Moon was at 19 degrees of Gemini in his natal 12th house. As we saw in chapter 2, in the 12th house we have the opportunity to transcend attachment to our personal identities. Here we are asked to surrender, to open ourselves to God or Spirit, to develop generosity, and to engage in service. This progressed New Moon in the 12th house initiated a new cycle in Kriyananda's life devoted to spiritual life, meditation, retreat, and monasticism, all of which were traditionally associated with the 12th house. With the progressed New Moon here, Kriyananda wanted to surrender his personal life and ambitions and to become a monk, aspiring only to God realization. He wanted to meditate, to pray, and to follow the spiritual path above all else.

At this time, transiting Uranus had moved from its elevated position in his 10th house into conjunction with the ascendant, the point of identity and dawning self-awareness. Thus, he experienced a need to break free of his old life and to establish a completely new identity. When Uranus transits the ascendant, your sense of who you are changes profoundly. Your identity is completely transformed, and you feel compelled do very unconventional things; you're not the same person thereafter. Events often unfold quite suddenly at such times, and one's actions can be very shocking to others. In Kriyananda's case, his parents and friends thought he was totally crazy and didn't know what to make of the new lifestyle he had adopted.

As we have noted previously, a crisis of severance is often required on the spiritual path. At such times, we are called upon to break free of our social conditioning, and our established modes of activity, and to do something to which we are called but which we may have never had the courage to pursue until Uranus comes along and says DO IT! Uranus teaches us to take chances, without regard for how one's actions will be judged by others. It bestows boldness and a willingness to experiment in order to bring about renewal. Kriyananda's life took a completely new turn during this transit. And as Uranus is also the planet associated with social experimentation and communities, Kriyananda now became a member of an unusual religious community.

There were other progressions operative at this time. Progressed Saturn, the planet of renunciation and ascetic effort, was exactly conjunct his Vertex during this period of dedication to spiritual discipline. Moreover, progressed Jupiter (the planet of the teacher or guru) had moved into an exact square with natal Sun, symbolizing his quest for expanded consciousness and the potential for him to come into contact with a great sage like Yogananda.

In addition, transiting Neptune was in Libra opposite natal Venus, and one could say that he fell in love with Yogananda. From the very first meeting they were completely devoted to one another. With Neptune opposite Venus he experienced an unconditional, spiritual love, a love of the Formless. Through this relationship, Kriyananda began to learn the love of God, in particular a love of God as embodied in his guru.

Kriyananda quickly became a central organizer and teacher in Yogananda's community, the Self Realization Fellowship (SRF). At the time he left home to seek out Yogananda, transiting Saturn was conjunct his natal Moon-Neptune, and activating his natal Grand Cross and all of its potentials for spiritual growth and awakening. When Saturn crossed over his Moon-Neptune he traveled across the country (the 3rd house governs travel, driving, taking a bus trip) and began reading, writing, and absorbing knowledge from his teacher (Jupiter in 9th opposite Moon-Neptune in the 3rd). Saturn brought him the realization that his main aspiration was to be a spiritual seeker and a member of a spiritual community. These major changes in his life were precipitated when Saturn activated his natal grand cross along with Uranus crossing his ascendant. He now knew what he wanted to commit himself to. Saturn's purpose is to bring about these kinds of choices and commitments that have long-lasting impact. He never wavered from his decision, and from that point on his life was completely devoted to God and the project of building community.

With Sun in the 11th house square Jupiter in the 9th, his path was to become a teacher within a community. When Saturn went 3/4 of the way around his chart by transit he changed his life dramatically to come into alignment with his true nature, in accordance with the symbolism of his birth chart. Then, when Saturn crossed over his nadir, he settled down and found a new home and a new family. He also had difficulties with his own parents at this time, as they did not understand his new pursuits (4th house: family of origin). Kriyananda then settled into a new cycle of activity as a teacher and writer, and was given the job of transcribing Yogananda's lectures and written lessons, commentaries on various scriptures, the SRF newsletter. With Saturn transiting through his 4th house opposite Mars in Pisces, he was also involved with construction projects on the SRF property (4th house), doing physical work (Mars) in a spirit of service (Pisces). This community was now his home.

Kriyananda stood out because of his youthful age and his enthusiastic devotion to Yogananda. While Saturn was opposite natal Mars and Uranus in his 10th house, he became a great organizer and had a spirited manner that marked him as unique. Progressed Venus had moved into conjunction with natal Mercury and he easily grew into the roles of an editor, a writer, and a lecturer.

Around 1950, he began to lecture and travel a lot for the SRF churches, while transiting Jupiter was passing over his midheaven. Jupiter's transit through the 10th usually brings some expansion in your career and public stature. Also, during the whole time he was undergoing his training with Yogananda, Neptune was opposite Venus, a transit that lasted three years. In this period, his heart opened, and he learned to love in a transpersonal way, a non-personalized and non-grasping expression of Venus. He wasn't just seeking to love one person; through his devotion to guru and God he was learning universal love. He enjoyed a very close, devotional relationship with his teacher during that period. However, Yogananda died on March 7, 1952, when Saturn transited opposite natal Venus. Unfortunately, Saturn transits do on some occasions correspond to painful times of sadness and loss in our lives.

Soon, Kriyananda began to travel all over the country conducting services and teaching Kriya Yoga at various SRF centers. Transiting Pluto had moved into the 3rd house, the realm of traveling, mobility, driving, and speaking. As noted earlier, the Moon-Neptune conjunction brings a longing for the infinite: The Moon symbolizes our longings and Neptune symbolizes meditation and the expansion of awareness. From the time when Saturn crossed these two planets he had been hungry for God realization, the transcendent experience of divine consciousness. Now when Pluto began to pass over natal Moon-Neptune that hunger intensified and his commitment to the spiritual path deepened. Pluto was activating Kriyananda's natal grand cross again, another symbol of this new phase of writing, teaching, and lecturing. With natal Jupiter square Sun and opposite Moon-Neptune, he was well suited for the role of a minister, exercising a priestly function (Jupiter), organizing the neptunian religous experience through ceremony and doctrine. He was a central figure within the SRF community.

Just before his Saturn return Kriyananda took vows of renunciation and was given the monastic name, Swami Kriyananda. Many years later, in the 1980s, he decided to marry, dropping the appelation "swami" and becoming known as Sri Kriyananda.

While Saturn was in Sagittarius and in his 7th house (realm of friendship and relationship) from 1958 to 1962, Kriyananda traveled extensively in India and began meeting many saints and yogis. Since he wasn't involved in romantic relationships or marriage at this time his interest was in meeting sages, spiritual friends. At this time, transiting Uranus was also in the 3rd house and was approaching his Moon-Neptune conjunction. A new phase of his spiritual journey was beginning, which he experienced at first as an intensification of his longing for meditation and God realization. While he traveled in India, Pluto was also making a major transit, going back and forth across his nadir: the foundation of one's sense of roots, family, national or racial heritage, or sense of connection to a particular cultural tradition. When Pluto was conjunct his nadir, Kriyananda discovered the mysteries of Indian civilization, connecting in the deepest sense with his lineage as a yogi by going to the source. However, this transit was also about to throw his personal foundations (especially in terms of residence) into a certain disarray for some time.

Transiting Uranus was very close to transiting Pluto at that time, nearing the conjunction that was the symbol of the great cultural and political revolution of the 1960s. These planets were conjunct throughout the sixties and corresponded to the psychedelic revolution, the political upheaval, the turbulent, eruptive forces, and the desire to radically restructure society that were all unleashed at that time. We're going to see these planets operating quite dramatically in Kriyananda's chart, completely altering the direction of his life.

Outer planet transits challenge us to relinquish our attachment to security and certainty. If our consciousness is bound by Saturn then we struggle to keep things safe and secure. But if we are consciously on the spiritual path then at some point we are asked to make an agreement to fulfill our role within the realm of Saturn — doing what we can to serve our people and our world — but giving our primary allegiance to the divine presence, which is often felt as a subtle, guiding, transforming force whose intention may not always be evident. The process of reorienting ourselves to welcome this presence into our lives is represented by Uranus, Neptune, and Pluto. These agents of spiritual transformation act in a series of tests, crises, or rites of passage, which traditionally was called the path of initiation. Initiation is sometimes turbulent and chaotic. The key is to cooperate with the process rather than to panic. Some part of us may feel, "I can't let my life fall apart like this, it's too awful." But we may also understand intuitively that a transformative process is operative, and that we should simply let go and allow things to change, however dramatically. It's important to go through such a process with the maturity and practical intelligence bred by attunement to Saturn — which enables you to cope responsibly and sensibly with the crisis. This kind of sensibility means that even if your life structure or internal equilibrium is temporarily disrupted by an outer planet crisis, you allow it to happen with equanimity, trust, and an effort to discern the underlying intention of the process.

We're about to witness Kriyananda going through a major spiritual crisis, very gracefully.

About the time that his travels in the East came to an end transiting Uranus formed a square to his natal Sun in the 11th house. Earlier, he had been named Vice President of the SRF, and was fairly powerful in the organization. However, when he arrived home from India, he was suddenly and unexpectedly ousted from SRF in July 1962. In plain language, he got kicked out of the group whose work he had spent years promoting. He was fully committed to the SRF's mission and teachings. But during this transit there was a rupture in his connection with this group. Uranus frequently brings about unexpected disruptions and disturbances. Its function is to stir things up and create change, movement, and new directions.

In addition, the progressed Sun was exactly conjunct Kriyananda's ascendant in July 1962. The progressed Sun crossing an angle is always momentous, signifying a milestone in one's life. In particular, when the progressed Sun crosses the ascendant it is a time of destiny with respect to the definition of one's identity as a distinctive person. Also, the progressed ascendant was trine natal Uranus, again suggesting that this was a time for him to express his individuality, his uniqueness, his own voice and gifts. But at first this was not an easy task. Often one feels the aftershocks of a Uranian earthquake for quite some time after the actual event that marks the rebellion or break from the established order of one's life.

Finally, transiting Mars was going through his 12th house and square his midheaven and natal Mars in Pisces when he was ousted. Although it is usually a relatively minor, short-lived transit, Mars's transit through the 12th house is often a period when feels one feels misunderstood or isolated from others, and can't control the course of events or get things to move forward. This transit may have corresponded to momentarily feeling sorry for himself or that God had forsaken him. It is to Kriyananda's credit that he demonstrated great strength of character and eventually overcame the pain and sense of betrayal this experience caused him. With his natal Mars in Pisces, the disruption of his involvement with the group that had been the center of his life for fourteen years led at first to confusion about what to do with himself or how to direct his personal energies.

Kriyananda's ouster from SRF appears to have been a purely political matter. The 11th house is where you deal with group politics. Thus, when Uranus squared his Sun there was a sudden "divorce" from this community. He was thrown out. He had to change his community, his affiliation; and he had to awaken to a new sense of futurity, a new vision, a new ideal that wouldn't have been possible for him to actualize within the structure of SRF. Uranus transits often correspond to developments that we are ready to have happen, even if were not consciously aware of it. He was ready to become the leader of a new and more revolutionary kind of community. And even though he was quite attached to SRF, Uranus' transit to his Sun uprooted him from it, as if to say, "No, you've got something very different on your agenda, something else is being called forth by the universe." Uranus enabled him to free himself of his existing involvement with SRF so he could move on to other tasks.

At the time when he was ousted, transiting Jupiter was conjunct his midheaven and natal Mars. This, too, was a sign that this event was a manifestation of grace, even though at the time he could not see this. The biggest crises in our lives are often the best thing for us, although we are unable to perceive the divine intention at the moment that our lives are being torn apart.

In addition, transiting Saturn was in the 8th house, the house of divorce, endings of relationships, and the hostilities and resentments that may result. This was clearly a period of interpersonal conflict, crisis, endings, and the "death" of an important set of relationships. In addition, transiting Pluto was opposite natal Mars, signifying a phase of his life in which there was bound to be interpersonal tensions or frictions. There was no getting around this difficult transit. Even an evolved, enlightened person has to live through, and exhaust, the same difficult karma that the rest of us experience. The question is, how does one meet the challenge of the outer planet transits: with bitterness, despair, and defeat, or with courage, faith, and hope?

At this time, Neptune was transiting opposite his Mercury, a symbol of the confusion he experienced in the aftermath of his split from SRF, his difficulty focusing his mind, and his inability to decide what he should do with himself. As Mercury rules his 4th house, Neptune opposite Mercury corresponded to a period in which he didn't know where to go. He was in all probability a bit mixed up and in a daze (Neptune).

Most importantly, however, Uranus was square his Sun and Pluto was still conjunct his nadir, the backbone of the chart. Thus, it is no wonder that he experienced a major crisis at this time. It happens to all of us sooner or later! This transit initiated a period of several years of real struggle for him, in which the most central difficulty was that he couldn't find a place to live. He wandered around for several years without a clear sense of where he was supposed to be. He tried living in monasteries of various religious orders because he was a monk. If you or I broke our connection with a group or community it would very likely be traumatic, but Kriyananda had renounced the world and made a complete commitment to spiritual life. To find himself more or less put out on the street by his religious order must have presented him with a great test of his faith and his equanimity.

As Uranus came into conjunction with transiting Pluto and they moved together into his 4th house, he went through a very painful period of not knowing where he belonged and what to devote his energies to. Uranus' transit through the 4th house often changes your location, but more importantly it profoundly changes how you organize your personal life.

Jupiter was transiting back and forth over his midheaven and conjunct natal Mars in Pisces. Thus, although he felt abandoned and victimized a bit at first, he soon began to receive lecture invitations. Jupiter doesn't let you down, unless you're totally lazy; and Jupiter's transit conjunct the midheaven and through the 10th house usually corresponds with some improvement in your profession, or at the very least, new ambitions and aspirations. At this time, he met Haridas Chaudhuri, a disciple of Sri Aurobindo and president of a graduate school of East-West studies, who invited him to speak. His lecturing expanded. At first, he didn't want to do it, feeling that perhaps he was unfit for teaching. But in his book, *The Path* (on which this present account of his life is based), he noted that when he became willing to serve others as a teacher many doors opened up for him. With Mars in Pisces in the 10th house, his calling in life was to be a mystic, a servant, motivated not by self-interest, but by generosity and altruism.

Soon things began to go his way again: in the mid 1960s, around 1966–1967, progressed Venus came into conjunction with his Sun, leading to harmonious expression of his identity as the leader of a community. He began to write books about the economics of communities and community life (Taurus Sun in the 11th house). As discussed earlier, Taurus is concerned with economics, money, substantial, tangible concerns. Kriyananada, from his youth, had been fascinated with the formation of spiritual communities and his teacher, Yogananda, spoke extensively about the importance of forming "world brotherhood colonies," spiritual communities. When progressed Venus came to conjunction with natal Sun, everything in this area came to fruition. He began to connect with people around whom the Ananda community would form. Transiting Jupiter crossed over the ascendant. The transiting north node passed over his natal Sun, which often brings a network of connections that enables one to fulfill the potentials indicated in the birth chart.

Transiting Uranus was opposite natal Uranus, a transit all of us go through in our late 30s or early 40s, which concerns freedom, taking risks and experimenting without holding back anything in order to be who we really are. Moreover, when Uranus and Pluto came together in his 4th house, Kriyananda gave expression to the revolutionary impulse of Uranus and Pluto through a completely new vision of community, family, and togetherness, as well as of the right use of land. Empowered by the conjunction of Uranus and Pluto, Kriyananda purchased land in the Sierra mountains of northern California, where he established the Ananda community, one of the most succesful, stable spiritual communities in the U.S., a living embodiment of the possibility for all of us to create a radically different way of life. Kriyananda can thus be viewed as a model for the changes many of us are currently passing through. For put quite simply, his life is an example of how to make the transition from self-interest and egoic striving to a life of service and sustainable community living, a path that many believe will become increasingly attractive and indeed necessary in the years to come.

CHAPTER 11
An Astrological Biography of Rabindranath Tagore

The incense wants to be one with the scent,
the scent to wrap itself round the incense.
Melody wants to take shape in rhythm,
rhythm turns to melody instead,
feeling looks for a body in form,
form can only find itself in feeling.
The infinite seeks the intimate presence of the finite,
the finite to disappear in the infinite.
I do not know whose scheme this is
in the eternal cycle of beginning and end
that between feeling and form should be this interchange,
that the bound should be on a search after freedom,
freedom asking to be housed in the bound.

Introduction

These words were written by Rabindranath Tagore one of the spiritual and literary giants of modern India, a poet, critic, statesman, playwrite, nature mystic, and educational reformer. Let us begin by looking at the general structure of his birth chart before examining his unusually rich and complex life in detail. I have made extensive use of a chronology of Tagore's life found in Radhakrishnan (1961). I have also been greatly assisted in my understanding of Tagore by Dan Johnson, a leading authority on Tagore's life and work.

Notice the Moon rising over the ascendant of Tagore's birth chartand exactly square to the midheaven and nadir. This is very important, for we will see that it refers to Tagore's patriotism, his love of his homeland, Mother India, as well as the importance of his family.

Mercury is also rising over the ascendant of the birth chart, in addition to which Uranus and Mars are in Gemini and in the 3rd house. Immediately we notice an emphasis on the communicative faculty, suggesting that this is someone who might ultimately become a speaker or a writer. Gemini and the 3rd house both concern a person's use of the narrative faculty; thus this natal emphasis suggests that this might be the chart of a person with a calling to tell stories or write poetry to express his ideas, his knowledge, and his infinite curiosity about life.

Tagore's chart features a very important conjunction of Pluto, Venus, and Sun in Taurus. The Venus-Sun conjunction in Taurus suggests that this may be someone who would have an appreciation for beauty and the material world. It could be a symbol of potential for wealth, even if that wealth derived from the family, as in Tagore's case. It might also signify the importance to this person of physical, sensate beauty and of nature.

Because the natal Sun is conjunct Venus, we can surmise that Tagore would be a relatively outgoing person, someone who likes people and is interested in the arts. Because the Sun-Venus are square to Jupiter, he enjoyed the things of the world. He wasn't an ascetic, by any means. This is illustrated in one of his poems, where he writes,

Rabindranath Tagore
May 7, 1861
4:02 AM LMT
Calcutta, India

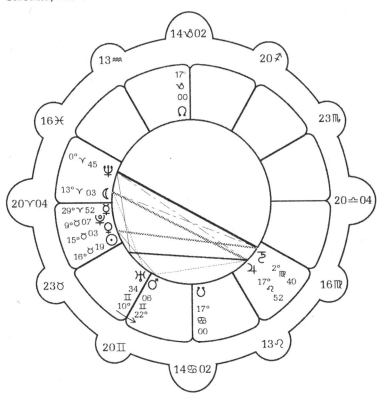

14♑02

13≈   20♐

17°
♉
00
☊

16♓   23♏

0°♈ 45   Ψ

13°♈ 03   ☽

20♈04   29°♈ 52
9°♉ 07   ☿ ♀
15°♉ 03
16°♉ 19   ☉   20♎04

♅   ♄ ♃   2°♏ 40
23♉   17°
34   ♌ 52   16♏
♂   ☋
II   06
10° II
22°   17°
♋
00

20II   13♌

14♋02

Source: B.V. Raman, *Notable Horoscopes*

Chart 23

> I shan't become an ascetic, I shan't. . .
> I tell you, I shan't become one, unless
> I find a lady to renounce with me.
> I have taken a vow. I shall not relent —
> if I do not find a bakul grove to sit in,
> do not find a mind after my heart and win it,
> I shan't become a renouncer, I shan't
> unless there be a lady beside me,
> sitting in penance as an ascetic.
> I shan't leave home and wander around,
> indifferent as a mendicant,
> if nobody smiles a charming smile
> that makes you forget the world. . .
> I shan't become an ascetic, I tell you, I shan't
> unless there be a lady with me doing her penance. . . .

Tagore embraced the world. He was a lover, as well as an artist, a poet, and a singer.

Tagore's artistic nature expressed itself a great deal through dramatic and literary work, writing plays, poetry and so forth. This is symbolized by the square of Venus-Sun to Jupiter, which is placed in the 5th house along with Saturn. Jupiter and Saturn are not in conjunction by sign, but they seem to work together as a unit. Because the 5th house is associated with creativity and self-expression, transits contacting Tagore's Jupiter and Saturn corresponded to periods in which he was engaged in artistic activities such as writing poetry and plays.

The Sun square to Jupiter often is the symbol of someone with intellectual interests and a yearning to comprehend the universal truths of religion, philosophy, and morality. Tagore was involved not just in Indian cultural affairs, but in international politics as well. This aspect also symbolizes his frequent travels abroad. The Sun-Venus square to Jupiter in the 5th house gave him the ability to create beautiful and dramatic works.

Uranus and Mars are widely conjunct in Gemini. Although Uranus is 10 degrees from the 3rd house cusp, I interpret Uranus and Mars as a unit placed in the 3rd house.[4] We will see repeated

---

[4] Different astrologers handle the matter of house cusps in various ways, and some might not agree with me on this point. I personally do not interpret house cusps strictly, preferring to look at the shape of the chart as a whole to determine the house placement of certain planets. There are no hard and fast rules here, for you simply have to *feel* the configuration of each chart individually. For example, if there was a planet two or three

evidence of the fact that Uranus expresses itself, with Mars, through the 3rd house activities of writing and speaking. Uranus in the 3rd also denotes sudden changes in travel plans, a repeated theme throughout Tagore's life. Frequently he would plan trips but would unexpectedly would turn around and go back. Uranus and Mars were also expressed through fierce expressions of criticism of other people's ideas and of governmental policies. Tagore's polemical writing and political activities were almost always associated with transits to natal Uranus-Mars in the 3rd house.

Neptune is the most elevated planet in the chart, placed in the 12th house, the house with which Neptune has the greatest affinity, and closely semi-square to Sun-Venus. This strong placement of Neptune signifies the centrality to Tagore of spirituality and the connection of his artistic expression (Sun-Venus) and his mystical orientation (Neptune). With this aspect, his essential life-purpose (Sun) was to create beautiful forms as the means of giving expression to his expanded consciousness, and his sense of beauty and wonder (Venus and Neptune). In time, it also gave him philanthropic interests, a concern with appropriate use of his money, and how to help others through charitable activities. With Sun conjunct Venus in Taurus, Tagore was a wealthy aristocrat, but the aspect to Neptune also gave him a sensitivity to the plight of those less fortunate.

With Neptune strongly placed in the 12th house, its own house, Tagore had a very strong yearning for God, for the experience of the infinite. Because it is connected with the Venus-Sun in Taurus, his connection to the sacred came though the beauty of the earth, of nature. Because he has those two Taurus planets, his spirituality involved a form of nature mysticism, an appreciation and worship of the divinity of creation. The Venus-Neptune contact also gave him a devotional nature, and an inclination toward romantic and spiritual love poetry. He wasn't into structured disciplines like *zazen* or

---

degrees on the left side of the nadir, I might consider it a 4th house planet. While the house cusps do mark significant points in the birth chart, planets near a cusp often affect the following house very strongly. Here the Moon is a few degrees above the ascendant, yet I place it in the 1st house because it is so close to the horizon. However, if the Moon was seven degrees above the ascendant but in a different sign, I would probably place it in the 12th house. I look not only at the mathematical position of the house cusp, but also at the signs. Tagore's Uranus and Mars are both in the heart of Gemini and feel to me like they are in the third "zone" of the chart.

complex philosophical systems. His was a path of the heart, with an emphasis on music, art, nature, and poetry. His favorite spiritual practice was to watch the sun rise and set every day.

Tagore's Youth

Tagore made his first attempts at writing poetry and translation when he was seven and eight years old. The boy was described as romantic (Venus-Neptune). In his ninth year he went to private tutors from whom he learned science, geometry, arithmetic, history, geology, physiology, anatomy, Sanskrit, Bengali, English, drawing, music, wrestling, and gymnastics. Progressed Mercury was conjunct his Sun-Venus conjunction, showing an early awakening of mental faculties.

In addition, at about the ages of 8 and 9, transiting Pluto and Jupiter simultaneously crossed over natal Venus and Sun, a major transit. At this time Tagore was absorbing all kinds of knowledge, including several foreign languages (Jupiter), and the principles of drawing (Venus). Pluto and Jupiter were bringing his essential identity to the surface. He learned many aspects of culture and the arts that he would later draw upon for creative activity and expression (Jupiter in the 5th house). With Jupiter square his Sun-Venus, Tagore demonstrated from an early age great intelligence, versatility of mind, artistic skill, and hunger for knowledge.

The natal Sun-Jupiter aspect symbolizes his early contact with pandits, learned people, and private tutors. But with Jupiter and Saturn placed in his 5th house (which rules recreational sports, athletics, and other fun activities) he was also practicing wrestling and gymnastics. Tagore's love of recreation manifested from his early youth.

Also, transiting Uranus was conjunct the south node in Cancer, in the 4th house. The south node of the Moon is generally considered one of the primary indicators of past karma, inherited influences, or areas of life with which we have much experience in previous incarnations and which we have fully developed. These become behaviors or skills that we rely upon, and that need to be complemented through new growth in the area of life symbolized by the north node's position. Transiting Uranus conjunct his south node in Cancer in 1869 may have symbolized his visceral affiliation with

Mother India, the traditions of the past, and a sudden awakening to his cultural inheritance.

Transiting Saturn was moving into the 9th house and opposing natal Uranus and Mars during this period when Tagore was immersed in a wide ranging education. Even though Tagore was only a young boy he was engaged in higher learning. With the Mars-Uranus conjunction in Gemini, he would prove to have a sharp, brilliant mind, an original way of using words, a unique literary voice.

In his tenth year, he was admitted to the Bengal academy, an Anglo-Indian school, but soon became a truant. He began to cut school while transiting Uranus was square natal Mercury. With Mercury on his ascendant, he was probably a very restless, lively, and playful child. Transiting Uranus aspecting Mercury apparently made the young boy discontented with formal education. During this transit of Uranus, Tagore became very active and curious, but very rebellious and unstable in school.

At age 11, due to an epidemic in Calcutta, he was removed to a garden house and became acquainted with the countryside of Bengal, giving him a new awareness of the beauty of the land. Transiting Saturn was square his Moon and conjunct the midheaven. In an older person this would relate to significant professional achievements or a period of focus on career. But in his youth, Saturn's transit over his midheaven brought a recognition of qualities or tasks that must later be achieved. The realizations he had now about the sacredness of his country foreshadowed his lifelong commitment to the nation of India. Subsequent transits to the midheaven, during which he received honors and traveled around the world, all, in a curious way, referred back to that moment when Saturn was conjunct his MC in 1879.

At the time of his Brahmanical initiation at age 12, he visited the family retreat, Shantiniketan, for the first time. He then accompanied his father on an extensive tour of North India, including three months of travel in the Himalayas. This was particularly significant for him, for his father was fairly reclusive and was widely regarded as a holy man. The fact that he had singled out Rabindranath to accompany him was quite significant (Johnson, 1989). At this time he received lessons from his father in Sanskrit, English and astronomy. During this voyage in North India and the Himalayas, transiting Mars was in the 9th house, opposite natal Mars and

Uranus. The 9th house often involves voyages to places of learning, sacredness, or holiness, such as this pilgrimage.

Transiting Saturn and Neptune were in a square, with Neptune in Aries and Saturn in Capricorn. Moreover, Saturn was square natal Mercury, and Neptune was conjunct Mercury: he was engaged in learning, developing his mind, and accumulating all kinds of knowledge. Neptune transiting natal Mercury corresponds to his contact with sages of the Himalayas and the instruction he received there from his father. It also symbolizes a potentially exhilarating, magical experience of travel, meeting spiritually oriented people, reading and conversing about spiritual and religious topics, and having his father teach him Sanskrit. Neptune began to awaken in him a yearning for the Absolute through contact with his father and his father's yogi friends.

At age 13 his poem "Desire" appeared anonymously in a publication. He went to a school in Calcutta and came in contact with Father Penerenda, a saintly Jesuit teacher. Transiting Neptune was still conjunct natal Mercury. He conversed with a holy man, a person consecrated to a spiritual life. He also wrote "Desire," which referred to spiritual desire, the longing for God.

In 1875, at age 14, Tagore made his first public appearance, reciting a patriotic poem at the Hindu Mela (a religious festival). Also, his mother died in March of 1876. At that time, there was an alignment of Uranus and Saturn in the sky, with Saturn in Aquarius and Uranus in Leo. Both planets were square Venus and Sun. Uranus had not quite reached conjunction to Jupiter, but it was, along with Saturn, in a direct aspect to Sun-Venus, across the 5th and 11th houses. Note that the poem was patriotic, and then that it was a public appearance, a performance (Uranus conjunct Jupiter in Leo).

We see here a 5th house activity: displaying himself in public, reading a poem. While transiting Saturn aspected his Venus-Sun Tagore began to express himself as an artist, demonstrating his capacity to create beauty. The transiting North Node was also conjunct the midheaven at this time, and the nodal axis was square to the Moon: he read a patriotic poem, and his mother died. Perhaps there was some connection between his feelings about his mother, and his powerful expression of love for Mother India. According to Dan Johnson (personal communication) the loss of his mother at an early age was a catastrophic event; for she had inspired in him a love for the humanities and throughout his life he was trying to compensate for that loss.

Here we see a number of developments related to his future success. When the north node crossed his midheaven, he made contacts that enabled him to show his talents and to receive acclaim to some limited extent. But it was focused through the Moon, through emotional expression, expression of his feeling for his country, his motherland. And he did this in an artistic manner, while Saturn and Uranus contacted natal Sun-Venus-Jupiter.

Turning to the death of his mother, transiting Saturn was square natal Sun and Venus, symbolizing a confrontation with the painful reality of time, aging, and death. Also, progressed Venus was square to natal Saturn, and although he wasn't old enough to experience this aspect through a mature love between man and woman, it did involve the love between a young man and his mother; he experienced great sadness of the heart over the loss of this beloved person. But simultaneously, the progressed Sun was sextile Neptune, the beginning of a deeper attunement to this expansive planet. At this time he publicly recited a poem entitled "Nature's Lament," in which he mourned the sad plight of Mother India. He then composed a song for a patriotic play, *Sarojini*, and a long narrative poem. He also left school without getting advanced to the next grade.

A lot was happening to him at age 14. With his progressed Venus-Saturn aspect and the nodal axis squaring the Moon, he was lamenting the loss of his mother and the sad plight of Mother India. While transiting Saturn and Uranus activated natal Sun-Venus-Jupiter, he wrote many poems, expressing himself as an artist, even though inwardly it was a time of sorrow, loss, and emotional pain.

However, because progressed Sun was sextile Neptune, Tagore was also expanding, opening and becoming more sensitive. Compassion is born from suffering. The 12th house, where Neptune is placed, is often associated with situations where you are powerless and feel self-pity because of circumstances beyond your control. But because of the intense transits of Saturn to Sun, Venus, and Jupiter, he used his intellectual and artistic resources to channel his suffering into creative activity.

A Young Social Critic

in 1876, Tagore joined a secret society, and published his first literary criticism. Transiting Saturn was opposite natal Saturn and had moved into the 11th house (group affiliations). Transiting Jupiter was in the 9th house (publishing), and opposite Uranus and Mars in the 3rd house (writing). With Mercury in Aries and Mars conjunct Uranus in the 3rd house, Tagore was a very passionate, dynamic speaker and a radical, revolutionary thinker and writer — whether it was through poetry, statesmanship, drama, or literary criticism.

At age 16, he composed and publicly recited a poem satirizing the Queen of England, the Empress of India. The poem was a severe indictment of the princely rulers of India who "hugged the golden chain" while the country was ravaged by famine. He also made a stage appearance in a comedy and contributed to a journal several poems and a scathing review of a novel. Then he wrote and published a long story, "The Beggar's Maid," and his first novel, *Karuna.* This very intense period was right before his progressed Full Moon, which would fall across his 3rd and the 9th houses — a significant indicator of his emerging capacity for literary expression of wisdom.

In 1877, Tagore's progressed Sun was square natal and progressed Saturn, symbolizing the seriousness with which he was attempting to accomplish things and to gain recognition for his ideas. The progressed Sun-Saturn square is often the symbol of a period when one feels compelled to achieve something tangible; it can promote hard work and discipline to cope with life's pressures and to attain excellence. Here the professional focus of Tagore's effort was intensified because Saturn ruled his 10th house, the house of career, public life, and social status.

The progressed chart shows what is going on inside the individual, ways in which he or she is growing and changing. Tagore's growth in maturity (progressed Sun square Saturn) meant becoming aware of the oppressive power of the State, and how it was impinging upon people's lives. He was becoming aware of harsh and difficult social realities and directly challenged the Queen of England, Empress of India, who, in his view, was exploiting his nation. His confrontation with Saturn manifested in his opposition to existing governing authorities as well as in his efforts to establish and assert his own authority.

Simultaneously, *transiting* Saturn was in his 11th house, which kept his attention focused on political activity, humanity's future, and joining with others to promote social and political change. Saturn also formed a square to Mars and Uranus, especially in the summer of 1877, symbolizing an activation of Tagore's mind, which was now on fire with revolutionary ideas. His poetic indictment of the British was a direct confrontation of the rulers of India. Note that with progressed Sun square Saturn, which natally was in the 5th house, he gained recognition in the world through his performances, by displaying his ideas publicly and dramatically.

Also, with transiting Saturn square Mars-Uranus, the variety of his writing was remarkable. Mars and Uranus were in Gemini, the sign of versatility and diversity. Tagore's plays, literary criticism, and poetry were all expressions of his Mars-Uranus conjunction, through which Mars magnified his uranian tendencies to be rebellious and radical.

Artistic Development

In 1878, Tagore was sent to Ahmedabad to study English. Here he set some of his lyrics to music. He traveled to Bombay, took English lessons, and composed articles on English life and letters and on the romantic love poetry of Dante, Tetrach and Goethe. At this time, transiting Jupiter crossed the midheaven, again foreshadowing his future literary achievements. The musical, romantic, and dramatic elements of his creative work are symbolized by natal Jupiter in the 5th house, square to Sun-Venus. Jupiter symbolizes the desire to travel abroad and to come into contact with places and people that expand our horizons. Thus, when Jupiter was conjunct his midheaven, Tagore went to Bombay, stayed with an anglicized family and studied English. The transiting nodes were square Sun-Venus and conjunct Jupiter, corresponding to this outpouring of music, poetry, and songs.

Also, transiting Saturn was in the 12th house, conjunct Neptune. Natal Neptune aspects Venus and Sun, which gave him the desire to implant his spiritual vision and yearning into music, to blend the devotional and the musical. Venus-Neptune combinations often signify the kind of awareness to which William Blake referred when he wrote, "Eternity is in love with the productions of time." Neptune represents eternity, an all-encompassing and timeless perspective, while Venus represents the creations of time. When they are in close aspect, as in Tagore's chart, the person may seek to cast a vision of perfection or the eternal into beautiful musical or artistic form. Transiting Uranus was conjunct his 5th house natal Jupiter, squaring Sun-Venus, during this period of creative activity, which must have marked him as an unusual and unique figure.

At around this time Tagore went to London and entered the University College, where he began to get some praise from Professor Henry Morley, a well known figure in British letters. Tagore attended a session of the House of Commons and began to get more sophisticated politically. Transiting Jupiter was in Aquarius and in the 11th house (social awareness), expanding his political consciousness. Jupiter isn't in itself a mystical planet but represents the desire to give meaning to life through learning and philosophical or conceptual doctrines. Also, with Jupiter squaring natal Sun-Venus and opposing natal Jupiter, he was learning Irish and English melodies and songs, exploring a foreign culture's (Jupiter) musical structure and popular styles (Venus).

Impatience with Schooling

Tagore returned to India in 1880 without completing any course of study. Transiting Jupiter was now squaring Mars-Uranus in the 3rd house; he was unable to stay focused on any one field of learning, and left England without a college degree. Also, transiting Uranus was conjunct natal Saturn. Uranus and Saturn are antagonists in the planetary drama, Uranus seeking freedom and experimentation that is often disruptive and threatening to Saturn's concern with stability and convention. Uranus-Saturn transits often bring deviations from socially sanctioned pathways such as attending college. In Tagore's case this transit may be viewed as one that liberated him to unfold his own genius. He later wrote that, "At this time the fountain of my song was unloosed at age nineteen." Tagore began to compose melodies and words while his brother played piano. The transiting North Node was conjunct the midheaven: he was following the path in life that was truly intended for him. Tagore was a free thinking person who was impatient with schools and unsuited for traditional, structured education. It was more important for him to let his own voice develop and expand without limitations.

Illumination of Identity

The transit of Saturn over his ascendant and Moon was crucial. The ascendant symbolizes the dawning of self-awareness. When Saturn comes to the ascendant, a person's identity begins to come into focus more clearly. In Tagore's case, getting praise and approval from his literature teacher may have been an important affirmation of his gifts as a writer. This major Saturn transit also correlates with Tagore's increasingly sober assessment of intercultural and international affairs, and his appraisal of English society. It is also very important that this was the period when he says, "the fountain of my song was unloosed." All of these developments mark a strengthening of his identity at age 19.

At age 20, Tagore composed his first set of devotional songs and his first musical play was staged, with the poet himself appearing in the title role. Some polemical writing condemning the opium trade appeared. He also gave a public lecture on music and healing with vocal demonstration. On the day after the lecture he sailed for England, but on the way he changed his mind and returned home to Madras.

Transiting Neptune was conjunct natal Sun-Venus, in Taurus, which rules the throat and singing, a beautiful symbol for his public lecture on music and healing. This significant transit awakened an outpouring of love and spirituality that got cast into artistic form.

Transiting Uranus was square to natal Uranus. During this transit he expressed his individuality, his uniqueness, his radical views. In addition, transiting Jupiter and Saturn were in conjunction at this time, in his 1st house and exactly conjunct natal Mercury. The house in which the conjunctions of Jupiter-Saturn fall and the planets they aspect are clear indicators of the direction, and the kinds of social activity, to which a person is called for a twenty-year period. With Jupiter-Saturn in his 1st house conjunct Mercury he awakened to his identity as a writer and began to publish his ideas. Tagore was absorbed in his writing. After turning back from his voyage to England, he started working on a series of essays and a novel, *The Young Queen's Market.* Although he had planned a voyage, with Saturn and Jupiter conjunct Mercury he didn't want to travel around; he wanted to stay home and do some constructive work as a writer. In addition, Mars was transiting through Gemini, conjunct natal Uranus and Mars. Again and again we will see that during major transits through Gemini and his 3rd house, Tagore wrote with great intensity.

A Mystical Experience

In 1882, Tagore established Sarasvat Samaj, an organization that was a precursor of the Academy of Bengali Letters. He also had his first glimpse of cosmic unity, a mystical experience he described in a poem entitled, "The Awakening of the Fountain." Then a musical play, *The Fatal Hound*, was performed and he appeared as a blind hermit. Transiting Neptune was still conjunct his Sun and Venus, an appropriate symbol for the occurrence of a religious experience. The potential to experience cosmic unity and Tagore's innate urge toward spiritual awakening and love of God was symbolized by the natal semi-square aspect of Neptune to Sun-Venus. Note that this mystical experience actually occurred when *transiting* Neptune was *conjunct* Sun-Venus.

Transiting Saturn and Jupiter were also both conjunct Sun and Venus within three months of one another. During January, February and March of 1882, transiting Saturn and Jupiter joined Neptune. The Neptune transit over Sun-Venus took about two years, but when Saturn and Jupiter linked up with Neptune, they intensified it. Lengthy transits of the outer planets represent significant developmental processes that get triggered and brought to a head by faster moving planets. Tagore experienced a major period of spiritual awakening during the combined transits of Neptune, Jupiter and Saturn over natal Sun-Venus.

When Saturn conjoined Sun-Venus, Tagore expressed himself with great clarity. Despite the adversity or difficulties a person may face when Saturn transits the Sun, it becomes clearer what one must do to express one's true nature. During this transit Tagore came to realize that he must create beautiful art, music, and literature (Sun-Venus square Jupiter in 5th). Thus his plays were performed and he played the part of a blind hermit, a neptunian, spiritual kind of role.

During the period when "The Awakening of the Fountain" was written, transiting Mars, Mercury, Venus and Mars were conjunct in his 9th house, opposite natal Mars in Gemini. Although his important mystical experience occurred while Neptune passed over his Sun, only during the 9th house transits did he come to understand the *meaning* of that experience. Only then could he cast it into a form that could be published and disseminated.

Marriage and Maturation

Tagore married in 1883 while progressed Venus was sextile his natal Moon, indicating a pleasant, harmonious time, a period of emotional happiness. His wife was born in 1873, so she was only ten years old at the time of their prearranged marriage.

In 1884 he was greatly saddened by the death of his sister-in-law, to whom he was deeply attached. This was just after transiting Saturn's third quarter square to its natal position, a transit that often signifies a period of encounter with the responsibilities and disappointments of adult life.

In 1995, Tagore was placed in charge of a new Bengali magazine for young people. Over the course of the year he contributed numerous poems, essays, and letters. He also had several books of his songs and serious essays published. This was during his Jupiter return, which intensified his aspiration to become a creative writer and dramatist (Jupiter in 5th).

Note also that the conjunction of Jupiter and Saturn had fallen exactly on his natal Mercury. The entire subsequent twenty-year cycle of Jupiter and Saturn was an outgrowth of all the writing he began doing at that time. This process continued now, as Jupiter and Saturn formed their first quarter square. Saturn was in the 3rd house conjunct natal Mars, while Jupiter passed through the 6th house, square to Mars. With both Jupiter and Saturn activating his 3rd house Mars, it not surprising that he did so much writing in this period, publishing essays, translations, and songs.

In 1886, he engaged in controversies over social and religious subjects, and composed and sang the inaugural song for the Indian National Congress. Transiting Saturn was conjunct the nadir and square natal Moon and ascendant. During this saturnian period, he was quite concerned about the affairs of the nation. The 4th house governs not only the family of origins but also our connection to our nation, our people, our heritage, and our ancestral roots. As Saturn crossed the nadir into his 4th house and squared his Moon, Tagore composed a song appropriately entitled "Gathered Are We Today at the Mother's Call." He was organizing his existence around his love for, and devotion to Mother India. The progressed Sun was conjunct

Uranus in 1886, signifying his involvement in social issues, becoming more politicized, radical, and outspoken.

In addition, while Saturn was square his Moon and conjunct the nadir, Tagore's first child was born, a daughter. He may have felt a great pressure to get his home organized for his family. He faced new responsibilities, perhaps a certain degree of anxiety, and a lot of "adult adjustment" issues. His mood was perhaps more one of seriousness and hard work (Saturn) than one of great joy and excitement.

Soon thereafter Tagore received a literary prize in the form of a large check from his father in appreciation of the devotional songs he had composed. With Saturn square Moon-ascendant and conjunct the nadir, his father was quite an important figure in his life. Perhaps his father's approval gave him a feeling of stability, a sense of getting his life together. This is what the nadir and 4th house are all about. He was trying to establish his home. The Saturn-father gave him financial assistance and helped him prepare for the arrival of his daughter.

A collection of his literary criticism appeared in 1888, and his first son was born on the 27th of November. Transiting Saturn had entered Leo and was conjunct natal Jupiter. This wasn't quite his Saturn return, but Saturn conjunct Jupiter in the 5th house in Leo seems to signify enthusiasm for children, enjoying being playful with them, and feeling very proud. While Saturn was conjunct natal Jupiter, Tagore also wrote *The King and The Queen*, considered one of his most important plays.

Transiting Pluto and Neptune were beginning to form the great conjunction of the early 1890s and both planets were square to Tagore's 5th house Saturn. He assumed the new responsibilities associated with fatherhood, and experienced the need to achieve, to be recognized and respected professionally. But his Saturn return would have a very distinctive quality, due to the concurrent transit of Neptune and Pluto square to natal Saturn during 1889 and 1890. He may have had great dreams of glorious accomplishments in the 5th house realm of drama and creative activity, as well as grand dreams for his children. Moreover, because his 5th house natal Saturn was being activated by two transpersonal planets, his personal self-expression was also addressing significant collective issues.

As we saw in Chapter 5, Dane Rudhyar (1977) described a transpersonal form of creativity that reveals a vision of the future and has a transformative influence upon the audience, reader, or witness. The transit of Neptune and Pluto square to Saturn evoked in him the urge to create such evocative, transformational art.

Tagore's Saturn Return

Tagore's Saturn return occurred in 1890. A play called *The Visarjan* was staged, and he read a paper at a public meeting in Calcutta protesting the reactionary, anti-Indian policy of the British. He advocated appointment of elected representatives of the people as members of the Viceroy's Executive Council. He then spent the summer months at Shantiniketan, took charge of management of the Tagore family estates, and attempted to read Goethe's *Faust* in the original German. Thus, during his Saturn return he was involved with politics, he took a vacation, he took charge of his family, and he read classics.

With natal Saturn in the 5th house, he was working constantly possibly making it difficult for him to relax and enjoy recreation. Nevertheless, with Saturn here, he needed to take a good rest and a vacation periodically. On the other hand, the time had come for him to take over the management of the Tagore estates, a big responsibility. He was, in effect, becoming the head of his family during his Saturn return.

He also confronted the State again, protesting against British policy in India and making a radical statement for appointment of elected representatives — while transiting Mars was in Sagittarius and the 9th house (March through August), opposing natal Mars and Uranus. Transiting Jupiter was in the 11th house, focusing him on political issues. There was also a major performance of one of his plays while Jupiter opposed natal Jupiter, square Sun-Venus.

Transiting Neptune and Pluto were squaring both transiting Saturn and natal Saturn. The Neptune-Pluto conjunction was the major symbol of the coming of the twentieth century and of new scientific discoveries that revolutionized and transformed the consciousness of humanity. Rudhyar (1969) wrote, "The rhythm of the cycle of relationship between Neptune and Pluto establishes the pattern of development in man's unceasing effort at emerging from the lesser to the greater social units" (p. 73). This conjunction augured new possibilities for the achievement of freedom, social betterment, and humanitarian goals on a global scale. New collective ideals were beginning to emerge; and because these planets squared his 5th house Saturn, Tagore attempted to focus this new social vision through his own creative expression. As we will soon see, he was becoming a mouthpiece for emergent collective trends.

A Fusion of Politics and Spirituality

Tagore sailed for England while transiting Uranus was opposite his Mercury in late August 1890. In 1891, his second daughter was born and a book of short stories was published. He also started a new Bengali monthly magazine, *Sadhana*, to which he contributed poems, short stories, essays, reviews, and political and scientific articles.

At this time, Jupiter and Saturn were in opposition, the climactic Full Moon phase of their cycle, and both were square to Mars. The last conjunction of these two planets had contacted his Mercury, corresponding to one of his most significant periods of literary activity. At their first quarter square, while Saturn was conjunct Mars, Tagore had engaged in intensive political activity, debates, lecturing, and writing. Now with Jupiter and Saturn opposing one another, squaring natal Mars, the cycle that received its initial impulse at the conjunction reached its culmination: the founding of *Sadhana*, a journal that was both political and spiritual in orientation, and which acted as a vehicle for both his romantic, mystical poetry and his critical, polemical essays. It was the means for Tagore to begin to define an all-encompassing form of spirituality that included politics and literature.

Educational Reform

In 1892, Tagore toured North Bengal and came into contact with the life of the local inhabitants. Transiting Jupiter was conjunct the Moon, and he became concerned with the welfare of the people, trying to gauge their needs and responding empathically to them. With transiting Neptune and Pluto now in exact conjunction, closely conjunct natal Uranus, Tagore engaged in a great deal of radical writing and anti-authoritarian social activism.

At this time, he wrote a major criticism of the education system introduced by the British. The 3rd house governs early education, the acquisition of basic skills and knowledge about the world. Tagore had predominantly negative experiences in schools, being a feisty, rebellious truant, and not graduating. Now he wanted to reform the educational system, and wrote an essay called "Tortuosities of Education," a plea for acceptance of the Mother Tongue as the medium of instruction. This occurred as Jupiter was conjunct his Moon: "Mother Tongue." He wrote and published this essay while transiting Mars was passing through the 9th house. While Jupiter was conjunct his Moon and ascendant, his second daughter was born and he was probably in a joyful, enthusiastic mood.

Change of Heart

In 1894, Tagore composed the poem "Turn Me Away Now," which was a call to his own self to turn away from a life of ease to a strenuous life of struggle dedicated to the service of humanity. Tagore's dedication to service is symbolized in his chart by the natal Sun semi-square aspect to Neptune. He was gradually becoming a transpersonal, self-consecrated individual. At the time he wrote this poem, Uranus opposed natal Venus in Taurus, symbolizing a critical reevaluation of his materialistic values and desires. With transiting Saturn opposite natal Mercury, he was thinking and writing in a serious, somber, renunciatory vein.

At this time, Tagore also collected folk rhymes and nursery songs. His interest in folk and folk culture, which remained strong throughout his life, was an expression of the prominence of his natal Moon conjunct the ascendant. Later on, he became fascinated with the folk cultures of Eastern Europe and other nations.

In the mid 1980s, while Tagore was managing the family estate, he sailed along the Padma river, a tributary of the Ganges. This brought him into contact with a lot of poor people and the middle classes of India. Many people viewed Tagore as an esoteric intellectual. But most people did not know that he was also very interested in the common people and folk cultures. According to Johnson (1989), nature now began to take on a new, symbolic significance for Tagore (Sun and Venus in Taurus). Whereas in his youth nature had been like a playmate to him, during this period nature became Tagore's teacher, revealing philosophical truths. For example, the river represented the passage of time, as well as the principle of continuity within change. Tagore began to view his own life as being like a river, with many sudden changes of direction, color, and speed, yet maintaining an underlying constancy. This awareness was expressed in a long poem entitled "The River."

A Period of Radicalism

In 1896, Tagore began expressing indignation at the insolence of British officers and the cowardly submission of the Indian people to it. With transiting Jupiter and Pluto conjunct natal Uranus in the 3rd house, he wrote critical reviews of contemporary publications, and he would soon initiate a variety of innovative social projects, focusing especially on educational reform. This was also the time of the Third Quarter square of the Jupiter-Saturn cycle. Saturn was opposite natal Jupiter in the 5th house, square natal Sun and Venus, while he was also experiencing his third Jupiter return. Thus he was inspired again to externalize his essential nature in poetry and other creative works.

In 1898, Tagore took over editorial charge of *Sadhana*, and contributed a large number of poems, short stories, and essays on political, literature, philosophical, and educational subjects. He initiated agricultural experiments and also wrote articles protesting reactionary government policies. Transiting Uranus and Saturn were conjunct in his 8th house (business ventures) in the early degrees of Sagittarius (the sign of publishing); Tagore responded to the turbulent political developments often associated with Uranus-Saturn conjunctions by taking charge of a radical, revolutionary publishing business.

During this period when Tagore was actively criticizing the government, and fighting reactionary political trends, he had the opportunity to sing the Indian national anthem before a government conference. Neptune and Pluto were in Gemini near natal Uranus, while transiting Saturn was moving into the 9th house, directly opposite transiting Neptune-Pluto and natal Uranus. On the dates of this conference, May 31 through June 2, the transiting Sun was conjunct Neptune and Pluto, thus acting as a trigger for the slower moving transit of the outer planets. During this transit of Pluto and Neptune conjunct his Uranus, Tagore was radicalized, becoming much more politically and socially active. He began to participate in efforts to create a more humane and free society, and contributed to this process of social transformation through literary expression of his radical ideas (3rd house Uranus).

When Neptune was conjunct natal Mars, Tagore became actively involved in organizing a relief effort for plague victims in Calcutta. The Pluto-Neptune conjunction was manifesting in India in the form of mass death, and the eruption of panic and hysteria, feelings of helplessness and victimization by conditions that were brutal, mysterious, and unfathomable. This mass calamity unleashed in Tagore a feeling of compassion, a desire to serve and relieve suffering. While Neptune was conjunct Mars, Tagore also delivered his first sermon at Shantiniketan.

With transiting Saturn in his 9th house, the house of meaning and wisdom, Tagore's understanding was deepening. And because of Saturn's opposition to Pluto and Neptune, he began to envision new evolutionary possibilities for humanity. He was becoming committed to the creation of a social order based on humanitarian principles and ideals. Thus, during a period in which all three outer planets, Pluto, Neptune, and Uranus were influencing Tagore simultaneously, he began to work toward the goal of uprooting and transforming entrenched aristocratic and reactionary attitudes and social institutions.

In 1900, Tagore wrote an inspiring exposition of the spiritual values of the Indian way of life. He read this work to his father, who gave him his blessing and some money for its publication. Increasingly Tagore began to uphold the historical foundations of Indian culture and to deplore the prevailing tendency toward blind imitation of the West. This was during the next Jupiter-Saturn conjunction, which fell exactly on his midheaven and conjunct his north node, between March and December of 1901. Appropriately enough, he received his father's (10th house) blessing. When the midheaven is contacted in this manner, one has the opportunity to accomplish whatever tasks one has set out to accomplish. During this period, Tagore gained recognition for his varied contributions to society as a patriot, poet, dramatist, and radical political journalist. Moreover, Tagore now founded a school based on the model of the ancient forest schools, himself teaching the boys and living with them. He must have felt a great sense of pride and accomplishment in being able to translate ancient values and knowledge into a meaningful form of contemporary social activity. In line with this conjunction in his 10th house, Tagore was concerned with social improvement, upholding the laws and values of the social order, and restoring the historic foundations of Indian culture.

Because the transiting Saturn-Jupiter conjunction fell on his midheaven, it was likely that Tagore would be entering a cycle of tremendous professional social influence and success. He now began to gain recognition for founding this remarkable school, attempting to implement the deepest spiritual values of the Indian way of life in the modern world. With Jupiter and Saturn conjunct his midheaven, Tagore's accomplishments were bringing him stature and acclaim. Later, Tagore would go into retreat, but for the moment he was out in the world, trying to make his mark. This culminated with his father's recognition of his work.

A Period of Sorrows

In 1902, Tagore faced severe financial difficulties. To cover the expenses of the school, he liquidated an unsuccessful business and had to sell his house, property, even his personal library. His wife was forced to sell jewelry to tide him over the crisis. He also had many problems with teachers at the school. Transiting Saturn was square the Moon and the ascendant during this difficult time. Transiting Neptune was square natal Neptune and aspecting natal Sun and Venus. All certainty and security in life had been undermined (Neptune), and he experienced confusion and tenuousness in his financial situation (Sun-Venus in Taurus). Because Saturn was conjunct the North Node and square the Moon and ascendant, it was a rough period of struggle, sadness, and austerity.

Added to this, Tagore's wife became seriously ill and died at the end of 1902, another manifestation of Saturn squaring the Moon and ascendant. Also, transiting Neptune was square Neptune and semisquare to natal Sun and Venus — the symbol of the wife in a man's chart, and the ruler of Tagore's 7th house. Tagore's wife died while Neptune aspected Venus, mysteriously undermining her health. During this transit, Tagore may have experienced a tremendous devotion to his wife and a sense of spiritual connection with her, a love that would endure even after her passing.

Subsequently, while transiting Uranus was exactly opposite natal Mars and transiting Pluto was conjunct the midpoint of Mars and Uranus, Tagore began to throw all of his energies into political and literary activities. This transit, a conjunction of Neptune and Pluto in Gemini opposite Uranus in Sagittarius, was a very rare and historically significant one. As it closely contacted Tagore's natal Mars the transformational energies of these planets were focused through him in powerful expressions of his ideas. He wrote an article in which he referred to the synthesizing genius of India and declared India's mission to be to establish unity in the midst of diversity. He also got involved in an agitation protesting a racist remark by a prominent British aristocrat, writing a bitter retort.

Tagore seemed to be very angry, and experienced many heated circumstances and hostilities during this period. For example, three teachers resigned suddenly from his school, leading to arguments, animosities, and sudden explosions of anger that got channeled through radical writing aimed against the British. Because Transiting Uranus was directly opposite the Pluto-Neptune conjunction, he seems to have sensed the incredible possibilities for social reform, yet he experienced great turmoil because these possibilities were not being realized. Nevertheless, he was working toward the eventual restructuring of social institutions, and for a rebellion against the racism and propaganda of the British aristocracy.

Transiting Pluto and Uranus were in exact opposition throughout 1902, especially in the summer when transiting Mars passed through Gemini along with Pluto, corresponding to this period of political struggle and personal crisis. The opposition of Pluto and Uranus directly contacted the volatile, explosive Mars-Uranus midpoint. As Mars symbolizes outbursts, fevers, and accidents, and Uranus represents sudden, unexpected developments, this too may relate to the sudden illness and death of Tagore's wife. Moreover, his daughter also got sick suddenly, deteriorated rapidly, and died when Uranus exactly opposed natal Mars. Mars rules Tagore's 8th house, the house in which we must confront the inevitability of death. Thus, when Uranus contacted Mars, there were two unexpected deaths in Tagore's life.

During 1904, Tagore's growing interest in the political problems of India found expression in a series of essays, in which he stressed the need for rural reconstruction based on mutual aid, and prepared a complete scheme for reorganization of village life. Saturn was moving into the 11th house, focusing him again on social dynamics and the need to respond to historical and collective conditions. He was preoccupied with politics, even in the midst of the chaos of his personal life caused by the sudden deaths of his wife and daughter.

Later in 1904, he wrote his first autobiographical article, interpreting his life as a poet. During this period of self-reflection and introspection, transiting Jupiter crossed the ascendant (awareness of self) and conjoined natal Mercury (writing). In 1905, while Jupiter was still conjunct Mercury, Tagore took up editorial charge of a new publication, creating a forum for discussion of important current topics. He also addressed a meeting of students, exhorting them to engage in first hand study of villages to be able to better serve the people.

This was while transiting Uranus was square natal Neptune from early Capricorn, corresponding to a sudden reawakening of his desire to consecrate his life for the benefit of others. Because Uranus is involved here, his focus was political, oriented towards social conditions. Tagore's passionate patriotism found expression in a large number of nationalist songs that he wrote when transiting Jupiter went through Gemini conjunct Uranus and Mars. He also began advocating a policy of noncooperation toward the British.

Dissatisfaction and Retreat

Tagore began to grow increasingly dissatisfied with the character of the political agitation in India, especially its narrow political aims and its disregard for the wider perspective of social and economic regeneration. He established another school and an agricultural cooperative bank, and initiated various rural reconstruction projects. This period of political activism occurred while transiting Uranus was still square to Neptune and while transiting Pluto was conjunct Mars. Tagore was troubled by prevailing conditions, and he acted vigorously to promote social change.

In 1907, perturbed by the growing alienation between Hindus and Moslems, and the sense of the utter futility of the resistance movement, Tagore withdrew from active politics. From his retreat at Shantiniketan, he wrote an article called, "The Disease and Its Cure," advocating acceptance of a radical social program for the attainment of freedom. However, he was severely criticized by many of his contemporaries for his sudden withdrawal from political activities (transiting Pluto conjunct Mars: under attack). Transiting Jupiter and Neptune were in conjunction and Jupiter soon crossed the nadir, again focusing him on national concerns (4th house), filling him with social idealism. But the reality in India at this time was quite different, pervaded by divisiveness and animosity between different religious groups. Both Jupiter and Neptune seem to have released in him an expanded comprehension of universal truths that he tried to express through the 4th house, the organization of personal and national life. During this period of disillusionment and retreat, transiting Saturn was in the 12th house, conjunct Neptune. It was an appropriate time for interiorization, solitude, turning to God in prayer (12th house).

At this time Tagore relinquished editorship of *Sadhana* and other publications, letting go of some of the major responsibilities of his outer life. It's a bit like when Sri Aurobindo was put in jail and held in solitary confinement, letting his whole political life go all at once. Similarly, when Neptune came into conjunction with Tagore's nadir in August 1907, he became disillusioned and began to long for retreat and meditation. Neptune also further undermined the stability of the family, as his younger son died suddenly from cholera when transiting Jupiter and Pluto were conjunct natal Mars — another rude shock. With Neptune conjunct the nadir and transiting Saturn in the 12th house (which is the death/8th house from the 5th house of children), there was nothing to do at such a time of personal tragedy but to relinquish control, to surrender. Tagore's life had changed greatly since the period a few years earlier when Jupiter and Saturn were conjunct his midheaven and he was at the peak of his public stature.

Service to Humanity

In 1908, Tagore delivered his first presidential address, reiterating his call to the young men of Bengal to dedicate themselves to constructive projects in villages with Hindus and Moslems working together. At this time, Uranus was conjunct his midheaven and once again he came into the public eye for his political activism. With Neptune still conjunct the nadir, Tagore had an idealistic vision of India's future. Both Neptune and Uranus were square to the natal Moon, an important indicator of his patriotism, his commitment to the betterment of the nation and its people. With Neptune and Uranus in exact opposition to one another, with Uranus on the midheaven and Neptune conjunct the nadir, Tagore was again focused on issues of social concern. Neptune bestows an all-inclusive perspective, for example, a vision of universal freedom, regardless of caste or religion. Uranus symbolizes the process of societal restructuring based on new technologies and political movements. During this transit, Tagore was dedicated to the implementation of new programs for social betterment, even while he himself was in deep sorrow and mourning stemming from his personal tragedies.

This is exactly the kind of crisis that Rudhyar taught could lead to a transpersonal metamorphosis. Tagore's personal life was in shambles, yet the call to service only grew stronger. He didn't dwell in self-pity, but rather responded courageously to the pressing needs of his community and nation. He became an agent of collective transformation, even though his own success and personal happiness were eclipsed at this time. Tagore transcended his own suffering, dedicating his life to a higher cause, self-consecration to humanity.

It is important to understand his actions in the context of the chaotic events in India at the time of this Uranus-Neptune opposition. The repressive policy of the government was so severe that idealistic young patriots were driven to desperation, setting off bombs in the middle of cities. People were going berserk and rioting, and an atmosphere of hysteria prevailed. It was in this context that Tagore attempted to define a program of social change, and a concept of non-violent non-cooperation as a political weapon. He was thus a predecessor of Gandhi and his tactics of nonviolent resistance.

Then in December of 1908, Tagore started delivering a series of daily sermons in which he upheld the ideals of universal religion, the synthesis of cultures, and the oneness of humanity. At this time, a T-square had formed right across the angles of his chart: transiting Saturn was conjunct natal Moon, and squared transiting Uranus on the midheaven and Neptune on the nadir. This represented for him a moment of destiny and dedication to social ideals, in which his humanitarianism and spirituality (Neptune) were translated into concrete plans (Saturn) for mass social transformation (Uranus).

Financial troubles plagued Tagore in 1911, when transiting Saturn was conjunct natal Sun and Venus in Taurus. Tagore had always lived off his family's money, but at this point in his life he was forced to confront some difficult economic realities. Also, plans for visiting abroad in October 1911 did not materialize as intended; transiting Mars was stationary retrograde exactly conjunct natal Uranus, leading to another reversal of his travel plans.

Acclaim

At the beginning of 1912, with Saturn still conjunct his Sun and Venus, Tagore received an unparalleled ovation at the town hall in Calcutta, the first time such time such an honor had been given to a literary figure in India. Saturn ruled his 10th house, thus its transit over natal Sun-Venus brought recognition for his achievements in drama, poetry, and music, as well for his social and political contributions.

Then, on November 13, 1913, Tagore received the news that he had been awarded the Nobel Prize for literature. A large number of people from Calcutta went to Shantiniketan to honor and congratulate the poet on November 23, the day that transiting Jupiter went stationary direct in exact conjunction with his midheaven. Subsequently, Tagore received tremendous public recognition and numerous awards, including honorary doctorates from universities, and traveled all over the world — all while Jupiter was conjunct his midheaven.

Finally, between 1913 and 1916 — especially in 1915 and 1916 while transiting Pluto semisquared Sun-Venus and Jupiter and squared Neptune — Tagore gave many performances and lectures. For the remainder of his life, although the demands of being a public figure reduced the time he had available for writing and reflection, Tagore continued to travel throughout the world and to express his devotion to God, nature, and nation, as well as his vision of intercultural unity and world peace.

With transiting Pluto aspecting natal Sun, Venus, Jupiter, and Neptune, Tagore became a beloved spiritual leader in India, a world renowned poet, and a prophet of a unified humanity. His life culminated in a synthesis of his spiritual, literary, and political talents and concerns, integrated into creative actions that addressed the pressing needs of humanity. In this way, Tagore radiantly fulfilled the complexities and responsibilities of the transpersonal life.

CHAPTER 12
An Astrological Biography of Ram Dass

In this final chapter we will examine the birth chart of Ram Dass (born Richard Alpert), famous american psychedelic researcher and popular guru of service and compassion. Ram Dass was born with a conjunction of Sun-Uranus in the 10th house, suggesting that he was born with the potential to become a highly original and unique personage with an unusual career, perhaps a revolutionary or radical figure of some kind. His chart suggests that he might become an agent of cultural change, an individual embodiment of collective trends toward transformation of consciousness (Sun conjunct Uranus). With Sun in the 10th house, Ram Dass has been a prominent public figure for most of his life. Even though he has periodically gone into retreat, when major transits aspect his 10th house Sun he has always returned to the public eye, bringing his unique spiritual perspective to large, receptive, and appreciative audiences.

With Sun square Jupiter in his 1st house, Ram Dass became a man of learning and education with a prominent position (10th house Sun) as a professor (Jupiter) at Harvard. Ram Dass is a man of stature, authority, and public responsibility (10th house). Yet with the strong Sun-Uranus conjunction, we might infer that something about his uniqueness could stir controversy.

Jupiter and Pluto are conjunct in Cancer on his ascendant, a symbol that has multiple meanings. On the most basic physical level, Jupiter on the ascendant signifies the fact that Ram Dass is quite tall; moreover, in his childhood he was somewhat overweight and was very emotionally sensitive (Cancer) about this as a youngster. With Pluto in Cancer, it is fitting that his career began as a psychoanalytic therapist trained to delve into unconscious memories and personality dynamics. Later he became a leader in the movement to provide more compassionate care (Cancer) for the dying (Pluto). As we will see shortly, Pluto in the 1st house also seems to refer to his commitment to continuously expose and uproot the impurities of his personality. The Jupiter-Pluto conjunction suggests power and influence, having a great impact on others, being a person of benevolent magnetism. With Jupiter amplifying Pluto's rays, Ram Dass has *shakti* and charisma. With Mars in Leo, trine the Moon in the 5th house, Ram Dass is a bit of a performer, a "stand-up comedian for God" as he was once called. He's a regal personality (Mars in Leo) who shines in the limelight, on stage (Moon in 5th house). With Mars in the 1st house, sexuality is likely to be a central evolutionary issue, and personal assertiveness would be marked. He also has Mars and Sun in mutual reception, a symbol of strength of character and personal power, and Jupiter and Moon in mutual reception, a symbol of emotional warmth and benevolence.

Saturn is placed in his 7th house, which suggests that relationships might be a major priority. Ram Dass's teachings emphasize the need to honor our human relationships and to serve our fellow human beings. He also feels a strong sense of responsibility to others and maintains stable, loyal, loving connections with a wide circle of spiritual friends. Ram Dass has never been married, and remaining single has been a matter of choice for him. Ram Dass has stated that relationships often become so absorbing or complicated that they get in the way of his relationship with God, thus he chooses to remain whole within himself. He has spoken quite a bit publicly about issues he has faced in relationships and friendships, and has used these personal experiences to give some of his most lucid spiritual teachings.

Ram Dass
April 6, 1931
10:40 AM EST
Boston, Massachussetts

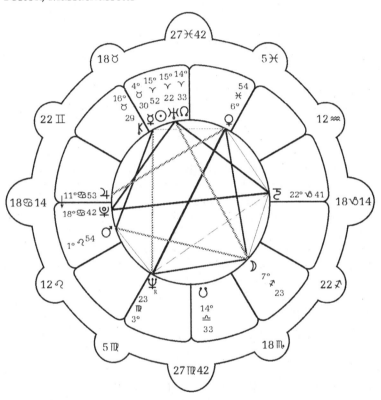

Source: Debbi Kempton Smith,
Secrets From a Stargazer's Notebook

Chart 24

Saturn's opposition to Pluto in the 1st house could refer to problems that arise with other people due to his charismatic and commanding personality — for example, negative projections that might be directed at him. It could also symbolize the fact that at times other people (especially older colleagues and mentors) have confronted him with his shadows.

Natal Venus is in Pisces opposite its ruler, Neptune, indicating a potential for devotional, unconditional love. This is the symbol of the fact that Ram Dass' spiritual path is *bhakti*, loving God, and awakening through love and service. Venus is exalted in Pisces, and its placement here gives a capacity to love freely, with a warm heart that is open to the world and to the suffering of others. With Venus in his 9th house opposite Neptune, love and service is the focus of Ram Dass' teaching.

With his Sagittarius Moon in the 5th house, trine Sun-Uranus, Ram Dass is constantly refining his understanding of the Dharma and expressing it through his unique teaching style. Neptune in the 3rd house symbolizes ecstatic, inspired speaking. Mercury is trine to Neptune, symbolizing a natural talent for, and abilities as a speaker. Moreover, Neptune's placement in Mercury's house symbolizes the fact that he speaks about spirituality, consciousness change, enlightenment, and meditation.

The Harvard Years

With Sun in the 10th house square Saturn, career would in all likelihood be quite important to this individual. During his twenties, Richard Alpert established himself in the world by being appointed to a position at Harvard, one of the most prestigious universities in the world. Saturn opposed natal Jupiter-Pluto in 1960, a period when he was enjoying prominence and success as a professor, a powerful man in the world, an influential teacher (Jupiter-Pluto).

At the time of his Saturn return in 1961, he took his first psilocybin trip and met Timothy Leary. His Saturn return coincided with a Jupiter-Saturn conjunction exactly conjunct his descendant. A new Jupiter-Saturn cycle was beginning with both planets entering the 7th house. Thus, it was quite significant for him to connect at that time with Tim Leary, a man who became his friend, associate, and teacher. This new friendship had a significant effect on his career (natal and transiting Saturn in 7th, square Sun in 10th) as they began conducting research and publishing papers together. The progressed Moon was also entering his 7th house. The progressed Moon shows the focus of one's emotional and inner life at a given time. In the 7th house, it symbolizes his inner focus on important friendships. With transiting Jupiter and Saturn and the progressed Moon in the 7th house, his alliance with Leary represented a lifelong bonding of their destinies. Leary and Alpert's active research into psychedelic drugs and their subsequent dismissal from Harvard were historic events. During the Saturn return important structures are built; in his case the bonds of friendship were formed. They had their fallings out but they always remained friends. The careers of Alpert and Leary are wedded in history.

When transiting Pluto came into contact with his natal T-square of Neptune-Venus-Moon, Alpert's life took a dramatic turn. When Pluto conjoined natal Neptune, he took psilocybin mushrooms and experienced a dramatic expansion of consciousness. His mind was opened to new realms of perception. With Pluto opposite natal Venus, he also had the experience of falling in love with everybody. Pluto's square to his 5th house Moon reflects a period of intense emotional experience as well as some heavy partying (Moon in 5th). Someone with a different natal chart or a different set of operant transits might take acid and have a total bummer. With transiting Pluto conjunct Neptune and square his Moon, Alpert was in ecstasy. This period was also characterized by travel, lecturing, publishing articles on the psychedelic experience, and taking the risk of expressing new theories (5th house Moon in Sagittarius) awakened by psychedelics (Neptune). Alpert and Leary didn't shut themselves up in libraries and laboratories. They were making wild pronouncements in their classes and articles, boldly voicing outrageous, neptunian ideas.

On the day of his first psilocybin trip in early 1961, transiting Venus was in Aries, exactly conjunct Sun-Uranus. Venus represents pleasant events, in this case, a nice experience that illuminated his purpose (Sun). That first trip showed him that his life was going to change. He reported standing outside of himself, seeing all of his identities as a professor, pilot, psychologist, and cellist all disappear until he experienced the pure, conscious witness that exists behind those identities. He began to undergo a transformation and mutation of his essential identity (Sun-Uranus).

Transiting Mars was in Cancer in the 12th house at the time of his first mushroom trip. The 12th house concerns altered states of consciousness; thus, this period awakened interests in psychedelics, meditation, enlightenment, and experiences of transcending the ego.

Transiting Uranus was in Leo, quincunx natal Saturn. I would speculate that this stressful transit might have shaken up his relationships with some of the stodgy professors in the Harvard Psychology department. Uranus-Saturn aspects are often struggles with authority and structure. Note that with Saturn squaring Uranus natally, Alpert might at some point in his life experience an internal conflict between the straight, conservative part of himself and the revolutionary side of his personality that would not be bound by social norms. The transit of Uranus to Saturn symbolizes a disturbance of the stability of his relationships with the saturnian authority figures that occurred when he started promoting the use of LSD. Neptune was also trine natal Jupiter, showing the potential for higher consciousness and new vision.

Two years later, in 1963, Alpert and Leary were fired from Harvard. A big press conference was held regarding the dismissal of these controversial professors. One might expect that the astrological symbolism of this event would portray the loss of his Harvard position as a great tragedy, the early end of a promising academic career. Surprisingly, however, transiting Jupiter, the traditional benefic planet of grace and opportunity, was conjunct the midheaven, near Sun and Uranus. We would expect this transit to bring improvement, expansion, and growth in his career. In this case Jupiter brought him into public prominence, but his notoriety had to be in alignment with the symbolism of his Sun-Uranus conjunction. Embodying the qualities of Uranus, the rebel, he was in public view as a radical, a bad guy who broke the rules by giving drugs to students.

Alpert conducted research projects in which he administered LSD to people from many walks of life, including prison inmates, to study the effects of these drugs. He did the research seriously, as part of a scientific effort to better understand human consciousness and behavioral change. But the changes of values, lifestyle, and behavior that often resulted from psychedelic use made his work a clear threat to the authorities. Jupiter brought him public visibility as a pioneer in psychedelic research, but also as a pariah in the eyes of the academic establishment. He was saddened that the people at

Harvard couldn't understand the exciting potentials of psychedelic drug research. He was probably quite shaken up by this event but he was also staying pretty high. The fact that these guys may have been taking LSD fairly often may have helped him maintain a somewhat wacky perspective on the whole episode. His progressed Venus was coming into conjunction with natal Sun-Uranus: Venus contacting Uranus could symbolize new and unusual friends and associations within the counter-culture.

In addition, the progressed Sun was exactly conjunct natal Chiron, the planet of the wounded healer. Chiron initiates you into new levels of consciousness, but some pain is usually involved in the initiatory ordeal. Being fired from Harvard was a rite of passage involving the stripping away of his comfortable personal and social identity and a bare confrontation with elemental forces; being ostracized and cast out by one's society is always unpleasant. At the same time, he was embodying the wounded healer, hurt because he had been fired from Harvard, but still wise and sharing knowledge freely with others.

Psychedelic Explorations

At this time Pluto and Uranus were coming into conjunction, the astrological event that corresponded to the cultural revolution of the 1960s — just as the impending social and spiritual revolution of the 1990s corresponds to the conjunction of Uranus and Neptune. At this time transiting Uranus was conjunct Alpert's natal Neptune. Uranus and Pluto were coming together in the early degrees of Virgo, near natal Neptune. Thus, first Pluto and then Uranus crossed his Neptune in close proximity. A lot of the guys who were enlightened in the 1960s experienced this transit. Da Avabhasa's main enlightenment experiences occurred during a similar series of transits over his 9th house Neptune (Chart 7). The same transit also brought about a major awakening of consciousness for Grateful Dead guitarist-sage Jerry Garcia. Alpert moved to the Millbrook, New York estate with Leary and other psychedelic associates, and spent days meditating, taking high doses of LSD, and reading mystical texts like the Tibetan Book of the Dead (3rd house Neptune).

Transiting Uranus was opposite Venus at this time and he continued to fall in love with everybody. He describes wandering around at the Millbrook mansion and seeing that there were lovers everywhere. This was his natal Venus-Neptune opposition being activated by transiting Uranus. He was stoned on love.

In the spring of 1963 transiting Uranus and Pluto both turned stationary direct equidistant from Neptune, i.e. the midpoint of transiting Uranus and Pluto was exactly conjunct his natal Neptune. He was getting really high during this period, experiencing states of higher consciousness. There may have also been a certain amount of confusion. He might have wondered what to do with himself now that he had been thrown out of Harvard. Neptune often brings experiences of disorientation, lack of form, fantasy, and living in the imagination. The folks at Millbrook were reading Herman Hesse's novels, especially the *Glass Bead Game,* and trying to recreate Hesse's mystical land of Castalia in their psychedelic mansion.

For the next several years (1964–1965), while transiting Saturn was in Pisces in his 9th house, conjunct natal Venus and opposite Neptune, Alpert used psychedelics extensively and lectured widely on their use. Also notice that transiting Saturn in Pisces was opposite transiting Uranus and Pluto, and all of them were contacting his Venus-Neptune axis, across his 3rd and 9th houses. He became a leading teacher of the burgeoning consciousness movement and became widely loved (Venus-Neptune). Between 1964–1966, while transiting Jupiter was in his 12th house, he was at Millbrook, sometimes staying high for days.

In 1966, while transiting Saturn crossed his midheaven, Alpert was a prominent spokesperson for the psychedelic movement, actively involved in publishing the *Psychedelic Review.* Saturn's transit over the midheaven was important, but not as important as its passage over his 10th house planets was subsequently to be. The transit of Saturn over the MC marked the beginning of a new phase of his career and a rise to public prominence; but only when Saturn contacted Sun-Uranus did the most significant events of his life begin to occur.

Meeting Maharaji

After the Millbrook psychedelic community was busted and shut down by the police, Alpert went on a trip to India with some of his friends. Having been forced to leave the Millbrook Estate, they were on a spiritual quest, a pilgrimage. Eventually Alpert met his guru,

Maharaji, as described in his book, *Be Here Now*. The ex-Harvard professor was quite suspicious upon first meeting Maharaji, who appeared to be just an old man lying on a blanket. But his attitude soon changed one day when Maharaji read his mind, recounting how Alpert had been thinking about his mother the night before, and how she had died of spleen failure the previous year. Alpert's mind was totally blown, because Maharaji had no apparent way of knowing these facts. It seemed that Maharaji was inside him and knew everything about him. Soon he was crying at the guru's feet. Shortly therafter Maharaji gave him the name Ram Dass, servant of God.

The transits operative at this important time are quite interesting: transiting Saturn was still in his 10th house (career); and even though he was going into retreat for a while, Alpert was still a public figure and was quite identified with his professional identity and social status. Also, transiting Uranus was crossing his nadir, symbolizing the dramatic changes he was about to experience in his life. Transiting Jupiter in Virgo was conjunct Neptune and opposite Venus. Jupiter's transits expand and augment whatever natal planets are contacted; and while Jupiter contacted natal Venus and Neptune he experienced a spiritual expansion and awakening of love for Maharaji. His 9th house Venus symbolizes both his love for his spiritual teacher, and meeting a teacher who was a being of love and who taught the path of love.

Ram Dass also had a progressed Sun-Chiron conjunction at this time. He was fired from Harvard when progressed Sun was conjunct natal Chiron; when he met Maharaji the progressed Sun was conjunct *progressed* Chiron. During this whole period he was being initiated by Chiron and met the embodiment of Chiron, which, according to Richard Nolle (1983), is the planetary symbol of the mentor, the spiritual master. At the same time, progressed Mars was trine his natal Sun-Uranus conjunction, symbolizing an intensified expression of his individuality. Ram Dass was not just going to stay in India, meditate, and disappear into the void. He was entering a period in which he would be more able than ever to express his uniqueness as a leader and an agent of cultural change (Uranus in 10th).

Transformation of Identity

In the spring of 1968 Ram Dass returned to the U.S. with bare feet and long hair. At the airport, his father told him to get in the car quickly before anyone saw him. Transiting Mars and Saturn were conjunct Sun-Uranus in the 10th house near the time his father was shocked to see him and became upset about Ram Dass' appearance and lifestyle. To his father he embodied the rebel because he looked weird and unconventional. With transiting Mars and Saturn conjunct his Sun, it was a bit of a harsh return, with his father (Saturn) openly expressing his disapproval.

Soon Ram Dass began talking publicly about his transformation and about the existence of a path beyond psychedelics, a path of yoga and purification, of gurus and mysticism. He assumed a new identity, began lecturing widely, and attracted a great deal of public attention upon his return from India. He was a changed man, with a new and unusual identity (Sun-Uranus in Aries). He was no longer Richard Alpert, Ph.D., clinical psychologist; he was now Ram Dass, the servant of God. With transiting Saturn conjunct natal Sun-Uranus, he now embarked on a socially unconventional path, using a Hindu name, wearing white robes, long hair, and prayer beads, and chanting in Sanskrit.

Also, the transiting north node was conjunct Sun-Uranus; the transiting nodes's contact with the Sun are always moments of destiny. Transiting Uranus was conjunct the IC, thus he was changing his lifestyle, diet, and personal habits, becoming more of a nomad, getting up early to meditate, doing all these unusual things. This transit also corresponds to his disheveled appearance (Uranus) and the disturbance this caused in his family (IC, 4th house).

Notice that natal Uranus is square to natal Saturn, showing an implicit tension between two sides of his nature: the part of him that is straight and conventional, that wants to fit in, and to have power in the world conflicts with his basic nature (Sun), which is uranian, unusual, or somewhat radical. During his Saturn return he became a prominent Harvard professor, embodying Saturn respectability and security. However, when Saturn conjoined his midheaven and Sun-Uranus he began to express his true nature as a yogi and a mystic, not a professor. He needed more room to evolve than he could have had as a Harvard psychologist. The Saturn transit activated the natal tension of Sun-Uranus and Saturn, thus he experienced a conflict about his profession, abandoning an old set of pursuits and career goals. Only when liberated from the tunnel vision of saturnian institutions, conventions, and norms was he free to be Ram Dass.

His progressed Moon was also conjunct natal Sun-Uranus at the same time. He had a new visibility, a career as a spiritual teacher, a new identity. There was also a progressed Mercury-midheaven conjunction, showing his constant travel, movement, and talking.

His progressed ascendant was trine natal Sun-Uranus, which illuminated his sense of purpose.[5] This important aspect signifies that was the stage of his life when he could begin to actualize his *dharma*, to express his true nature and calling to the spiritual path.

In 1970, he returned to India to look for Maharaji, feeling lost in the world and in his desires, seeking more training. He spent time with Maharaji over the next year or so, doing meditation retreats and yoga. With transiting Saturn in the 11th house he also lead groups, and was looked to as a leader by many young Westerners who had followed him to India. A spiritual community (11th house) was forming around Maharaji, and Ram Dass had a central role in this group as a teacher.

With transiting Pluto conjunct his IC, this period was one in which Ram Dass was confronted more directly with his desires and attachments. Pluto brought to the surface many of his impurities, such as hidden power and sexual motives. With natal Pluto on the ascendant, Ram Dass has alot of power, but he also freely admits that he has a shadow and has had to work to uproot his hidden attachments and drives for power and control. When Pluto transited over his IC Maharaji exposed his desires, his anger, and his pride (natal Pluto conjunct ascendant, square Sun). Pluto's passage over the nadir also signified a reconnection with his ancient spiritual roots (4th house) in the yogic traditions of India, especially his specific lineage of devotional yoga. He was in the balsamic progressed Moon phase at this time, the ending of a progressed Moon cycle. A cycle was coming to a close, and a new cycle was about to begin.

---

[5] The progressed ascendant is calculated as follows: first, calculate the solar arc midheaven, by adding the distance between the natal Sun and the secondary progressed Sun to the natal midheaven. Then look in the table of houses for the latitude of birth and find the ascendant corresponding to the progressed midheaven. This is the progressed ascendant.

Struggles With Trungpa and Joya

In fall of 1973, after he returned to the US and began teaching again, Maharaji left his body. With transiting Saturn going through Ram Dass' 12th house, he went into retreat and meditated trying to contact his guru on inner planes. Then his progressed New Moon occurred, at 26 degrees of Taurus, in his 11th house. A new period of personal evolution was beginning that might focus on the practical dynamics of groups and communities. His progressed Mars and progressed ascendant were conjunct; Ram Dass was having some difficulty reconciling his efforts to be a very pure, holy man with his strong desires for power, adulation, and sexual gratification. He was also about to have some unpleasant, abrasive interactions with others (progressed Mars-Ascendant conjunction).

In the summer of 1974, Ram Dass taught a course at Naropa Institute on the *Bhagavad Gita*. Chogyam Trungpa was reigning over Naropa and he and Ram Dass got involved in a not-too-subtle power struggle. Transiting Jupiter was in his 9th house and conjunct his Venus at that time; he was doing a magnificent series of lectures on the *Gita*, on *bhakti* and *karma yoga*, and the love of God. They were some of his best lectures, great expressions of wisdom. Jupiter was very strongly placed natally, close to the ascendant, squaring his Sun. When Jupiter passed through his 9th house (its own house) and contacted Venus, he was lecturing and teaching.

However, with transiting Saturn conjunct his ascendant and natal Jupiter-Pluto, Ram Dass got involved in a very complex interpersonal conflict (Pluto opposite Saturn in 7th house). He and Trungpa engaged in a kind of competition with one another and the Naropa community became somewhat divided in its allegiances toward the two teachers. Trungpa took it upon himself to try to expose Ram Dass' limitations as a spiritual teacher. Moreover, with Saturn conjunct his ascendant, Ram Dass himself felt that he was not living up to his own ideal. Saturn's transit over the ascendant is often difficult because it requires a clear reevaluation of identity, and questioning of whether or not you are embodying the truth you have defined for yourself. He felt that he was impure and recognized that he still had much inner work to do. He became discouraged because of his continuing entanglement in worldly desires and considered returning to India again for an extended period of meditation.

Before he could do so however, Ram Dass had a vision in which Maharaji told him not to go back to India because he would soon be guided to his next teacher in America. Soon thereafter he met a woman named Joya who seemed to be the teacher Maharaji had indicated would appear. She was very powerful, seemed to have psychic or telepathic communication with Maharaji, and channeled information from various other spiritual guides. Ram Dass moved to New York City to become Joya's student and proclaimed that she was enlightened and an embodiment of the divine Mother. Many of Ram Dass' students followed him to New York to study with Joya. Transiting Neptune was conjunct his Moon: he was idealizing (Neptune) Joya as the Great Mother (Moon). Also, he was experiencing expanded consciousness through meditation and worship of the divine Mother. Because his Moon squares Venus and Neptune natally, this was a critical transit that opened his heart and his capacity for devotion. He was doing high spiritual practices and often spoke about various gurus and ancient masters being present in the room during his lectures. But with Saturn still conjunct his ascendant, Jupiter, and Pluto and opposite natal Saturn during this period, interpersonal power struggles were soon to reemerge.

In 1975 he studied intensely with Joya and was at the center of a spiritual community that gathered around himself, Joya, and another teacher, Hilda Charlton. Transiting Jupiter was conjunct the midheaven and his Sun-Uranus. Just as when he was fired from Harvard, this was a very public period in which Ram Dass conducted many public talks and intensive classes in New York, and acted as a spiritual guide for many students.

October 1975 through July 1976 was the most intense period of his training under Joya, who began initiating him into Tantra, through devotional and sexual practices. During this period, transiting Saturn was conjunct Ram Dass' Mars (sexuality). Joya was an extremely intense teacher whose spiritual awakening occurred suddenly but seems to have had an inadequate foundation; for eventually she became psychologically imbalanced and appeared to burn out. But at that time she did wield a great deal of spiritual power. She also created alot of difficulty for Ram Dass, waking him up at all hours of the night with repeated phone calls, not letting him sleep, hassling him, keeping him off balance, all in the name of loosening his attachments.

Ram Dass tried to view this fierce teacher as the embodiment of the Goddess Kali and honored the intense fire of purification he was experiencing under Joya's guidance. However, as he became more deeply involved with Joya, Ram Dass began to perceive that she was not above attachments and lust, and thus not so liberated as he had thought. The reality was that Joya had some very human problems of her own, and was also quite manipulative. Ram Dass then began a painful process of severing this relationship, which was complicated by their public visibility and his prior endorsement of Joya. As Ram Dass struggled to free himself from Joya he began to unravel a web of lies she had woven around herself and began to question her motives and purity. This required some unpleasant confrontations with Joya and her followers, and the assertion of his own will to address the situation (transiting Saturn conjunct Mars in the 1st). Ram Dass had been wielding a lot of *shakti*, drawing spiritual power from his meditation and tantric practices. Now he was also expressing anger and confronting people who were angry with him. While Saturn passed over natal Mars he evolved greatly through intensive work in the areas of power, anger, and sexuality. Transiting Neptune was quincunx natal Jupiter during this period: receiving distorted teachings, and feeling deceived by a teacher.

Finally, in September 1976, Ram Dass published an article in which he admitted that he had been wrong about Joya, that she was not in fact an enlightened being, and took responsibility for leading other people to her. This period was one of intense struggle with Joya and her followers, some of whom made life quite unpleasant for him. Transiting Uranus was conjunct the south node, leading to unexpected problems. But Ram Dass' progressed MC was sextile Jupiter, while progressed Jupiter was exactly conjunct the natal ascendant, symbolizing his own moral courage (Jupiter) in confronting this situation honestly, despite the embarrassment this caused him. Uranus was also trine Jupiter, perhaps signifying the way that Ram Dass was acting as a spokesperson for the truth (Jupiter) above all else. He cited Gandhi, who, after changing his mind on an important decision, stated that his commitment was to truth, not consistency.

Ram Dass' Yoga of Service

Ram Dass emerged from this period more independent and more able to serve others without glamor or subtle desire to be worshipped as a spiritual teacher. From this metamorphosis was born his later involvement with the SEVA Foundation, a non-profit organization that carries out a variety of human service projects. SEVA has implemented programs to fight disease and preventible blindness. Ram Dass has also worked extensively with prisoners and with Cancer and AIDS patients, and supported various progressive political causes. Through his tireless efforts, Ram Dass has embodied love in action, contributed significantly to the eradication of human suffering, and taught and exemplified the yoga of service. His lucid teachings continue to influence thousands of people. He has also been a model of candor, and of socially engaged spirituality. He has also never rested in his search for liberation, continuing to study and practice meditation. Ram Dass' life vividly demonstrates the positive social impact that can result from one person's commitment to the path of spiritual awakening.

CONCLUSION
Writing Your Own Astrological Biography

Each of the lives you have just studied is a perfect expression and manifestation of the individual's birth chart. Know that your own chart accurately portrays the kinds of experiences and activities that are right for you, just as it did for these famous spiritual teachers.

Now the time has come for you to apply all that you have learned in this book to your own life. Meditate on your birth pattern, with its unique configuration of planetary placements and aspects. Determine which of the twelve yogas of the zodiac are highlighted both by your natal chart and by current or upcoming transits. How does your birth chart suggest that you might best proceed on your path of spiritual growth? How could you apply the principles of the six shaktis to further your own evolution?

Begin writing your own astrological biography by making a list of the most memorable and important events of your life thus far. Try to recall the dates of these occurrences, and then investigate the transits and progressions operative at those times. Note how the planetary symbolism illuminates the significance of events and enables you to harvest meaning from every stage of your life-cycle. Pay attention to repeating themes and relate these to the symbolism of your natal chart. Keep a record of your discoveries.

Note what transits and progressions lie ahead and reflect on the kinds of tasks and challenges they herald for your near and distant future. Imagine who you will be in one year, five years, and ten years by meditating on these planetary symbols, and contemplate how your own actions will help shape the outcome. Ask yourself what are the optimum ways for me to utilize these transits and progressions?

Exploring your own astrological biography will reveal the nature and direction of your unique spiritual path. It will enable you to perceive that your life is unfolding in a coherent manner, in accordance with planetary symbolism. It will also help you perceive what steps need to be taken now or in the future to fulfill the potentials of your birth chart. Remember that to make your studies of planetary symbols truly fruitful you must go *beyond* astrology by taking the concrete steps needed to transform your life.

Reflection on the birth chart should awaken not fear but faith, which is the certitude that our lives are unfolding according to a hidden pattern or intelligence — what some would call the divine intention. May this realization awaken in you a profound inner peace, the ultimate goal of astrology. May the spirit of guidance illuminate your path!

References

Arroyo, S. (1978). *Astrology, Karma, and Transformation*. Sebastopol, CA: CRCS Publications.

Arroyo, S. (1989). *Manual of Chart Interpretation*. Sebastopol, CA: CRCS Publications.

Baigent, M., Harvey, C., and Campion, N. (1984). *Mundane Astrology*. Wellingborough, Great Britain: Aquarian Press.

Bogart, G. (1993). *Culture, Crisis, and Creativity: The Prophetic Vision of Dane Rudhyar*. Berkeley, CA: Dawn Mountain Press.

Braha, J. (1986). *Ancient Hindu Astrology for the Modern Western Astrologer*. North Miami, FL: Hermetician Press.

Deutch, E. (1969). *Advaita Vedanta: A Philosophical Reconstruction*. Honolulu: University Press of Hawaii.

Dobyns, Z. & Roof, N. (1973). *The Astrologer's Casebook*. Los Angeles: TIA Publications.

Dyczkowski, M. (1987). *The Doctrine of Vibration: An Analysis of the Doctrines and Practices of Kashmir Shaivism*. Albany, NY: State University of New York Press.

Eliade, M. (1981). *Autobiography*. New York: Harper & Row.

Forrest, S. (1984). *The Inner Sky*. New York: Bantam Books.

Frawley, D. (1990). *The Astrology of the Seers*. Salt Lake City, UT: Passage Press.

Gauquelin, M. & Gauquelin, F. (1982). *The Gauquelin Book of American Charts*. San Diego, CA: Astro Computing Services.

Gawain, S. (1978). *Creative Visualization*. Tiburon, CA: Whatever Publications.

Greene, L. (1984). *The Astrology of Fate*. York Beach, ME: Samuel Weiser.

Greene, L., and Arroyo, S. (1983). *The Outer Planets and Their Cycles: The Astrology of the Collective*. Sebastopol, CA: CRCS Publications.

Grof, S. (1992). *The Holotropic Mind*. New York: Harper Collins.

Harding, M., & Harvey, C. (1990). *Working with Astrology: The Psychology of Harmonics, Midpoints, and Astrocartography*. London: Penguin.

Hopkinson, T., and Hopkinson, D. (1982). *Much Silence: The Life and Work of Meher Baba*. Australia: Sheriar Press.

Inayat Khan, H. (1978). *The Complete Sayings of Hazrat Inayat Khan*. New Lebanon, NY: Omega Press.

Johnson, D. (1989). *The Role of the River in the Life and Work of Rabindranath Tagore*. Ann Arbor, MI: University Microfilms International.

Jonas, H. (1958). *The Gnostic Religion*. Boston, MA: Beacon Press.

Jung, C.G. (1961). *Memories, Dreams, and Reflections*. New York: Vintage.

Kempton-Smith, D. (1982). *Secrets From a Stargazer's Notebook*. New York: Bantam.

Kriyananda, S. (1979). *The Path: Autobiography of a Western Yogi.* Nevada City, CA: Ananda Publications.

Muktananda, S. (1974). *Play of Consciousness.* South Fallsburg, NY SYDA Foundation.

Muktananda, S. (1980). *Secret of the Siddhas.* South Fallsburg, NY: SYDA Foundation.

Muller-Ortega, P. E. (1989). *The Triadic Heart of Siva: Kaula Tantricism of Abhinavagupta in the Non-Dual Shaivism of Kashmir.* Albany, NY: State University of New York Press.

Nolle, R. (1983). *Chiron: The Key to Your Quest.* Tempe, AZ: American Federation of Astrologers.

Radhakrishnan, S. (Ed.) (1961). *Rabindranath Tagore: A Centenary Volume.* New Delhi: Sahitya Akademi.

Raman, B.V. (1981). *Notable Horoscopes* (5th printing). Bangalore, India: IBH Prakashana.

Raman, B.V. (1972). *Three Hundred Planetary Combinations.* Bangalore, India: IBH Prakashana.

Rael, L. (1983). *The Essential Rudhyar.* San Francisco: Rudhyar Institute of Transpersonal Activity.

Reynolds, J. (1989). *Self-Liberation Through Seeing with Naked Awareness.* Barrytown, NY: Station Hill Press.

Ricketts, M. (1988). *Mircea Eliade: The Romanian Roots.* New York: Columbia University Press.

Rodden, L. (1979). *Profiles of Women.* Tempe, AZ: American Federation of Astrologers.

Rodden, L. (1980). *The American Book of Charts.* San Diego, CA: Astro Computing Services.

Rodden, L. (1986). *Astrodata III*. Tempe, AZ: American Federation of Astrologers.

Rudhyar, D. (1968). *The Practice of Astrology as a Technique of Human Understanding*. Baltimore, MD: Penguin.

Rudhyar, D. (1969). *Astrological Timing: The Transition to the New Age*. New York: Harper & Row.

Rudhyar, D. (1973). *An Astrological Mandala*. New York: Vintage.

Rudhyar, D. (1973). *Rania*. San Francisco: Unity Press.

Rudhyar, D. (1975). *The Sun is also a Star: The Galactic Dimension of Astrology*. Santa Fe, NM: Aurora Press.

Rudhyar, D. (1976a). *Person-Centered Astrology*. Santa Fe, NM: Aurora Press.

Rudhyar, D. (1976b). *Astrology and the Modern Psyche*. Sebastopol, CA: CRCS Publications.

Rudhyar, D. (1977). *Culture, Crisis, and Creativity*. Wheaton, IL: Quest Books.

Rudhyar, D. (1979). *Beyond Individualism*. Wheaton, IL: Quest Books.

Rudhyar, D. (1980). *The Astrology of Transformation*. Wheaton, IL: Quest Books.

Rudhyar, D. (1982). *Beyond Personhood*. Palo Alto, CA: Rudhyar Institute for Transpersonal Activity.

Rudhyar, D. (1983). *The Rhythm of Wholeness*. Wheaton, IL: Quest Books.

Ruperti, A. (1978). *Cycles of Becoming*. Sebastopol, CA: CRCS Publications.

Sannella, L. (1987). *The Kundalini Experience*. Lower Lake, CA: Integral Publishing.

Saradananda, S. (1952). *Ramakrishna, The Great Master*. Calcutta, India: Advaita Ashrama.

Scott, M. (1983). *Kundalini in the Physical World*. London: Routledge & Kegan Paul.

Tierney, B. (1983). *Dynamics of Aspect Analysis*. Sebastopol, CA: CRCS Publications.

Tyl, N. (1991). *Prediction in Astrology*. St. Paul, MN: Llewellyn Publications.

Vissell, B. & Vissell, J. (1984). *The Shared Heart: Relationship Initiations and Celebrations*. Aptos, CA: Ramira Publishing.

Index

Also by Greg Bogart

Finding Your Life's Calling:
Spiritual Dimensions of Vocational Choice

This book combines practical, down-to-earth suggestions, psychological theory, and lively case histories to teach readers how to find and fulfill their life's central work. The book begins by tracing the history of the concept of vocation in Eastern and Western religions. The author then illustrates the varied ways in which a person can gain illumination—such as vision quests, dreams, and inner voice experiences. Describing how an individual moves through the various stages of confirming and developing a life's work, Bogart suggests ways to navigate the interpersonal struggles and internal conflicts that may be confronted along the way.

The author recounts a number of instructive, often humorous, anecdotes about his own search for a vocation. His adventures take him from travels in India, to a vision quest in Oregon, to time spent as a street musician and poet, to his current work as a psychotherapist, yoga teacher, and spiritual counselor. He also tells the stories of numerous individuals pursuing unusual career paths. This is not just another book about how to find a job, but rather a unique perspective on the search for a meaningful vocation.

"This excellent book lucidly discusses religious, psychological, and spiritual issues involved in defining one's calling, including a transpersonal aspect that is usually overlooked."

Stanley Krippner, Ph.D.

$14.95. Mail check or money order to Dawn Mountain Press, P.O. Box 9563-A, Berkeley, CA 94709-0563. Shipping charge: add $2.00 for first book, $1.00 for each additional copy. Canada: $19.00 (us). Europe: $20.00. California residents add 8.25% sales tax.
A quality paperback. 176 pages. ISBN # 0-9639068-4-4.
Retailers order from SCB Distributors: 800-729-6423.